WOMEN WHO *MEAN* BUSINESS

WOMEN WHO *MEAN* BUSINESS

Success Stories of Women Over Forty

A. MIKAELIAN

William Morrow and Company, Inc., New York

It is the policy of William Morrow and Company, Inc., and its imprints and affiliates, recognizing the importance of preserving what has been written, to print the books we publish on acid-free paper, and we exert our best efforts to that end.

LIBRARY OF CONGRESS CATALOGING-IN-PUBLICATION DATA
Mikaelian, A.
    Women who mean business : success stories of women over forty /
  A. Mikaelian. —1st ed.
      p.   cm.
    ISBN 0-688-15677-0
    1. Businesswomen—Biography. 2.Women executives—Biography.
  I. Title.
  HC102.5.A2M55 1999
  658.4'09'0820922—dc21
  [B]   99-27429
                                        CIP

Printed in the United States of America

First Edition

1　2　3　4　5　6　7　8　9　10

BOOK DESIGN BY CHERYL L. CIPRIANI

www.williammorrow.com

INTRODUCTION

NOTHING HAS TRANSFORMED the business world in the past thirty years more than the women who entered it. Those at the forefront of this change, now in their forties and early fifties, can look back on careers that helped rewrite the rules of business. The women who got started in the seventies and early eighties succeeded in a male-dominated environment, and created a nation where we are increasingly less surprised to find a woman in a position of wealth, respect, and power. They brought to the workplace values and concerns that companies had rarely tackled before, and are still learning to manage today. They watched business and government respond, however slowly, by addressing discrimination, wage gaps, family leave, and sexual harassment. Businesses were placed in a position they hadn't faced since the rise of the labor unions—addressing the needs of their employees rather than focusing only on the needs of the marketplace. In return, they gained some incredibly talented people. The number of working women rose from 30 million in 1970 to 60 million in 1997, at which point they accounted for 46 percent of the labor force.

The women in this book all joined the workforce as this change was getting under way. Other than that, they have very little in common. Every state of the union—and Canada—is represented here, showing how women have blazed trails from the Deep South to the Pacific Northwest. They've succeeded in incredibly diverse industries—from high technology to construction. Many have stood on their own as entrepreneurs, many others are taking on the still male-dominated upper echelons of the Fortune 500. How they've approached their careers, the values they give to success, and the obstacles they've overcome are as varied as where they live and where they've chosen to make their mark.

Some chose so-called nontraditional fields, accepting the fact that they would often be the only woman in the room. Others faced single motherhood as they built their careers. A surprising number succeeded without ever getting a college degree, and would never recommend their route to anyone. Many have faced more personal obstacles—a lack of confidence that might have killed their careers early on, a battle with life-threatening illness, fear of what might happen if they didn't succeed. Everyone in this book, looking back over twenty to thirty years of their working lives, feels fortunate. No one in this book says it was easy.

Incredibly, they all took time from their schedules to share those experiences. As the last generation that faced a male-dominated workforce, their lives are a record of that time and an inspiration to anyone who is building a career. Few of these women had female mentors early in their careers, and said during the interviews that made this book possible that they would like nothing better than for younger women to take some teachings and guidance, however small, from their experiences. If that happens, then this collection will be a success.

The profiles you are about to read are in two parts. Each woman was asked a set of standard questions about their greatest rewards, achievements, and challenges. Each one gave advice to women just getting started, and each one offered her personal definition of success. The answers reflect just how diverse these women are. Their answers are followed by a short—in every case too short—biography that outlines their careers, using as many of their own words as possible. These biographies are brief attempts to honor these women and give them a platform for their thoughts, reflections, and stories.

This is not a scientific study, and it would be difficult to find common threads in such a diverse group. But as these women generously lent their life stories to this book, one theme was struck repeatedly, and it had little to do with business. Regardless of their profession, education, or background, all of these professionals share a commitment to improving their world through community service. Whether that be through volunteer work with charitable organizations, mentoring younger professionals, hiring from empowerment programs, or working to bring jobs into their regions, the desire to see others succeed is undeniably strong in this group. They weren't selected for their community involvement, but as this project progressed, it became evident that this spirit would be found in every candidate uncovered, and it was. Nothing was more satisfying in gathering these stories than this discovery. If this group is truly representative, then the transformation women have created in the business world will continue into the world at large. If it does, we will all be better for it.

WOMEN WHO *MEAN* BUSINESS

Martha Warren Bidez, Ph.D.

CHAIRMAN AND CHIEF
EXECUTIVE OFFICER

*BioHorizons Implant Systems
Incorporated*

Birmingham, Alabama

WORK HISTORY

1981–1997   Numerous University of Alabama at Birmingham (UAB) professorships, directorships, and research positions: Department of Biomedical Engineering, Department of Electrical Engineering, Department of Mechanical Engineering, Center on Aging, Injury Control Research Center, Department of Biomaterials.

1991–1995   Assistant Professor (Adjunct Appointment), University of Pittsburgh School of Dentistry.

1997–present   Adjunct Associate Professor, Department of Biomedical Engineering, UAB.

1990–present   President and Owner, BioHorizons, Inc.

1995–present   Chairman and CEO, BioHorizons Implant Systems, Inc.

EDUCATION

1979   B.S. (with high honors) in biology/pre-health, Auburn University, Auburn, Alabama.

1985   B.S. (cum laude) in mechanical engineering, UAB.

1983   M.S. in biomedical engineering, UAB.

1987   Ph.D. in biomedical engineering, UAB.

FIRST JOB

Assistant bookkeeper in my parents' trucking company.

ASSOCIATIONS AND NETWORKS

Founding President, Implant Dentistry Research and Education Foundation; Academy of Osseointegration; American Academy of Forensic Sciences; American Society of Mechanical Engineers; Association for the Advancement of Automotive Medicine; Biomedical Engineering Society; International Congress of Oral Implantology, Society for Biomaterials; Society of Automotive Engineers; Society of Women Engineers.

COMMUNITY SERVICE

Alabama Civil Justice Foundation; The Women's Fund of Greater Birmingham; Birmingham Partnership Assistance to the Homeless (PATH) program; St. Mary's Center (for homeless women); The Old Firehouse (for homeless men); Birmingham Shelter Task Force; Southside Ministries Policy Board; United Way Community Research Committee; Rotary Club of Birmingham; The Women's Network; Women's Business Ownership Council.

AWARDS AND HONORS

Unsung Hero, U.S. Department of Transportation (for leadership in improving the safety of children in car crashes), 1997; Kellogg National Fellow, 1993–1996; Top Ten Women in Birmingham, *Birmingham Business Journal,* 1995; Leadership Birmingham, 1995; PATH Building dedicated to Martha Warren Bidez, 1995; Outstanding Woman Faculty Member, The

Women's Center, UAB, 1995; Woman of Distinction, Cahaba Girl Scouts Council, 1995; Top 40 under 40, *Birmingham Business Journal,* 1992; Young Engineer of the Year, Engineering Council of Birmingham, Inc., 1988–1989; numerous academic and graduate school honors.

FAMILY

Married eighteen years.

PERSONAL GOALS

I want to make a difference in our world and be remembered for freeing and empowering the human spirit.

PROFESSIONAL GOALS

To lead BioHorizons into global market leadership and to become known as the founder of a visionary company that exemplifies corporate social responsibility.

WAYS OF DEALING WITH PRESSURE AND STRESS

Quiet reflection. Sometimes exercise. I also cry. It's important to know that it's okay for strong leaders to cry.

ADVICE TO ASPIRING BUSINESSWOMEN

Hold tight to your dream, don't give it up, don't let others place limitations on it.

*a*s I've moved through my engineering career, I've faced virtually all of the old-school attitudes about women in engineering, and I've either tried to reeducate them or, when I hit a brick wall and couldn't go through it, I'd go around it.

Even as she went around the occasional obstruction, Martha Warren Bidez never deviated far from her path. Research that she began with colleague Dr. Carl Misch in the early eighties has resulted in two patents that now form the backbone of BioHorizons Implant Systems. Martha's small start-up is poised to compete with global leaders in the industry, and she says they will not be going around obstacles the competition might create. "We did not tiptoe into the market. We got into the arena in a very big way."

Martha can't remember a time when she wasn't interested in science, particularly in biology and the human body. But when she was an undergraduate at Auburn University, she met her husband, Earle, who was studying mechanical engineering. "Because I tended to be a bookworm," Martha remembers, "our dates primarily consisted of studying together, and I found that mechanical engineering fascinated me." But she didn't see herself studying anything other than biology and "the human machine" until she graduated: "I then learned for the first time of biomedical engineering, and it was a ray of sunshine. Suddenly it wasn't an either/or proposition."

At the University of Alabama at Birmingham, she and Dr. Misch collaborated on solving a problem that had been around for decades—giving patients new sets of teeth that stayed in place. "There are four different strengths of bone in the human mouth," she explains, "but every implant on the market was the same design irrespective of the type of bone quality and density." When Martha and her collaborator were finished with devising a new system, UAB had two patents, and BioHorizons was formed with the exclusive right to sell them.

Transitioning into the business world from the academic wasn't as hard as it might seem. "There hasn't been a dramatic difference," Martha says, citing her experience in establishing a new research laboratory at UAB. "It was up to me to recruit the best students and raise all the money to fund the research. I was in fund-raising mode all the time. Now I'm doing the same things on a broader, grander, and global scale." The genesis of the implant company was in UAB's business incubator facility, where Martha and her partner raised seed capital, developed prototypes, and got through FDA clearance. The company then specialized in computer animation models, and it wasn't until four years later, in 1994, that the actual implant company was formed.

It took another three years before the product was ready to be introduced to the market. "This was a challenging time," Martha remembers. "We knew we would be a major threat to all the global market leaders, and indeed we were. Their competitive response was fairly vicious. Responding required enormous cash reserves, and a real fortitude to stand up against the response in print and being criticized from the podiums at professional meetings." BioHorizons has not shied away from the big boys, and Martha adds that they really are boys: "There's no other company in this industry led by a woman."

Martha's dedication has made her a leader in the community as well. Although she has served several causes, she says, her most enduring commitment has been to alleviating the problem of homelessness, particularly as it affects women and children. Through her church, she and a small group of women established a day center for homeless women that has since expanded into PATH, a comprehensive, interfaith organization. In 1995, the building that houses the project was dedicated to Martha, who says that when she started working with homeless women as a graduate student, she realized how lucky she had been: "As I got to know these women, I began to understand how similar they were to me. But for the privileges and blessings I have been afforded, I could be in a similar situation. The Fridays I sat having coffee with these women changed my life."

Robin Ann Schafer, L.M.T., N.C.T.M.B.

PRESIDENT AND OWNER

Advanced Neuromuscular Therapies

Alabaster, Alabama

Melissa E. Wertz Photography

WORK HISTORY

1972–1977   YCC Camp Member, Park Aid, then Park Ranger, Pennsylvania and Florida.

1987–1992   Self-employed Massage Therapist, Atlanta, Georgia.

1994–present   President, Advanced Neuromuscular Therapies.

EDUCATION

1983   B.A. in art, Penn State University, State College, Pennsylvania.

1987   Certification, Atlanta School of Massage, Atlanta, Georgia.

FIRST JOB

Member, 1st Youth Conservation Corp Camp, GNMP, Gettysburg, Pennsylvania.

ASSOCIATIONS AND NETWORKS

Member, American Massage Therapy Association (AMTA); AMTA Chapter past President and Government Relations Chairperson; National Certification for Therapeutic Massage and Bodywork; AMTA Foundation 2000 Charter Member; Penn State Alumni Association; Government Relations Chairperson, Hoover Chamber of Commerce; National Association for Female Executives; past President, North Atlanta Female Executives.

COMMUNITY SERVICE

Mentor, Hoover High School ACE Program; Neighbors Who Care.

AWARDS AND HONORS

AMTA—Alabama Chapter Government Relations Award, 1997; AMTA—Alabama Chapter Meritorious Awards, 1994, 1995, 1996; Network Birmingham Professional Award, 1995; Top 40 Under 40, *Birmingham Business Journal,* 1994.

FAMILY

Married.

PERSONAL GOALS

My future health is in my own hands—through knowledge, and taking preventative measures now, I can improve my own quality of life, translating practical information into everyday behavior changes. I can only help others as far as I've helped myself.

PROFESSIONAL GOALS

To be a Massage Therapist in the Sydney, Australia, Olympics in 2000.

DRIVING FORCE

My clients.

DEFINITION OF SUCCESS

Restoring a smile to someone's face, putting hope in their hearts, comfort in their bodies, and dreams in their minds.

BUSINESS MAXIM

You never know when a moment is going to become a memory or when you will witness a miracle.

GREATEST REWARD FROM CAREER

My appointment to the 1995 World Cup Synchronized Swimming Team Event in 1995, and the medical staff for the 1996 Centennial Olympic Games.

GREATEST DOWNSIDE TO CAREER

My work is very physically, mentally, emotionally, and spiritually challenging.

ADVICE TO ASPIRING BUSINESSWOMEN

Choose a mentor you respect and admire. Pick a cause greater than yourself—get involved in creating the world you want to live in. Take someone under your wing and let him or her learn from your successes as well as your mistakes.

*E*very client that comes through my front door is an influence on my life and my practice. Each one is a unique learning experience that leaves me transformed.

Robin Ann Schafer was thirty before she transformed her own life by attending the Atlanta School of Massage. She had been a ranger at national parks in Pennsylvania and Florida, never quite connecting the work to her own life, when she was encouraged to attend the massage school through her high school mentor at her tenth annual reunion. Robin had a leg injury that therapists at the school gradually repaired, and when they were finished, she had a new life course. "It worked for me," she says, "so for the last fourteen years now, I've been working on others."

Robin has given therapy ever since, and hasn't stopped there. As President of the American Massage Therapy Association's Alabama Chapter, she led a drive to establish laws and regulations for massage therapists in Alabama where there once was nothing. "What led me to create the Massage Therapy Licensure Bill for Alabama was the belief that massage therapy is health care," she says. "In the past, the word 'massage' was abused. The law restored our traditional 'massage therapy' name as well as our professional reputations." Over two years, Robin wrote and visited each state representative and senator to educate them about therapeutic massage, stressing the need for certification, ethics, and standards: "We work with people who have been injured, stressed, or are in acute or chronic pain. This takes training and continuing education."

Massage therapists in Alabama must now go through a program similar to that of the Atlanta School of Massage. "I had no idea what I was getting into when I enrolled," she says, stressing that beyond intensive human anatomy and physiology courses, she was required to take classes in body-work, ethics, wellness/holistic health, personal skills development, and business. She explains, "You have to learn people's boundaries and respect their bodies, values, and beliefs. They have to understand why you are touching them before you work on an area. As for business, not many therapists are good at promoting themselves. I've been lucky in that I'm a good networker. I've always had more business than I know what to do with."

Much of her business has come through referrals from physicians, chiropractors, and other professionals. After lugging around her massage table on house calls for years, she established Advanced Neuromuscular Therapies. This gave her a base and allowed her to bring in other therapists to offer one-stop integrative health care: "My goal has always been to have more modalities and different types of therapies, even acupuncture and nutrition, under one roof." Robin herself has the tools to do this. In addition to reconstructive and pain-fighting neuromuscular massage, she's been trained in advanced Pfrimmer deep muscle therapy, lymphatic drainage, Jin Shin Do acupressure, sports massage, Reiki, CORE myofascial therapy, and therapeutic touch. She's continuing to learn by attending dissection labs, graduate school, and regular conferences. "Continuing education is part of our state law," she says. "We have to communicate with other therapists."

After she wrote the state law and got it passed, the way was paved for Robin to join the Olympic Medical Services Team in 1996, a great reward for her years of work and a further legitimizing of her profession. But the clients she sees day to day are still, she says, the greatest reward of all. She mentions a current client, a fifty-year-old heart bypass patient and right leg amputee. "It is my pleasure to work with him. He was almost completely wheelchair-bound a year ago. Now he can walk forty feet without the use of crutches or a cane. He has been the perfect example of how when you restore structure to the body, function will follow." Robin doesn't take complete credit for this transformation—it's as much due to his positive attitude and efforts as hers. "When I started in this business," she says, "I thought healing was up to me. This isn't true. People heal themselves."

Linda J. E. Henrikson

PRESENT AND CHIEF
EXECUTIVE OFFICER

Linder Construction, Inc.
Anchorage, Alaska

L.I.P.S.

WORK HISTORY

1972–1973   Secretary, National Weather Service, Engineering Division,
Anchorage, Alaska.

1975–1977   Administrative Assistant, National Bank of Alaska,
Anchorage, Alaska.

1977   Contract Instructor, Martin Explosives Corporation,
Anchorage, Alaska.

1977   General Office Manager, Bridges-Monsarrat Architects,
Anchorage, Alaska.

1977–1979   Office Manager, Marston Real Estate, Anchorage, Alaska.

1980–1986   Owner/Manager, Horizon Construction, Inc., Kenai,
Alaska.

1987–present   President/CEO, Linder Construction.

EDUCATION

1973–1976   Attended Whitman College, Walla Walla, Washington, and University of Alaska, Anchorage.

1998   Selected to attend minority executive training program at the Amos Truck School of Business, Dartmouth College, Hanover, New Hampshire.

FIRST JOB

While still in high school, secretary for the Engineering Department of the National Weather Service.

ASSOCIATIONS AND NETWORKS

Alaska 8(a) Association; Member and Chair of regional conference committee, Society of American Military Engineers; Board of Directors, Associated General Contractors; past President, Alaska Native Contractors Association; Landfill Committee Chair, Adak Restoration Advisory Board.

COMMUNITY SERVICE

Volunteer, Alaska Native Youth Leadership Council; Anchorage School District Mentorship Program; Junior Achievement; Speaker, Small Business Development Center Women's Networking Breakfast; Trainer, Small Business Development Center; Resource Development Council; Commonwealth North; Masque Ball Chairman, Anchorage Fur Rendezvous; Volunteer Projects at Children's schools.

AWARDS AND HONORS

Golden Spike Award, Kenai Peninsula Home Builders Association, 1984; Certificate of Appreciation, U.S. Commission on Minority Business Development, 1992; Outstanding Women Business Enterprise, U.S. Coast Guard, 1994; Outstanding Sustaining Contractor, Society of American Military Engineers, 1994; Alaska Representative, President's Conference on Economic Development, 1995; Athena Award Nominee, 1995; Outstanding Contractor, U.S. Army Corps of Engineers, 1996.

FAMILY

Married, three children.

GREATEST OBSTACLES OVERCOME

Being a woman in a man's field—learning not to engage when I encounter bias, but to rise above it and conquer it.

PERSONAL GOALS

Living to see the growth and personal and business development of my children and of their children.

PROFESSIONAL GOALS

To be recognized as a professional in my field who can compete at any level, as a role model for women and minorities, and as an outstanding small business entrepreneur.

DEFINITION OF SUCCESS

Being a successful mom and a successful businesswoman.

WAYS OF DEALING WITH PRESSURE AND STRESS

Great marriage, children, cooking, sewing, gardening, boating, fishing.

ADVICE TO ASPIRING BUSINESSWOMEN

Never ever give up—you can be anything you want as long as you don't ever compromise your family, principles, ethics, integrity, and goals. Remember that you can be a successful mom and a successful businesswoman. Organize!

*W*ay back when I was in sixth grade, I knew I wanted to have my own business. We had learned the requirements for becoming president— you had to be born in the U.S., you had to be over thirty-five—and I thought, if that's all it takes, why can't I be anything I want to be?

❋

She didn't know it at the time, but Linda Henrikson would need to hold this question in the forefront of her mind as she ventured into the clearly male-dominated world of construction. Her company, Linder Construction, is her answer, and no, there's no reason she couldn't be anything she wanted.

But if there was anything she could have changed, Linda says, it was not finishing her college education, something she impresses on the younger generation through mentorship programs and speaking engagements. At the time, however, she says it made sense: "I was extremely frustrated with my education. I was working at the same time, and learning infinitely more at work than I was at school. Their examples were so theoretical, and when I was at work I was doing the real thing." With the desire to get into the business world overwhelming her, Linda left after her third year and started her career.

Linda's first job was with the National Weather Service in an office devoted to building weather stations throughout Alaska. Here, she says, she became convinced that her future was in construction. Later, she worked for an architectural firm and then a real estate company that built residential housing. Working at a bank for two years gave her a background in finance, and she started a commercial and residential construction company with her future husband. Six years later, after oil prices took a plunge, Alaska fell into a serious recession.

"People were leaving Alaska by the tens of thousands," Linda remembers. "The state was completely overbuilt." Incredibly, she was able to find her silver lining by focusing on government contracts, and founded Linder Construction as a sole proprietorship. "Because of the military presence here, government construction never felt the same depression that commercial and residential construction did. That's why I started Linder." The work was very different and demanding, and a host of new regulations demanded her attention, but now Linda also had to face new problems associated with running a woman-owned business.

Government agencies were required to make certain jobs available to women and minority-owned businesses, a benefit Linda, a Native American, is ambivalent about, but being recognized as such was a job in itself. The problem seemed to be that agencies assumed she was a front for her husband, and attempting to take advantage of set-asides. "I was turned down for every single certification I applied for," Linda says. Her appeals opened her up to "inquisitions," where she remembers being asked "all sorts of technical questions, but also what I would do if my husband died. It was just bizarre." She usually won, but her business was meanwhile growing beyond needing special assistance.

Linder Construction now employs seventy-five in the field and twenty-five in administration, and takes in over $11 million a year. With the shutdowns of military bases and the cleanup involved, environmental remediation has proven lucrative, and Linda has opened a branch in Washington State to keep the business active throughout the year. "We can't work through the winters," she says, "and employees who need to make money throughout the year can work in Washington. So we can maintain our workforce, the biggest asset this company has."

Linda's community involvement has given her a hand in standardizing policies of the Bureau of Indian Affairs toward Native American–owned businesses, developing younger women's business sense through mentoring programs, and changing perceptions about what the construction industry is and does. But while moving bureaucratic mountains, her fondest accomplishment was taking a girl into her meetings and onto her job sites for high school credit: "I feel I have to be a positive role model," Linda says. "Construction is challenging and rewarding, but participation in the trades isn't what it used to be. Children, especially girls, need to be exposed to the fact that this is a very sophisticated career choice."

Carrie Abraham Martz

President and Chief Executive Officer

The Martz Agency

Principal

Martz & Goldwater Public Relations

Scottsdale, Arizona

WORK HISTORY

1977–1979   Account Executive, Greyhound Bus Lines, Phoenix, Arizona.

1979–1980   Account Executive, Bowers & Associates, Scottsdale, Arizona.

1980–present   President and CEO, The Martz Agency.

1996–present   Principal, Martz & Goldwater Public Relations.

EDUCATION

1977   B.S. in Marketing, Arizona State University, Tempe.

FIRST JOB

Tray carrier at Bishop's cafeteria, Omaha, Nebraska.

ASSOCIATIONS AND NETWORKS

Governor, Transworld Advertising Association Network; Member, National Association of Women Business Owners.

COMMUNITY SERVICE

Honorary Chair, Sojourner Center's Capital Campaign; Board of Directors, Phoenix Suns Charities; Chairman, Home of Miracles; Member, National Charity League, Scottsdale Chapter.

AWARDS AND HONORS

Golden Heart of Business Award, *Today's Arizona Woman,* 1997; Most Distinguished Alumni Award, Arizona State University Marketing Department, 1997; Athena Award, Arizona Chamber of Commerce, 1998; Phoenix Chamber of Commerce Athena Award, 1996; Woman of Distinction Award, Chrohn's & Cloitis Foundation, 1998; World of Today and Tomorrow Award, Arizona Cactus-Pine Girl Scout Council, 1995.

FAMILY

Two children.

GREATEST OBSTACLES OVERCOME

Lack of financial expertise. Being taken seriously as a young woman when I started my business.

DRIVING FORCE

Fear has been a big driver. I grew up sharing a room with three sisters and one bathroom, and I didn't like it. As soon as I started to be able to acquire some things and have some success, I really enjoyed my new lifestyle, so I'm always afraid that if I don't continue to work as hard as I do, all this will go away or I won't be able to provide options and opportunities for my children.

DEFINITION OF SUCCESS

Balance. Having a respected business in the community. Being able to find time to contribute to that community. Bringing up your children so they are driven by strong values.

GREATEST REWARD FROM CAREER

Being recognized by the community for all that we have done for the non-profit sector in Arizona. Motivating others to follow suit and get involved. Having people know that our business isn't just about making money.

WAYS OF DEALING WITH PRESSURE AND STRESS

I surround myself with very competent people to delegate to. By being very organized. By trying not to let myself be down for too long. If I'm down for one afternoon, I work hard the next day to find something to be excited about.

ADVICE TO ASPIRING BUSINESSWOMEN

Don't expect too much in the beginning. Be patient. Listen and watch successful women around you. Always volunteer.

*R*eally, I've had a lot of blind luck, but when opportunities have been given to me, I've always said, "Yes, I can do it." I then surround myself with experts in the field, and just listen.

Carrie Martz was twenty-four, and already a refugee from corporate America, when she started her advertising agency. After a brief stint at Greyhound after college, and an even shorter-lived job at a small agency, it seemed that starting her own company was the only way to go. "I knew I didn't fit in a corporate environment. I moved a bit more quickly than they wanted," she explains. "Ever since I was very young, I'd always been creating something, and I'm probably a little hard to manage in that regard." One of the people who realized that was her last boss, who released her from her noncompetition agreement and told her she should, and had to, make it on her own.

After eighteen years of determined work and "blind luck," The Martz Agency is the fourth-largest women-owned business in the state, and among Arizona's top ten advertising firms. The Martz & Goldwater public relations offshoot is the largest PR firm in the state. Through these two entities, Carrie is able to offer full-service advertising, marketing, and publicity to her clients, which include Arizona's largest developers and the Scottsdale Convention and Visitors Bureau. She also served as marketing co-chair for Super Bowl XXX.

But as a twenty-four year-old attempting to start a business in a competitive field, Carrie had to learn not just how to make money, but to recognize when she had succeeded. Doing all her own accounting on a system new to her, she once struggled all weekend to figure out why she was $1,400 off: "I couldn't figure out what it was. I called my accountant on Monday, and he said 'That's your retained earnings. That's the money you made.'" Learning the business side was technique, but getting clients was, she says, sheer determination: "I just made sure I stayed in contact with everyone I'd met. I gave myself a guideline—ten cold calls a day. Building a client base is not a tough thing, if you're disciplined."

Carrie's first big break, however, was an exercise in confidence. Her business was in the beginning devoted to promotional items, but when a client with a start-up semiconductor company asked if she could do a brochure as well, she didn't hesitate to say yes. She completed the job by freelancing out every component, and delivered in four weeks, just in time for their trade show. They were so impressed and appreciative that they gave her their entire $250,000 advertising budget, and she was on the way to becoming a full-service agency.

Carrie isn't surprised that she and other women have made it in the advertising world: "Being female can be a distinct advantage in this business." After all, women are involved in most buying decisions, and advertisers too often repel these buyers by either portraying them as hapless housewives or flawless superwomen. Carrie's middle ground is a more realistic representation: "It doesn't necessarily affect women's self-esteem if everything isn't perfect. The to-do list doesn't get completed every day." But even as advertisers learn to cope with powerful women, Carrie sees too many successful women losing touch with themselves and other female colleagues: "We have a lot to learn about how to be better mentors," she says, "on how to support other women in leadership positions, and how to just be who we are—to accept that how we work is different."

Once in the upper echelons of Arizona's business community, Carrie started looking for ways to give back. The most noted of these was the Home of Miracles program, started in 1993 when The Martz Agency teamed up with developer Greg Hancock. Hancock built and donated with his subcontractors and suppliers a 3,300-square-foot home, which was then raffled off at $100 a ticket. The Martz Agency promoted the raffle, which raised $1.4 million for the Phoenix Children's Hospital. In 1995 the same plan brought in $1.7 million, and expectations for the 1998 raffle are around $1.6 million. Everything is donated, Carrie says, so the children's hospital gets every penny from the raffle, money they've put toward a neuroscience center and an endowment.

Not so long ago, Carrie took her first afternoon off—just left the office without telling anyone where she could be found and hit golf balls for a few hours. She remarked to a friend that she'd better not say where she'd been, but was corrected: "I was told that I have to let my employees know I have fun, because if all they can see is that working for twenty years only leads to more work, why would they want to be like me? The next time I went out to hit golf balls, I came back with my golf clothes on. There are rewards from hard work."

Kay A. Fulkerson

FINANCIAL PLANNER
AND OWNER

Swipe This, Inc.
Phoenix, Arizona

WORK HISTORY

1973–1974 Cottage Parent, Lutherbrook Children's Center, Lombard, Illinois.

1974–1976 Infant and Preschool Teacher, Chicago, Illinois.

1976–1978 Program Facilitator, Institute of Cultural Affairs, Peoria, Illinois, and Salt Lake City, Utah.

1978–1980 Trainer, Adult Education and Preschool, Institute of Cultural Affairs, Western Samoa.

1980–1982 Program Developer, Institute of Cultural Affairs, San Francisco and Los Angeles, California.

1982–1987 Director of Program Marketing, Institute of Cultural Affairs, Zambia.

1987–1993   Registered Representative, Waddell & Reed, Inc.,
Oklahoma City, Oklahoma and Phoenix, Arizona.

1993–present   Independent Financial Planner with Sun America
Securities, Phoenix, Arizona.

EDUCATION

1973   B.S. in Family Services, Eastern Illinois University, Charleston,
Illinois.

FIRST JOB

At age sixteen, arts and crafts leader for children, City of Naperville, Illinois.

ASSOCIATIONS AND NETWORKS

Past President, Board Member, Impact of Enterprising Women; Member,
past Board Member, Entrepreneurial Mothers Association.

COMMUNITY SERVICE

Assisted in Children's Walk-a-Thon fund raising; volunteer for "Christmas in
July" community renovation; "town meeting" facilitator in Utah and Southern Illinois.

FAMILY

Married, one daughter.

DEFINITION OF SUCCESS

Enjoying your life and listening to spiritual needs while accomplishing your
tasks and projects.

BUSINESS MAXIM

Integrity and honesty in all your dealings.

WAYS OF DEALING WITH PRESSURE AND STRESS

Staying organized, doing tai chi, going for walks, water aerobics, pulling up weeds in the garden, watching my daughter's sports games.

ADVICE TO ASPIRING BUSINESSWOMEN

Be persistent, pick a business you are willing to discipline yourself to do, even if you are not in the mood. Stay involved in professional and personal activities outside of your business.

FAVORITE PART OF THE DAY

Morning. It's a brand-new day.

i spend my day working with people, not so much working with numbers.

Kay Fulkerson's approach to finance is firmly rooted in her background of social service. From Chicago's West Side to Zambia, and finally to Phoenix, Arizona, Kay has chosen paths that allow her to empower others. Whether dealing with a group or an individual, Kay sees her current role as an independent financial planner as that of troubleshooter, counselor, and inspiration: "All of my experiences have trained me for being a problem solver," she says.

In 1976, Kay put her degree in family services to work with the Institute of Cultural Affairs, developing and facilitating programs in Chicago, Salt Lake City, Los Angeles, San Francisco, and Western Samoa. At each location, she worked with communities to establish their needs, helped individuals to discover a sense of self-determination, and help them act on their newly discovered power. "People too often feel victimized. They feel they're weak, that everyone else is in charge—the landlord is in charge of the house, the city's in charge of the streets. That's what we tried to change."

Kay's last assignment with the organization took her to Zambia, where she served as ICA's Director of Program Marketing. Hitchhiking from village to village with her daughter (who was only two when they arrived), she met with residents, developed a program, and helped secure funding to make their plan a reality. ICA's effort touched the lives of residents in over two hundred villages during her five-year tenure, and left a legacy of new wells, irrigation systems, schools, and a sense of self-determination.

Returning to the United States, Kay and her husband, also with ICA, found themselves in the midst of a restructuring program, and embarked on a career change. Kay began searching for a career that would be "people-related," and would allow her to continue to be of service. She obtained financial planning certification, and became a representative of Waddell & Reed Financial Services in Oklahoma City, where she found that the career change wasn't going to happen easily: "Figuring out employee benefits in third-world countries is nothing like it is in the United States," she says. But there were more challenges to come. Her husband obtained his degree in computer science, and the Fulkersons moved to Phoenix, where Kay was faced with building a new list of clients.

To keep "debt and hunger away from the door," she took up substitute teaching in Phoenix, which gave her the afternoons and weekends to drum up business. Kay attended trade shows, joined organizations, and gave seminars, leaving her card wherever she could: "Every time I'd go into a restaurant, I'd leave with a business card." After a year, she was able to cut her time substituting to just a few days a week. A semester later, she was able to devote herself entirely to financial planning. Last year, she launched Swipe This, Inc., a company devoted to helping small businesses minimize costs associated with credit cards through new equipment and financial systems.

Kay's business has grown to over one hundred clients, most of them women or women-owned businesses. She thinks this reflects the organizations she joined in the beginning, such as Impact for Enterprising Women, a local network that promotes, educates, and honors women business owners. In 1997, Kay served as president of the organization, and put forth a program to restructure the organization's goals and operations, successfully boosting membership, and cutting operating costs. Here again, her experience in working with groups and establishing their needs was essential to her success.

Still driven by a need to be of service and to help work out thorny group dynamics, Kay has embarked on perhaps her most ambitious program yet: a co-housing project in metropolitan Phoenix. If it is successful, thirty families will act together to buy land and design a community that meets all their needs. "We really would be living in a community, we'd know our neighbors, because our neighbors helped build it," Kay speculates. She sees this project, for which she has helped select land and secure a mortgage broker, as final culmination of all of her experience in business and social work, where she learned, she said, to ask the tough questions: "How do you want to live, and what value do you really place on how you live?"

Judy R. Loving

CHAIRMAN, PRESIDENT, AND CHIEF EXECUTIVE OFFICER

The Bank of Yellville
Yellville, Arkansas

WORK HISTORY

1977–1987   Teacher, Reading Specialist, Yellville-Summit School District, Yellville, Arkansas.

1987–present   Management Trainee, then Executive Vice President and Chairman, then Chairman, President, and CEO, The Bank of Yellville.

EDUCATION

1977   B.S. in Education, University of Arkansas, Fayetteville.

1982   M.S. in Education, University of Arkansas, Fayetteville.

FIRST JOB

Working in the box office in a movie theater in Coral Gables, Florida.

ASSOCIATIONS AND NETWORKS

Director, Bank Services Subsidiary and Member, Government Relations Committee, Arkansas Bankers Association; Privacy Board and past Education Foundation Trustee, American Banker Association; Board Member, Northwest Arkansas Economic Development District, Inc.; Board Member, Information Network of Arkansas; Advisory Board, State Bank Department; Board Member, Yellville-Summit School Board.

COMMUNITY SERVICE

Mid-Marion County Rotary Club; Advisory Board Member, Baxter Regional Hospital; National Kidney Foundation of Arkansas; Yellville Area Chamber of Commerce.

AWARDS AND HONORS

Top 100 Women in Arkansas, *Arkansas Business,* 1995–1998; Mid-Marion County Rotary Club Wheelhorse Award, 1996, 1997; District Service Award, National Kidney Foundation, 1995; Distinguished Service Award, Yellville Area Chamber of Commerce, 1994; Recognition of Service Award, Northwest Arkansas Economic Development District, 1993; Dedication Award, Yellville-Summit School District, 1987.

FAMILY

Four children.

GREATEST OBSTACLES OVERCOME

Most obstacles reside within myself—my strengths have a counterside and can become weaknesses which impede progress.

PERSONAL GOALS

My personal goal is to overcome my fears so that I am able to more fully participate in motherhood, in friendship, and in enjoyment of life.

DEFINITION OF SUCCESS

Success is the freedom, ability, and wisdom to create your own definition of success and to know when you've achieved it.

BUSINESS MAXIM

"What are we here for if it is not to make life less difficult for each other?"
—George Eliot

WAYS OF DEALING WITH PRESSURE AND STRESS

By remembering to nourish all aspects of yourself—keep a firm grasp of the long-term aims and purposes of your work, retain your sense of humor, eat and exercise with vigor, save time for introspection and friends.

ADVICE TO ASPIRING BUSINESSWOMEN

Face your fears.

*O*ne of my very favorite parts of this job is participating in bringing new industry, development, and progress to the community. I love to watch things change.

Marion County, Arkansas, is changing and Judy Loving thinks it's her privilege to make sure the changes are for the better. The former teacher is now Chairman, President, and CEO of the independent Bank of Yellville, and has seen enough changes in her bank and her own career that it's not surprising she can see great things for her community.

The Bank of Yellville was founded in 1946 by Bernice Berry, and experienced problems after the founder's death in 1982. Judy's husband held a percentage of the bank's shares and Judy, who held a position on the board, became increasingly fascinated with returning the institution to safety and soundness: "I started to research what was going on before I went to teach in the mornings, and when I got home I started playing with the problems again. I found that one of my strengths is asking questions, and when the answers didn't make sense, I started looking for solutions." When she shared her ideas with the board, they liked them, the State Banking Department liked them, and the board asked her to start working at the bank. "So through working and reading, I taught myself banking," Judy explains. From Management Trainee, she became Executive Vice President in 1987, and President in 1991.

No one who witnessed the turnaround can question that Judy was a banker waiting to happen. The bank was losing money in 1986. It is now in the top 25 percent of banks statewide in terms of growth and return on equity. Assets doubled between 1995 and 1998, and the bank grew from two offices to five in three counties. Working with the Yellville Chamber of Commerce and the Arkansas Economic Development Commission, she's helped develop existing industry in the area and attracted new industry to an area which is ripe for development. "I don't know what people think driving through here," Judy says. "It's not wealthy, but it's deceptive in that there's a lot of manufacturing, very low unemployment, and very low crime." A sign of change recently popped up on a local street corner—the county's first stoplight.

But another sign that things are moving forward was the successful wooing of St. Louis Music to establish a speaker and amplifier plant near Yellville. "It was thrilling to tackle each issue, piece by piece, and to see it all come together to everyone's advantage." The 50,000-square-foot plant employs over one hundred, and plans to expand even further. It's just the sort of clean manufacturing that Judy wants for Marion County: "We really don't want to see industry that will pollute the water or the air. This is a beautiful area, with mountains, rivers, and lakes, and we can't see that destroyed."

Judy credits her employees, family, and loyal customers for making her career a success, but she also recognizes the bank's founder, Bernice Berry, as a role model. Born at the turn of the century, Berry assumed her husband's check-cashing service after he died of cancer, and it evolved into Yellville's first bank in 1946. Like her eventual successor, Bernice was a self-taught banker. "I think her formal education was only to the eighth grade, but she had a lot of common sense. It's amazing how far you can go in this business just on that."

When the time came to follow in these "mighty big footsteps," Judy was, for a moment, overwhelmed: "It was intimidating at first, but you can't let role models intimidate you. You have to emulate them as best you can. I think what I learned from her, because she was so tolerant and accepting, was that I have to accept my own weak spots and keep going anyway."

Mary Jean Connors

SENIOR VICE PRESIDENT
HUMAN RESOURCES

Knight Ridder, Inc.
San Jose, California

WORK HISTORY

1974–1980   Reporter, Assistant City Editor; then City Editor,
              Cincinnati Enquirer, Cincinnati, Ohio.

1980–1988   Urban Affairs Editor, Suburban Editor, Executive Business
              Editor, then Assistant Managing Editor, Personnel,
              Miami Herald, Miami, Florida.

1988–1989   Assistant to the Senior Vice President, news and
              operations, Knight Ridder, Inc.

1989   Vice President, Human Resources, Philadelphia
              Newspapers, Inc.

1990–present Vice President, Human Resources; then Senior Vice
              President, Human Resources, Knight Ridder, Inc.

EDUCATION

1973   B.A. in English, Miami University.

FIRST JOB

Reporter, *Cincinnati Enquirer.*

ASSOCIATIONS AND NETWORKS

Society of Human Resource Management; Newspaper Personnel Relations Association; Newspaper Association of America; Senior Personnel Executives Forum; National Association of Minority Media Executives.

COMMUNITY SERVICE

United Way of Dade County Trustee; Society of Human Resources Management Board; Knight Center / Journalism Advisory Board.

AWARDS AND HONORS

Catalyst Award, Newspaper Personnel Relations Association, 1977.

GREATEST OBSTACLES OVERCOME

Self-doubt, prejudices of colleagues, others.

PERSONAL GOALS

To be supportive of my family, friends.

DRIVING FORCE

The will to excel, the desire to serve, a sense of responsibility, the desire to be a role model for other women.

DEFINITION OF SUCCESS

Making a real contribution to the company and its people.

BUSINESS MAXIM

Act with honor and truthfulness. Place principles above personalities in all dealings.

WAYS OF DEALING WITH PRESSURE AND STRESS

Keeping it in perspective, having gratitude for the wonderful things and people in my life.

ADVICE TO ASPIRING BUSINESSWOMEN

Believe in your worth. Don't derive your sense of self from others, but from doing what you think is right and honorable.

FAVORITE PART OF THE DAY

At home, in bed, with a good mystery, just before dozing off.

i think it's wonderful that women today are impatient with a world that is already so much better than the one I entered. Change doesn't happen if people don't start with today and look for something better.

Mary Jean Connors entered the workforce as a reporter for the *Cincinnati Enquirer,* and before long worked her way up to city editor. Two incidents from those days stick in her mind: "I was walking across the newsroom, and a copyeditor at the state desk yelled across the room to a copyeditor at the business desk, 'Hey, Burt, now you'll have two woman bosses, one at home and one at work.' " When she became city editor, a local station thought that this appointment was unusual enough to run a feature on her: "I'll always remember the tag line," she recalls. "It said, 'She's been City Editor for two weeks, and the paper hasn't missed an edition yet.' In that kind of environment, it takes confidence to say 'I'm in a role that's appropriate for me. I'm not a misfit,' despite what others may say or the looks you may get." Mary Jean isn't exactly sure where her confidence came from, but it must have come from a reliable source.

Later in her career, she was lucky enough to have a female role model, Janet Chusmir, then editor of the *Miami Herald,* who expanded the confidence she had acquired. "It was very liberating to work for a woman," Mary Jean explains. "I had a self-consciousness about being female around a bunch of men, while she was unabashedly female. She would even pull out a compact in the middle of a meeting and put her lipstick on—and that was shocking to me. But it was also very liberating. It was okay to have female mannerisms in a male setting and not be fearful about it."

Eight years after moving to Florida, Mary Jean had the confidence to start on a career change from the editorial side to the corporate side, even as her mentor advised against it: "People thought I was crazy, but it was a risk I felt was worth taking." By the time the transition was complete, Mary Jean had found a position devoted to what she loved best about being an editor— developing employee's careers and skills: "My interest had always been on the people development side. I love journalism, but I also love developing journalists." Now, as senior vice president of human resources, she is involved in every area of Knight Ridder's operations in addition to working out some very "thorny" issues: "A lot of what I do involves me in people's lives at interesting moments. Sometimes they're painful, but there are windows of opportunity where you can make a difference in people's lives. That's very rewarding."

Mary Jean and her immediate employees are going to have more opportunity to have an impact on people's lives in the coming year. Mary Jean is in the process of outsourcing benefits programs, which will allow the human resources department to devote more time to strategic planning. And then there's the move—in fall 1998, Knight Ridder relocated its corporate offices to the heart of Silicon Valley as part of a strategy to further develop its online services. A move on this scale always makes great demands on all departments, but none more so then human resources. Mary Jean will have her hands full of fascinating people problems long after the move is complete.

As a woman who turned a career path on its head and was still able to take it to the top, Mary Jean now advises people to take risks: "You always grow and learn when you put yourself in a new setting. You're always better for the experience and you can always move on from that." In her case, she has no doubt that the choice was the right one, leading her on to new challenges, while her original love for journalism is still fed daily: "I enjoy the newsroom and journalists—my husband is a journalist—I'm around them all the time, and my business has that as its core. I don't really feel I ever left."

Patty DeDominic

CHIEF EXECUTIVE
OFFICER

PDQ Personnel Services, Inc.
Los Angeles, California

WORK HISTORY

1972–1975   Area Operations Manager, Task Force, Los Angeles, California.

1975–1978   District Sales Trainer/Manager, Avon Products, Pasadena, California.

1975–present   Chief Executive Officer, PDQ Personnel Services, Inc.

FIRST JOB

Working part time in my father's office.

ASSOCIATIONS AND NETWORKS

Los Angeles Area Chamber of Commerce; California State Chamber of Commerce; National Association of Women Business Owners.

COMMUNITY SERVICE

Board Member, American Red Cross—Los Angeles Chapter; former Vice Chair, Los Angeles Private Industry Council; Board Member, St. Vincents Medical Center Foundation; former Board Member, Salesians Boys and Girls Club; former Board Member, Los Angeles Urban League; Board Member, Southern California Foster Family Agency; leadership positions in National Association of Women Business Owners; State and Greater Los Angeles area Chambers of Commerce; Leader, U.S. White House Conference of Small Business, 1995; Leader, U.S. Business Delegation to the United Nations Fourth World Conference on Women, 1995.

AWARDS AND HONORS

Honorable mention in the U.S. Department of Labor's "Glass Ceiling Report"; Business Woman of the Year on three separate occasions.

FAMILY

Married, three sons.

GREATEST OBSTACLES OVERCOME

Starting my own company from scratch.

PERSONAL GOALS

Balance, health, and time to enjoy family, friends, pets, and flowers.

PROFESSIONAL GOALS

To help my company grow past the $100 million mark.

DRIVING FORCE

I have a strong sense of purpose and need to achieve. I set greater goals along the way.

DEFINITION OF SUCCESS

Having plenty of options, the accomplishment of financial goals, good friends and family.

BUSINESS MAXIM

Have high integrity, tenacity, and deliver value.

GREATEST REWARD FROM CAREER

Seeing my employees develop and become financially successful, creating wonderful career options for a variety of people.

WAYS OF DEALING WITH PRESSURE AND STRESS

Seek balance, live and deal with people honestly and with integrity.

ADVICE TO ASPIRING BUSINESSWOMEN

Set high goals, surround yourself with achievement-oriented friends and colleagues, and go for it.

*i*t's really important to have a variety of resources. Those networks one establishes as one is growing up need to be continually replenished, so while it's important to keep the old advisors, it's even more important to have a continuous stream of current, state-of-the-art business resources.

PDQ Personnel Services, Inc., founded by Patty DeDominic in 1979, is itself a resource for thousands of job seekers at all levels, hundreds of temporary employees, and, of course, the corporations that take them on. So it's not surprising that the CEO would place such an emphasis on contacts, networks, and advisors as the key to survival and growth. In her case, it's been much more about growth than survival.

After eight years in business, PDQ was an $8 million company. It was already a success story, but Patty knew, looking at all the changes that had happened in the staffing industry already and looking forward to the changes that were to come, that there was an inherent danger in staying on that level. "We've had to reinvent ourselves many times over," she says. From where they started, with secretaries and office help, today PDQ offers computer systems integrators, telecommunication specialists, medical assistants, accountants, and graphic artists, just to name a few. "We are many more things to many more clients nowadays. And clients are much more discerning, so it's important to be able to be a professional partner with a client rather than simply a supplier."

Six years after the reinvention that took her over the $10 million mark, PDQ was making over $20 million a year, and in 1997, they placed more than three thousand employees. Now, Patty says, they are positioned to move beyond the state of California, and move above $100 million in sales by the end of 1999. All this started when Patty, a former trainer for Avon, was out looking for work. "As I talked to people who I felt should have been very knowledgeable about what was happening in the search business and employment services, I realized that there weren't a lot of those people who were more knowledgeable than I. It became clear to me that there was a market to start a company like mine."

With the help of a partner, personal savings, and a incubator-type relationship with an existing company, Patty launched PDQ. After only a few months they were paying rent on their small office space. Two years later, Patty took off on her own, taking out a $50,000 mortgage on her home to buy out her partner. Like so many entrepreneurs, she's had to learn along the way, and credits outside help as key to helping her move forward: "We used the best resources we could, outside professionals like CPAs, lawyers, and businesses advisors, people who have done this or similar things before."

To make sure that her employees, both the core staff and temporary employees taking assignments, are as up to date as possible, PDQ offers in-house tutorials on computer programs and systems, gets employees into outside training programs for more specialized knowledge, and works with community colleges to develop a curriculum that will give graduates the skills they need. Field employees not on assignment can use the office computers to train for their next assignment, and PDQ is in the process of co-creating a "university environment" for management development and executive training.

Policies like these, and the opportunities they have created for women and minorities, earned PDQ an honorable mention in the U.S. Department of Labor's famed "Glass Ceiling Report." Patty herself, while downplaying the importance of her gender as regards her management style, has been a key player in promoting women in business. During her two years as president of the National Association of Women Business Owners, she oversaw a period of immense growth in local chapters and members, helped form an agenda for the 1995 White House Conference on Small Business, and led the delegation for the United Nations conference on women in Beijing. This conference, she notes, was the first time the topics of women and business had ever come together on a U.N. agenda.

Giving back in this way is to Patty an integral part of doing business: "To this day," she explains, "I feel like I'm a beneficiary of a fabulous country and a great society. If I can do things that will contribute to the society or community, I will always try to do that."

Anna Garcia

PRESIDENT

ANKO Metal Services, Inc.
Denver, Colorado

WORK HISTORY

1971–1975   Gate City Steel, Denver, Colorado.

1975–1979   Reliance Steel and Aluminum, San Diego, California.

1979–1981   Reynolds Aluminum, Denver, Colorado.

1981–present   ANKO Metal Services, Inc.

EDUCATION

Coursework, San Diego School of Engineering and Drafting.

FIRST JOB

Inventory control clerk for steel distribution center.

ASSOCIATIONS AND NETWORKS

Denver Hispanic Chamber of Commerce; Denver Metro Area Chamber of Commerce; Minority Enterprises, Inc.; Colorado Women's Chamber of Commerce; Colorado 8A Association; Women's Forum of Colorado.

COMMUNITY SERVICE

Governor's Small Business Advisory Council, State of Colorado; Board of Directors, Mile High United Way; City of Denver, Mayor's Affirmative Action Advisory Council; Planned Parenthood, Rocky Mountain Region; Hispanic Women's Caucus.

AWARDS AND HONORS

Hispanic Business Woman of the Year, U.S. Chamber of Commerce, 1991; Small Business of the Year, Minority Enterprises, Inc., 1996; Business Woman of the Year, Colorado Women's Chamber of Commerce, 1998; Entrepreneurial Woman of the Year, YWCA, 1992; Excellence Award, Small Business Administration, 1995; Minority Business of the Year, The Denver Post, 1994; Distributor of the Year, Minority Enterprise Development, 1994.

FAMILY

Married, two daughters, two stepchildren, one granddaughter.

GREATEST OBSTACLES OVERCOME

Getting construction companies to take a Hispanic woman in the steel industry seriously. Obtaining credit liens with steel mills. A minority female in a male-dominated industry has double the odds against success in my business, but that's okay . . . it's just made ANKO twice as good!

PERSONAL GOALS

To continue to grow in my marriage and my relationship with my children, and to support the community where I live. As my business grows and demands less of my time, I go into schools and tell children that they matter, they are loved, and we're counting on them.

DRIVING FORCE

The desire to succeed in an industry that has only known minorities as laborers, not as executive decision makers.

DEFINITION OF SUCCESS

Sleeping at night. Knowing that, as part of your daily activities, you have done something to enrich your life and the lives of others.

BUSINESS MAXIM

Steel is not just my business, it's my heritage.

GREATEST REWARD FROM CAREER

Looking around Denver at the numerous projects ANKO has participated in and saying to my granddaughter, "We are a part of this."

WAYS OF DEALING WITH PRESSURE AND STRESS

Silent prayer. Getting down on your knees helps keep you up on your toes.

ADVICE TO ASPIRING BUSINESSWOMEN

Select a business that you have a passion for. Be prepared to SHOW UP.

*M*inorities have always been in the steel industry, as support, as laborers in the steel mills, at the blast furnaces, or operating cranes, but seldom in a management position or an executive position. I never thought when I was growing up that I would be an executive in the steel industry.

❧

Raised in Pueblo, Colorado, Anna Garcia's entire family worked in steel in some capacity, and there was little doubt that she would join them when she left high school. But it was surprising that her first job, as an inventory control clerk, put her in the office rather than on the line. It was there that Anna saw the benefits and possibilities of challenging the white and male status quo that permeated the entire industry. Six months after starting, she told her boss that she wanted to move into sales.

"My manager at that time took it very, very lightly," Anna remembers. He first told her that to become a sales person, she would first have to become familiar with the customers by working in billing. After she excelled in the billing department, he told her that she would now have to first do a stint in purchasing. "He kept putting me off," she says, knowing that this was not a normal route to sales. Finally, she was allowed to take overflow calls in the afternoon, but only if she completed all her other tasks in the morning. But she was certain, after she had built a customer base of her own, that the next opening in the sales department would be hers.

The opening arrived, and was filled by someone from outside. Anna says she had never been more frustrated; "I'd been overworked and jumped through hoops that I'd never seen anyone jump through in my entire time with the corporation. I knew something was not right." In her frustration, Anna mentioned to someone "off the cuff" that she should go to the EEOC. This idle comment found its way to corporate headquarters, and the decision makers now decided, Anna says, that she should have gotten the job. She was a salesperson within a week.

Ten years later, Anna was suddenly caught up in downsizing when her employer closed its Denver branch. Anna still had customers who still needed metals, and hit on the idea of drop-shipping materials—holding no inventory and keeping no warehouse. Her customers were so eager to keep working with Anna that they agreed to pay her ten days net, rather than the standard thirty days. With this concession, Anna had nineteen days to work with receivables as capital. It was a risky juggling act, but after being refused for a bank loan, she knew it was the only way. "My customers really did walk their talk about their dedication to minority business development," Anna says, and adds that their commitment paid off: "After eighteen months, I was able to extend net thirty days to my original customers, with a thank-you letter."

ANKO Metal Services now ships over one million tons of metal a year, and has been involved in some of Denver's highest-profile projects, including the new international airport, the Museum of Natural History, and the home of the Rockies, Coors Field. Her original customers are still with her after eighteen years, a loyalty Anna attributes to ANKO's bend-over backward approach to service. "We do business the way our customers want us to do business," she says. Her team is structured to return quotes within an hour, and will find a supplier for any request, whether it's in the database or not.

With the local community giving her so much business, Anna is determined to give back. Her employees are almost all graduates from local welfare-to-work programs who have received basic clerical training, but who are otherwise novices: "I've never hired anyone who has been a veteran of the steel industry. Everybody I hire, I hire on potential. I want individual thinkers, who haven't been in a cookie cutter–type atmosphere, which I think a lot of corporate America is."

Known at the local chamber of commerce as "Colorado's Woman of Steel," Anna is in a unique position to see the fruits of her labors all around her, and share her pride with future generations. Her granddaughter knows that the signs at the zoo, the handrail at the natural history museum, and the metal braces at the stadium came from her own family. "My goal is to make sure that our children, Hispanic children, know that there are unlimited opportunities," Anna says. "When you help build your community, even in the small way ANKO has, you get that much more strength knowing your work went into it. Twenty years ago, we didn't even have a part in that."

Laura K. Bradford

CHIEF EXECUTIVE OFFICER

Pro-Safe / Clinicovers, Inc.

Grand Junction, Colorado

WORK HISTORY

1979–1982   Real Estate Agent, Ground Junction, Colorado.

1982–1985   Medical Office Receptionist, Surgical Assistant to a
periodontist, Grand Junction, Colorado.

1985–present   Owner, CEO, Pro-Safe / Clinicovers, Inc.

EDUCATION

Colorado Real Estate Institute.

FIRST JOB

Working in a Minnesota beet field.

ASSOCIATIONS AND NETWORKS

Parent's Organization of the U.S. Air Force Academy Cadets; Junior Service
League of Grand Junction; Vice President, Republican Leadership Program

of the State of Colorado; Women's Business Network, Mesa County, Colorado; Regional Representative, Business Network of Entrepreneurial Women; Toastmaster's International.

COMMUNITY SERVICE

Appointed Member of Women's Economic Development Council by Governor Roy Romer, 1995 and 1997, appointed to Council Chair, 1998; Member, Board of Directors, Mesa County Revolving Loan Fund Administration; Board Member, President, local Swim USA club; instructor, facilitator, and mentor for the high-school age instruction program, Young Women of the West; Delegate, State House Conference on Small Business; Delegate, Western National Conference on Small Business Incubator Tenants.

AWARDS AND HONORS

Member, Rotary International Group Study Exchange Program to Southeast Asia, 1991; Toastmaster's International Regional Champion Speakers Contest, 1998; Outstanding Young Women of America, 1987; Nominated "Mother Cheerleader of the Year" by regional swim clubs, 1986; scholarship recipient, Leading in a Changing World Seminar, Daniels Leadership Institute, Daniels School of Business, University of Denver, 1998.

FAMILY

Remarried, three children.

PROFESSIONAL GOALS

To eventually sell company and pay back investors, prepare for a new career.

DEFINITION OF SUCCESS

The ability to choose what I do with each day. Being solely responsible and accountable for the achievements and failures of that day. To realize the rewards of hard work, whether that is money or self-satisfaction. To pass those values on to my employees, my mentees, and my children.

GREATEST REWARD FROM CAREER

Buying and merging an existing company into Pro-Safe. Attaining my father's respect as a successful mother and business owner.

WAYS OF DEALING WITH PRESSURE AND STRESS

Gardening, talking to Lady, my Shetland sheep dog. A really good Manhattan, made with the best possible bourbon, helps too.

ADVICE TO ASPIRING BUSINESSWOMEN

Work hard. Never give up. Read all you can to learn what you need to know. Make money *with* people, not *off* them.

*t*urning forty for me was the beginning. Now I have freedom *and* confidence at the same time.

⁂

In 1985, Laura Bradford was a receptionist at a dentist's office when opportunity appeared seemingly from nowhere. With the spread of HIV in the headlines, her boss was wondering how he could create a more sterile environment for himself, his staff, and his patients. Laura's solution, and her future, was created that night on her sewing machine when she whipped up a set of customized linen covers for her employer's equipment.

They were just what was needed, and apparently not just in that office. It wasn't long before other doctors showed interest, and some very positive words from the sales rep of a medical supply distributor finally convinced Laura that she could make it on her own.

Laura turned to the phone book for help launching Pro-Safe, and found it in the Western Colorado Business Development Corporation. They were just starting their "business incubator" program, whereby fledgling businesses could take up residency and entrepreneurs receive vital training. "They made me develop a business plan, analyze the numbers and develop cash flow projections. I hated every minute of it—and if I hadn't done it, my business wouldn't have survived," Laura said of those lessons.

They were especially helpful because Laura, who didn't attend college, spent her twenties focusing on "being a mom and raising a family," a role she filled alone. Finding a career without having a college degree was a major obstacle, but one Laura says she has overcome: "The older I get the more I think that it's not such a disadvantage. Not having a lot of stiff, academic book learning has allowed me to be very flexible and spontaneous where others might have been deterred because they knew it couldn't be done. I never knew it couldn't be done. I had a naivete about me that I think was an advantage."

Pro-Safe / Clinicovers now manufactures a wide variety and steadily changing line of covers for hard-to-sterilize medical equipment, as well as garments for hospitals and other institutions. Competition has picked up as demand for safer medical environments has increased, and Laura has found herself revisiting her niche markets to find "niches within niches." When she learned that many major suppliers were simply not producing extra-large and small-size gowns, she quickly focused on this area. When ski season is on, the local hospitals know they can count on her to rapidly fill orders for extra supplies as soon as injured skiers flood the emergency rooms. Laura has built a business on flexibility.

With her business firmly established and two of her three children out on their own, Laura has celebrated her accomplishments by establishing a fresh set of goals. After buying a related company and merging it with her own, Laura is now poised to take her company over the million-dollar mark in annual sales. She is bringing supervisors into management positions, which will allow her to get back into design, and may, in time, even sell the company in order to launch another business, career, or perhaps even a bid for public office. "I've come to realize I'm in a huge benefit period of my life," she says. "I've got everything going for me."

Brenda J. Culpepper

PRESIDENT

PepperCo Music Group
Stamford, Connecticut

WORK HISTORY

1969–1986   Started as a Clerk, left as Division Credit Manager, The Continental Group, Stamford, Connecticut.

1986–1991   Director, Corporate Relocation, Century 21 Gold Coast Realtors, Monroe, Connecticut.

1991–present   President, PepperCo Music Group.

EDUCATION

1984   *GRI* Connecticut Realtors Institute, Danbury, Connecticut.

1988   Certified Financial Analyst, New York Institute of Credit, New York City.

1989   Certified Financial Analyst, Dun & Bradstreet Institute of Credit, New York City.

Pending B.S. New York Institute of Technology, New York City.

FIRST JOB

Clerk.

ASSOCIATIONS AND NETWORKS

Past President, National Coalition of 100 Black Women, Bridgeport Chapter; former Chair, Gospel Music Executive Committee; Member, United Gospel Industry Council; National Conference of Community and Justice, Fairfield County; Chapter Leader, Edwin Hawkins Music and Arts Seminar, New England Chapter.

COMMUNITY SERVICE

Department of Social Services Regional Advisory Council; Permanent Commission on the Status of Women, Congressional District 4; Allocations Council, United Way of Eastern Fairfield County; past Vice President, Jack and Jill of America, Bridgeport Chapter; Women in Partnership Scholarship Fund—Bridgeport University; Founder, Kingdom Builders Youth Association; Policy Committee, YWCA—Greenwich, Connecticut.

AWARDS AND HONORS

Entrepreneur of the Year Award, National Association of Black Accountants; Award for Outstanding Community Service, United Way of Eastern Fairfield County; Leadership Award, National Coalition of 100 Black Women; 20 Most Noteworthy Women Award, *New Haven Business Magazine;* Woman of Distinction, *Connecticut Post;* Business of the Month, *Business New Haven;* 1994 Woman of the Year, *Connecticut Post* (first African American to receive award); Centurion Award, Century 21; Certificate of Achievement, U.S. Treasury Department, for raising the most money during a savings bond campaign; Vision Award, John P. Kee convention; Arkansas Travelers Award, awarded by then-governor Bill Clinton; Keys to City—Little Rock, Arkansas; Buffalo, New York; Dallas / Fort Worth, Texas.

FAMILY

Married, two children, one stepson.

GREATEST OBSTACLES OVERCOME

Being an African-American female in the male-dominated music business.

PROFESSIONAL GOALS

To be the "Motown" of Gospel music.

DRIVING FORCE

God.

DEFINITION OF SUCCESS

To have prevailed, not just persevered.

BUSINESS MAXIM

If the dream is big enough, the facts won't matter.

GREATEST REWARD FROM CAREER

To have impacted the lives of so many other women and teenage moms. To have been able to be a light for all to see. To have overcome adversity.

ADVICE TO ASPIRING BUSINESSWOMEN

Prevail, stay in the race. A quitter never wins and a winner never quits.

i never let my wallet go empty. I keep a crisp fifty-dollar bill—it was a two-dollar bill, now I'm up to fifty—so that feeling of lack doesn't come over me. I don't let my gas tank go below half full. Those are some of my idiosyncrasies. It's an attitude, a mind-set.

Brenda Culpepper herself thinks some of these habits are "weird," but she's not even close to giving up ways that have served her so well. It all amounts to living in the present and looking toward the future, because the past for her was a treacherous time. Brenda is now one of only two African-American women owners of gospel music labels, and has made a permanent mark in a volatile business both with established artists—such as three-time Stellar Award–winner Lucrecia Campbell and Billy Preston—and upcoming artists like Shontae Henry. At the same time, she's an involved community activist, and an inspiration to women facing the same difficulties she faced twenty-nine years ago.

Brenda was a high school senior in Queens, New York, with a full scholarship to Cornell when she made a "calculated mistake." She became pregnant at the age of nineteen and, determined to "accept responsibility for the choices I had made," had the child, took a job as a clerk for the Continental Group, married the child's father, and moved to the South Bronx. A year and a half later, she reevaluated her choices. Her husband, she says, was addicted to drugs, and the neighborhood wasn't the place to raise a child. "One day," she says, "I said enough was enough, left her father, moved back home, and started going to school at night to improve my situation." At each turn in this story, Brenda says her eyes were set ahead, never letting her mistakes drag her down: "I'm not one of those who spends a lot of energy on coulda, shoulda, woulda. I'm more of a 'next thing' person.

By the time she left her job at the Continental Group, she was a credit manager with 1,200 accounts. Along the way, she met her future husband, investment banker Irvin Culpepper, on the Long Island Railroad, and then got a job as relocation manager for Century 21. Things seemed settled, and Brenda even had a second child, something she thought she would never do. But the world had other plans: "I didn't choose the music industry," Brenda says. "It chose me."

While doing financial consulting for churches, Brenda explains, "someone said to us that we were so organized, had we ever thought of moving into the music business." Not thinking they would make any real money, they agreed to manage a concert by Tramaie Hawkins. In her band was Joel Bryant, former music director of the Stylistics and the O'Jays, who asked them to manage another concert in New York, featuring the

East Coast Regional Mass Choir. When they took the master to record companies and saw how interested they were, Brenda decided she would found her own record company instead. "Wow, did that decision change my life," she says.

This first release was a hit, landing on *Billboard*'s top twenty-five gospel chart, but Brenda was far from being home free. Even after learning firsthand the complexities and overwhelming expense of the music industry, she was unable to get an SBA loan or any backing from major labels. "They called me the one-hit wonder," she says. "So we limped along for five years without money." Paying for everything out of pocket, Brenda still managed to put out twenty-two albums, "which is supposed to be phenomenal."

Help came at first from music veterans such as former Motown producer, Frank Wilson, who serves on her advisory board. After five years, PepperCo finally showed a profit, got an SBA loan, and started getting serious offers from major labels. An inspirational video produced for the Department of Social Services, "I Believe I Can Fly," was born of Brenda's social commitment. It helped her form a film division and has been a big seller. A strategic partnership with BMG, now in the works, will complete the picture. "For the first time," Brenda says, "I can play the game for real."

These days, the only time Brenda looks back at the tough times and hard choices is when she thinks she can help someone else. An active speaker and mentor to teenage mothers, her message is that no matter what your circumstances or past mistakes, change is always possible. And once change is accomplished, the past is past.

Linda C. Drake

CHIEF EXECUTIVE
OFFICER

TCIM Services, Inc.
Wilmington, Delaware

WORK HISTORY

1973–1977   Marketing Representative, IBM, Wilmington, Delaware.

1977–1982   Vice President, Relocation Patterson-Schwartz,
Wilmington, Delaware.

1982–1984   Manager, Communications and Public Affairs, Chemical
Bank, Wilmington, Delaware.

1984–1987   Director, Corporate Relations, Blue Cross / Blue Shield,
Wilmington, Delaware.

1988–present   CEO, TCIM Services, Inc. (formerly TeleCall).

EDUCATION

1970   B.S. (magna cum laude) in education, Kent State University, Kent,
Ohio.

1972   M.A. in communications, University of Massachusetts, Boston.

FIRST JOB

Legislative researcher for the Ohio Legislative Service Commission, Columbus, Ohio.

ASSOCIATIONS AND NETWORKS

American Telemarketing Association; Direct Marketing Association; Wilmington Women in Business (Founder and President 1980–1982); Forum of Executive Women.

COMMUNITY SERVICE

Board of Directors, Mid-Atlantic Region, American Cancer Society; Board of Directors, Delaware State Chamber; Board of Directors, United Way of Delaware; Honorary Co-chairman, Juvenile Diabetes of Delaware Monopoly Tournament, 1999; Board of Directors, Family Business Council, University of Delaware; Treasurer, Mid-Atlantic Chapter American Telemarketing Association (ATA) 1990–1992; Co-chairman National Conference ATA 1992.

AWARDS AND HONORS

Delaware Alliance for Professional Women Trailblazer Award, 1983; Delaware Women's Hall of Fame nominee, 1984; Entrepreneurial Woman of the Year, State of Delaware, 1994; Blue Chip Enterprise Initiative Award, 1994; Delaware Valley Entrepreneur of the Year, Finalist for Service Organization, 1996.

FAMILY

Married, two children.

GREATEST OBSTACLES OVERCOME

Only one: fear of failure.

PERSONAL GOALS

World travel, to become a pilot, to learn conversational Italian, to continue to support my community.

PROFESSIONAL GOALS

To double the size of our existing business in the next five years.

DEFINITION OF SUCCESS

It's a different definition than ten years ago. Success in middle age looks like balance: balance between financial freedom and personal freedom.

GREATEST REWARD FROM CAREER

Observing and experiencing the development of loyal employees. Financial freedom.

ADVICE TO ASPIRING BUSINESSWOMEN

"You are your deepest driving desire. As your desire is, so is your will. As your will is, so is your deed. As your deed is, so is your destiny."

*W*hat I like about this business is that where you stand is highly measurable. It involves a lot of people, a lot of activity, and a lot of intensity. In the end, I was drawn to it because it is the business that is most like myself.

Working as a marketing executive for companies such as IBM, Chemical Bank, and Blue / Cross Blue Shield was certainly active and intense, but Linda Drake always harbored an independent streak and dreams of running her own show. Finally, a situation arose at her last job where she knew that her career within a particular company had reached a dead end. "My husband looked at me," she remembers, "and said, 'If you're ever going to do this, you're going to do it now.' " With that, she founded TeleCall in 1988 with forty ordinary telephones and three full-time employees.

The activity and intensity now took on a new meaning: "I had leveraged both my home and my kids' education," Linda says, "and that's what I saw written behind my eyes every day. I had no choice but to be successful." Success came, but it didn't happen overnight. Depending on just one client for 80 percent of her business put Linda's start-up close to the edge for the first few years. But sticking with that client, and serving it well, allowed both companies to grow. Ten years later, Linda's company has a new name, eleven locations, over three thousands employees, and a track record that draws clients from the Fortune 1000 to her door.

TCIM has evolved from a "simple" telemarketing services company into a highly complex and dynamic service. "It used to be that you could simply present something to a customer or receive a call on behalf of a company. Things have changed," Linda explains. "Now corporations are trying to augment what they're doing through by-products of the selling process." TCIM uses each contact with a customer—and Linda says they've interfaced with over 100 million of them—to develop and refine their database, and results are available to clients every morning. So selling is often research, and research directs their sales efforts. "What we're trying to do," Linda says, "is make the most out of every interaction and extract the most value for the client and customer from each contact."

As TCIM is getting to know its customers on a massive scale, Linda says there's even more value in getting to know her employees on a personal level: "There are people who work for us who will see us through, and have, in good times and bad. That loyalty not only emanates from rewarding people financially, but from having a sensitivity to who they are and caring for them as a whole person." Linda is especially proud to be in a business that employees can easily transition into after a layoff, during college, or as any form of reentry into the workforce. As she told a group of telemarketing executives, "The communication skills they acquire in the industry training programs will serve them well throughout life, in future jobs, in parenting, in any of life's many communication challenges."

In 1978, Linda felt she was facing a communications challenge of a different sort. While she watched local business clubs and organizations repeatedly vote to exclude women, she became frustrated over being denied access to networking. At the same time, she says, "I was in a position where I was calling on many local corporations and meeting these phenomenal women who had no way of coming together other than for dinner after work or a lunch. There was no connection." So Linda founded Wilmington Women in Business. As women's role in business and the community has evolved, so has this organization: "We now have all kinds of offshoots—a mentoring group, a women entrepreneurs group, a corporate group, a women in transition group, all kinds of fabulous subgroups that have started as a reflection of our times."

With so much success in selling the products of others, Linda is looking into diversifying her company by developing products of its own. It may be an unusual approach, but she says it's clearly a fit: "We have an absolutely fine-tuned distribution system, and it clearly needs to be matched with our own product at some time in the future." That product is undecided, but regardless of the changes her company will experience, Linda asserts she will never diverge from her original passion for this business: "I love clients," she says. "I love being able to serve and serve well."

Laurie Silvers, Esq.

PRESIDENT

Big Entertainment, Inc.

Boca Raton, Florida

WORK HISTORY

1983–1989   Co-owner, CEO, Flagship Cable Partners, Boca Raton, Florida.

1981–1989   Partner, Rubenstein & Silvers, Boca Raton, Florida.

1989–1992   Co-founder, CEO, The Sci-Fi Channel, Boca Raton, Florida.

1993–present   President, Big Entertainment, Inc.

EDUCATION

1974   B.A., University of Miami.

1977   J.D., University of Miami School of Law.

FIRST JOB

Assistant programmer at a radio station.

ASSOCIATIONS AND NETWORKS

Member, Economic Council of Palm Beach County.

COMMUNITY SERVICE

Board of Directors and Board of Advisors, Pine Crest Preparatory School; former Member, Executive Advisory Board, School of Business of Florida Atlantic University.

AWARDS AND HONORS

Co-Business Person of the Year, City of Boca Raton, Florida (with partner and husband Mitchell Rubenstein), 1992.

FAMILY

Married, three children.

PERSONAL GOALS

I never want to lose the ability to be the person I am. I never want to do anything that would compromise my values, or what I think is right.

PROFESSIONAL GOALS

To identify industries that are growth-oriented, and figure out how I could get in and make a difference—how I could change the landscape. That is the only thing I want to do.

MENTORS

I've had quite a few mentor-like situations early in my career, although I've never had a traditional mentor. I've always tried to learn from the people I've met and worked with, especially from those people who have gone out of their way to help me along. I like to think that I have learned something from the professional men and women with whom I have worked and I hope to be able to pass some of that knowledge on to others. One of my goals, as a businesswoman, is to be a role model for young women.

WAYS OF DEALING WITH PRESSURE AND STRESS

When I'm under stress, I try to identify and work toward definite goals. I identify what has to be done, prioritize, and go after it.

*t*he people that I deal with exist in such a creative world. They create all the time. They create entire worlds, entire universes. I'm humbled before talent like that.

Laurie Silvers is in the midst of building a very innovative business—Big Entertainment. Established in 1993, it's only the latest chapter in a powerful partnership with her husband, Mitchell Rubenstein. This couple, who once gave us the Sci-Fi Channel, now works with products and projects from authors like Anne McCaffrey, Arthur C. Clarke, Gene Roddenberry, Isaac Asimov, Leonard Nimoy, and Mickey Spillane.

Combining her background in the cable industry with her background and training in intellectual property law, Laurie is constantly in the market for ideas. Many of her authors, she says, come to her with an idea or a character that they have been either too busy or two distracted to fully develop. "What we do best," Laurie says, "is build relationships and create products based on that relationship." The products can be as varied as the idea will allow. So far they include television miniseries, movies, toys, books, comic books, video games, and new media formats. Now Laurie is aggressively moving her company into the emerging realm of e-commerce.

The e-commerce division, she says, "is as exciting, if not even more exciting than the early days of cable television. There are daily opportunities here to do great, great things in an environment that did not even exist five years ago." She has the perspective to know whereof she speaks: her father, Gordon Sherman, was a broadcaster and "cable pioneer" at a time in the industry when "cable was perceived to only be the solution to help bring broadcast signals to televisions with poor reception." With this pioneering spirit in her blood, Laurie ran several cable companies with her husband. The pair then embarked on a project with a real future, in more ways than one—the Sci-Fi Channel.

Laurie says she entered this project as a businesswoman and not as a science fiction fan, but exposure to the brightest lights in the genre brought her around: "I had an opportunity to meet creative people like Gene Roddenberry and Isaac Asimov, and those encounters made me a huge fan." Both aficionados and viewers with a tangential interest in science fiction were drawn to the channel, which Laurie and her husband later sold to USA Networks. The relationships they formed while building the channel were instrumental in the creation of Big Entertainment.

In a company built on relationships, Laurie's most important relationship is the one she shares with her business partner and husband. They've been in business together for seventeen years. "We've been doing this a long time," Laurie says, "and unquestionably we had a learning curve on how to separate business from our personal relationship. I think you need to learn to shut down the business side, just like you would when you're leaving the office." Not that business doesn't get discussed outside the office, Laurie explains, it comes up just as it would in any home where both parties work. But there are special requirements of both partners in order to make this happen: "There has to be mutual respect and very little competition. Both parties have to have very strong egos and have to be very confident in what they do."

In a forward-looking and diverse company like Big, driven by talented and creative authors, Laurie has also learned to temper her confidence with modesty in the presence of genius. She says its a requirement of the job: "Working with some of the major creative figures of our time, such as Gene Roddenberry and Isaac Asimov, is a very humbling experience. I'm not only not in the same ballpark with these men, I'm not even sure I'm on the same planet." At the same time, she seems to have found a comfortable place between these alternate universes and the business world: "I consider myself lucky to be a part of all this."

Rebecca Graham Paul

PRESIDENT AND CHIEF
EXECUTIVE OFFICER

Georgia Lottery Corporation
Atlanta, Georgia

WORK HISTORY

1978–1985   Community Affairs Director/Account Executive, WICS-
TV, Springfield, Illinois.

1985–1987   Director, Illinois Lottery, Chicago, Illinois.

1987–1991   Inaugural Secretary, Florida Lottery, Tallahassee, Florida.

1991–1992   Director of Lottery Consulting Services, Ernst & Young,
Tallahassee, Florida.

1992–1993   President, Strategic Support Associates, Inc., Tallahassee,
Florida.

1993–present President and CEO, Georgia Lottery Corporation.

EDUCATION

1970   B.S. in education, Butler University, Indianapolis, Indiana.

1974   M.S. in education, Butler University.

FIRST JOB

Gymnastics coach.

ASSOCIATIONS AND NETWORKS

Past President, National Association of State and Provincial Lotteries; past President, International Association of Lotteries.

COMMUNITY SERVICE

Board of Directors, Georgia Chamber of Commerce; past Board Memberships include: Aid to Retarded Citizens; American Heart Association; Butler University Alumni Board; Illinois Governor's Council on Health and Fitness; Indiana Society for Prevention of Blindness; Sangamon Valley Red Cross; Sangamon County Teenage Substance Abuse Council; Springfield Ballet Company; United Way.

AWARDS AND HONORS

Keough Award for Marketing Excellence, *Georgia Trend Magazine* 1993; Marketer of the Year, Stanford Business School Alumni Association 1994; Georgian of the Year, Georgia Association of Broadcasters 1998; Peter O'Connel Lifetime Achievement Award, Public Gaming Research Institute 1998.

FAMILY

Married.

GREATEST OBSTACLES OVERCOME

Being a woman in male-dominated industries.

PERSONAL GOALS

To stay healthy so I can enjoy the rest of my life.

DRIVING FORCE

My mother and my husband. My desire to succeed.

DEFINITION OF SUCCESS

Having a career in which you are respected by your peers and having a happy, healthy family.

BUSINESS MAXIM

Stay focused on where you've been and where you're going.

GREATEST REWARD FROM CAREER

Sending students to college on lottery scholarships, students who might not otherwise have been able to go. That is the ultimate reward.

WAYS OF DEALING WITH PRESSURE AND STRESS

Knowing that all storms will pass and nothing is usually as bad as it seems.

ADVICE TO ASPIRING BUSINESSWOMEN

Be confident. So many young women lack confidence, but have the ability to do what they want. Don't be afraid to be yourself!

*t*he programs we fund really make a difference in people's lives, and make me feel great about getting up in the morning and coming to work. At the same time, I have the challenges of managing what would be a Fortune 500 company.

Georgia's state lottery, started in 1993 with Rebecca Graham Paul as President and CEO, has become a model for other state lotteries, not only in terms of how the money is raised but in how the money is spent. Georgia high school students with a B average are guaranteed a full college scholarship, as long as they stay in Georgia. Ninety-seven percent of the 1997 University of Georgia freshman class is on lottery funding. Every four-year-old in Georgia is eligible for a prekindergarten program funded by the lottery. Every Georgia classroom is being wired to every other classroom in the state through computers and satellite dishes, all on lottery funds. "Nothing," Rebecca says, "has changed education this much in Georgia since the G.I. Bill."

As President and CEO, Rebecca's job is to make sure that money will continue to be there, and if her past successes are anything to go by, the lottery will only continue to grow. From the time she was asked to build the new company, the Georgia Lottery has exceeded all expectations, setting a record for the most successful state lottery start-up ever, passing the original goal of $463 million in sales in just five months, and finishing the first year with $1.13 billion in sales. So far, this success has translated into a $2.7 billion return for the State of Georgia's educational programs. Each year only gets better.

Rebecca was working for an NBC affiliate in Illinois when she was introduced to the lottery industry by the Governor of Illinois. As the Republican State Chairwoman, she had known the Governor for some time, and he was already familiar with her management and marketing skills. With no direct experience, but plenty of confidence, she quit her job, resigned her post, and became Director of the Illinois State Lottery. "If I had known then how little I knew, I would have been scared," Rebecca remembers, "but I was young enough that I thought I could do anything." The folly of youth was never better placed: sitting in the Director's chair less than two years, Rebecca oversaw record sales of $1.34 billion.

After serving as secretary in the Florida Lottery, followed by two years on the private side of the industry, Rebecca was asked to take on the challenge of running Georgia's new lottery. The statewide referendum had passed by an extremely narrow margin, and she was being asked to build the company from scratch in five months, with no appropriation from the state legislature. In a state with no previous lottery, there was the problem of finding employees with experience. Finally, there was Rebecca's concern over whether she was the politically correct choice when the Governor and a majority of the legislature were Democrats. "When the Board offered me this job, I said, 'You can't hire me. I'm a Republican.' They looked at me like I was from Mars, and asked, 'Why would we care how you vote? You know how to start a lottery.' "

The Georgia Lottery is a state instrumentality, rather than a state agency. Rebecca explains, "I report to a seven-member Board of Directors, just like I would do if this were a private company. The only difference is that our profits go to defined educational programs in the State of Georgia." Rebecca took some new strategies to this new lottery, introducing scratch cards before introducing the lotto and taking advantage of new technologies that speeded up sales and made the games more entertaining. It was an example of shrewd marketing and teamwork among lottery employees, vendors, and suppliers, but to Rebecca, it means more than that: "People who work here know that they make a difference. You can speak with pride in Georgia when you tell somebody you work for the lottery. You're making kids' lives better."

The former Miss Indiana (and very nearly Miss America) also gets to meet the other beneficiaries of the lottery—the winners. But unlike the lives of children that the lottery dollars are changing, she says that the winners' lives are surprisingly unaltered. For example, the lawyer who won $30 million agreed to do a press conference, but only if he could keep it down to fifteen minutes. He had to meet with a client. As she often remarks during her speeches, "If you shopped at Kmart before you won, you probably still will. You just won't look for the blue light specials."

Jane Edwards Shivers

PARTNER/DIRECTOR

Ketchum Public Relations
Atlanta, Georgia

WORK HISTORY

1980–1985   President, Shivers Communications, Atlanta, Georgia.

1985–present   Partner, Ketchum Public Relations.

EDUCATION

1965   B.A. in American Studies, University of Maryland, College Park.

FIRST JOB

Reporter, Williamson County Sun, Georgetown, Texas, while in high school.

ASSOCIATIONS AND NETWORKS

Board of Directors, Atlanta Chamber of Commerce, Georgia Chamber of Commerce, Peachtree Club and Crown Crafts, Inc.; Fellow, International Society of Business.

COMMUNITY SERVICE

Board Member of the Woodruff Arts Center, Emory School of Public Health, The Alliance Theatre, and Central Atlanta Progress. Board of Councilors, Carter Center; past Commissioner, Governors Commission on Economy and Efficiency in State Government.

AWARDS AND HONORS

PRSA Order of Phoenix, 1993; Georgia Hall of Fame, 1993; George Goodwin Award for public service, 1997; "100 Most Influential Georgians," *Georgia Trend,* 1998. Ketchum Atlanta has won five Silver Anvils from the Public Relations Society of America and 75 other industry awards.

FAMILY

Two children.

GREATEST OBSTACLES OVERCOME

My own self-doubts.

PERSONAL GOALS

To have time, time, time. To travel, for my sons and my friends, and to continue to give back through community service.

PROFESSIONAL GOALS

To continue to grow what is now the largest PR agency in the south. To continue to diversify. To continue to attract smart, talented people.

DEFINITION OF SUCCESS

Being rewarded for doing what I love and what matches my innate abilities. Having a well-rounded life of family, friends, hobbies, and sports.

BUSINESS MAXIM

Treat people as I want to be treated.

GREATEST REWARD FROM CAREER

Working in the agency business and being surrounded by high-energy, smart young people. It is never, ever boring.

WAYS OF DEALING WITH PRESSURE AND STRESS

Keeping a sense of humor helps. Regular exercise and dancing. Having many friends and colleagues who are good sounding boards.

ADVICE TO ASPIRING BUSINESSWOMEN

Focus. Don't be overly sensitive and uptight. Only take jobs that utilize your true abilities and aptitudes. Respect your boss and co-workers. Be sure to have a life.

I'm just not happy if I don't have a set of problems to solve. In this business, I get them—new clients with new opportunities, old clients with new challenges. That keeps a mind like mine busy.

When Jane Shivers took her first job in public relations, it didn't go by that name. She says she didn't even know what she was applying for: "I'd heard of this little college program called Semester at Sea, and I just had to work there, so I marched in and said, 'Hello, I'm here to get a job.' " She was immediately told they didn't have anything for her on their floating classroom, so she waited in the hall for six hours. Finally the director came out to see who was "causing all the trouble," and asked her what she could do. "The only thing I knew how to do was write press releases," Jane says, "and he asked, 'Well, why didn't you say so?' " He introduced her to the director of information and she was hired on the spot.

Jane took a lesson in determination from that day: "I've always thought that was a good technique. I've hired many a person who's just chased me down." Since then, she's had to hire many a person. Her small advertising and PR firm was joined with the global Ketchum Public Relations in 1985, and she's made her branch the largest PR company in the south, with $13 million in billings and over 130 employees. She oversees Ketchum's Miami, Dallas, and half-dozen Latin American offices, and throughout her career has watched public relations grow from an obscure discipline into a necessity: "In the time I've been in the business, there's been a general recognition that public relations is real. I still have to explain what we do, but at least now I don't have to explain to clients that they need it."

At age thirteen, "back in the days of cold type and cut-and-paste," Jane started writing for her local Texas paper. "As I grew up," she remembers, "I thought I was going to be the next Bob Woodward, so I went to the University of Maryland near Washington, D.C., where I thought it was all happening." After traveling in Europe she relocated to California to help a relative and worked with an ABC affiliate before she found a home for her skills on the high seas. Then, after working for four L.A. area weeklies, she married and moved to Atlanta.

Jane worked briefly for the Atlanta Arts Alliance before she was asked to build a public relations division in an existing advertising agency. "Then, in 1985," Jane recalls, "everyone in the northeast woke up and discovered there was a place called Atlanta." She was contacted by three national organizations looking to bring her company into their fold, and Jane had a sense that the future lay with global firms: "I had a premonition that being part of a larger agency was the way to go. I saw more reach for our clients and more opportunities for our staff, and my instincts were right. I've never regretted it for even one instant." Beyond the growth possibilities, Jane saw a sincere synergy between her and Ketchum's corporate culture: "Culture is everything. If that isn't a fit, your life will be miserable."

Jane says she was prepared for the new demands on her management skills that arrived with becoming a branch of Ketchum. Her travels alone and with Semester at Sea had given her a global perspective, while her motherhood had brought her back to the here and now: "Being a mother was probably as good a training as a lot of the management courses I've taken. It makes the rest of this look easy." While working on a global level, "dealing with our people in Hong Kong as much as with someone down the hall," Jane volunteers on a local level, with business and arts organizations committed to sustaining Atlanta's rebirth.

But Jane's favorite part of the job are those occasions when her business sense meets her civic sense. In her field, she says, the two can come together in unexpected ways. "We do a lot to hook up our clients with health or education programs that need a boost. It's an amazing part of our business, when you can use your skills to do something that really improves society, and see the for-profit and nonprofit worlds come together in a way that helps everybody."

Pam Chambers

OWNER AND PRESIDENT

Pam Chambers & Associates
Honolulu, Hawaii

WORK HISTORY

1975–1980   Manager, San Francisco Branch, Actualizations, Inc., San Francisco, California.

1981–1990   Director, Winner's Circle Breakfast Club, Honolulu, Hawaii.

1985–present   Owner and President, Pam Chambers & Associates.

EDUCATION

1972   B.A. in English Literature and Communication Disorders, San Francisco State University, California.

FIRST JOB

Working on an assembly line at age sixteen with twenty other women of all shapes, sizes, values, numbers of teeth, and musical tastes. We made cassette tapes. I was the one who inserted the tiny square sponge that holds the tape in place.

ASSOCIATIONS AND NETWORKS

Sales and Marketing Executives of Honolulu; Chamber of Commerce of Honolulu; Rotary Club of Honolulu.

COMMUNITY SERVICE

Board Member, Winners' Camp (for teenagers); Editor, newsletter of the Sales & Marketing Executives of Hawaii; frequent gratis speeches for not-for-profit organizations.

AWARDS AND HONORS

Two-time recipient, The First Lady Volunteers of the Year Award; Runner-up, Hawaii's Toastmasters Speech Contest, 1987.

FAMILY

Two sons.

PERSONAL GOALS

To have the best relationship possible with my boys. To continue to live with integrity, to respect myself always.

DRIVING FORCE

The desire to bring out the best in others.

BUSINESS MAXIM

Discover what you love to do and find a way to make it beneficial to others.

GREATEST DOWNSIDE TO CAREER

Having no "security." I don't get a paycheck, I have no pension plan. Everything depends on others believing in me. My reputation is everything. I have to "walk my talk."

WAYS OF DEALING WITH PRESSURE AND STRESS

Searching the thrift stores to find the perfect men's tuxedo shirt for $3.50. By reading *Simple Abundance* when everyone else is working. By listening to Vivaldi at six A.M. or midnight. By reminding myself that I chose this life.

ADVICE TO ASPIRING BUSINESSWOMEN

Discover your unique talents and gifts. Serve others. Keep the faith.

*I*n my line of work, I get to see diamonds in the rough, show people a reflection of what they could be, and help them experience that. And I get to do it in a way that is visible to everybody. Everyone sees the transformation.

Part motivational speaker, part counselor, and part critic, Pam Chambers works on her clients' fears of public speaking. It's not an easy task—surveys repeatedly place speaking to groups at the top of people's personal horrors. "Drowning is something like number three, and public speaking is number one. Snakes and spiders and such are way down the list," says Pam. So business has been good: since she hung up her own shingle in 1985, Pam has built a client list, mostly from word of mouth, that includes many of Hawaii's major financial institutions, the Army Corps of Engineers, GTE Hawaii, Chevron, and even a submarine tour company. In her spare time, she's written four books based on her training seminars, the last of which made the regional bestseller list. She's done it all from home, and never looked back:

"I am so grateful that I can do what I want to do, work from home, and get paid for it. I can't have it any other way at this point."

Pam works with regularly scheduled open seminars, corporate clients, and individuals, but what her students go through is remarkably similar. There are often tears and jitters at the beginning, followed by a building of self-confidence, and finally, an ironing of rough points. Even those experienced with public speaking can learn something from this training, according to Pam. There was, for example a minister who automatically put his hand in his pocket whenever he mentioned monetary gifts to the church. His bold goatee, Pam says, probably wasn't the right choice for a man of his profession. His rhetorical questions lost their impact, she claims, when he failed to pause to give his congregation a chance to reflect. Like many other public speakers, he had no one to tell him about these little details. "And I cover everything," says Pam. "If somebody has body odor, I even have to tell them that."

Although she was lured into a training job out of a speech pathology M.A., Pam claims she was once "terrible" at public speaking. Since she was working for a company that provided seminars for "personal and professional growth," she had to train herself in public speaking very quickly. Five years later, she realized two things after a trip to Hawaii. First, that she had gone about as far as she could in her company, and second, that although she had always thought of herself as a "city girl," Hawaii was where she wanted to live. With nothing but a dozen boxes, she and her future husband settled in Hawaii. The transition to paradise wasn't all smooth. "It's like another country, the culture is so different. And sometimes mainland people are perceived as know-it-alls, with mainland ideas that they want to cram down local people's throats. You really have to prove yourself before people will listen."

So it's quite an accomplishment, she notes, that she now gets paid to teach people how to get others to listen to them. The greatest transformation Pam witnessed was the massage therapist who had broken down in tears during her first public speaking class, only to give a direct and inspiring talk in her last class while passing out her business cards. Pam says she lives for results like this: "I hope I'm able to give people access to a part of themselves that's lying dormant, and show them how to use it. It's a great sense of satisfaction to be able to be a part of that, and to see more beauty and expertise around me because of that contribution."

Carol Gerber Allred, Ph.D.

PRESIDENT / DEVELOPER

Positive Action Company

Twin Falls, Idaho

WORK HISTORY

1972–1981   High School Teacher, Twin Falls School District, Twin Falls, Idaho.

1977–1981   Director of Special Programs, Twin Falls School District, Twin Falls, Idaho.

1982–present   President, Positive Action Company.

EDUCATION

1971   B.A. in English and psychology, Brigham Young University, Provo, Utah.

1980   M.Ed., College of Idaho (now Albertson College), Caldwell, Idaho.

1984   Ph.D. in educational administration and psychology, Brigham Young University, Provo, Utah.

FIRST JOB

High school teacher.

ASSOCIATIONS AND NETWORKS

Advisory Board Member (1987–1989), Western Center for Drug-Free Schools; Governor Appointee (1979–1983), Idaho Commission for Children and Youth; Association for Supervision and Curriculum Development; National Association for Elementary School Principles; American Association for Career Education; American Association of School Administrators; American Counseling Association; American Psychological Association.

AWARDS AND HONORS

Idaho Governor's Award for developing an exemplary program for alcohol and drug abuse prevention, 1981.

FAMILY

Three sons.

DRIVING FORCE

The dream that the goals of the community and school can be wider.

DEFINITION OF SUCCESS

Feeling good about who you are and what you're doing.

GREATEST REWARD FROM CAREER

Visiting the schools we've served and knowing that there are hundreds of thousands of kids out there whose lives are improved as a result of what we do.

WAYS OF DEALING WITH PRESSURE AND STRESS

I recognize it and take some downtime. The best thing for me to do is get rested and then get involved in something creative. I also see a massage therapist regularly.

ADVICE TO ASPIRING BUSINESSWOMEN

You have to persist. You just have to keep taking the next step. Don't quit until there are no more steps to take.

*t*he big picture is that we're creating a more positive society, but most of the time I'm thinking about how to solve this or that problem, how to get this work done, and how to make the best decision. Then, seeing the results, I know I have to keep going.

The results, Carol Allred says, are more attentive students, improved test scores, grateful teachers, and appreciative parents. Carol's Positive Action Company is devoted to promoting a program used by schools to teach life skills, character, and values to students. So far, seven thousand schools have adopted her program, and they depend on Carol's company to supply curriculum materials and consulting.

Teaching high school English and psychology in Twin Falls, Idaho, Carol thought something was missing: "I felt like our graduates weren't quite prepared for life, for becoming successful and reaching their goals. I thought these were things we should be teaching them, in addition to English, math, and science." She started collecting her ideas into a curriculum, and finally got permission to start an elective class in "Positive Action." The students responded enthusiastically. "We could never add enough sessions," Carol says. "Every semester we would add more, but it was never enough." Before long she was approached by the governor's office and asked if she could adapt her program to catch kids' attention at a younger age.

Positive Action is a comprehensive method with a very simple premise. Actions influence feelings, which develop thoughts, which then direct actions. Injecting positive actions—whether directed at one's self or the community—into this cycle gives children not only a sense of self-esteem, but a sense of responsibility. "As you incorporate these skills into your life," Carol explains, "you gain control over areas of your life. So the students are empowered, and gain a good sense of the consequences when they choose negative actions." The program goes far beyond the individual, according to Carol. "It creates a climate of encouragement and friendliness. In that kind of environment, children thrive and learn. When they're learning, teachers do a better job. They're not dealing with management issues and discipline all the time. The kids are able to manage themselves."

The program, however, isn't just directed at the children. Schools that adopt Positive Action make a commitment to involving parents, teachers, and administrators, and allow the idea to touch every part of the organization. "Positive Action totally restructures the school," Carol says, "and organizes everyone into the activities and philosophy. It's asking for a lot, but it's easy to do, it's all pretty commonsense, and it works." Carol points to an independent study, commissioned by the Idaho governor's office, that showed not only dramatic improvement in test scores after implementation of the program but also a marked drop in discipline referrals and absenteeism in each school studied. These secondary effects are more to Carol than icing on the cake: "The point is that this works for just about everything you are trying to do in a school."

Carol developed and refined this method through her tenure at the Governor's Commission for Children and Youth, and through her doctorate. All the while, she was starting her company as a nonprofit with federal funds. She soon found, however, that she could get much more accomplished as a private company: "It's so much easier to get decisions made and move forward. You don't get caught up in the bureaucracy." Further streamlining her organization, Carol opted to buy her own printing equipment, rather than continue to outsource her rather large manuals and kits. "It got to be such a headache—contracting everything out and losing that control. I finally thought there had to be an easier way." Now she has a full printing company, including a four-color press and a bindery.

Positive Action had already been adopted by schools in Russia, Germany,

Egypt when Carol was invited to present her program to the United Nations Fourth World Conference on Women in Beijing. Taking her idea beyond the national borders is a natural step for Carol, who says, after returning from one school's celebration of ten years with her program, "Every child deserves to be in a Positive Action school. I just have to keep going and make it happen for as many kids as I can."

Suzanne Locklear

OWNER AND FOUNDER

Suzanne's Sensational Foods
Boise, Idaho

WORK HISTORY

1975–1982   Flambé Captain, Waitress, various restaurants and
locations.

1978–1980   Art Salesperson, Monterey, California.

1984–1985   Furniture Salesperson, Boise, Idaho.

1986–1993   Auto Salesperson, Boise, Idaho.

1993–present   Owner and Founder, Suzanne's Sensational Foods.

EDUCATION

Continuing education at local colleges.

FIRST JOB

Burger King, so I started in foods, in a way.

ASSOCIATION AND NETWORKS

Member, National Women's Business Council; Member, Idaho Specialty Foods Association.

COMMUNITY SERVICE

Member, National Breast Cancer Coalition; Co-President, Idaho Breast Cancer Coalition; Member, National Association of Breast Cancer Organizations; Volunteer, Cancermount program, American Cancer Society.

AWARDS AND HONORS

Best New Product, Idaho Specialty Foods Association, 1994; Governor's Marketing Award, 1994.

FAMILY

Married, three children.

GREATEST OBSTACLES OVERCOME

That's easy: getting through breast cancer twice. That helps my perspective when a trucking shipment is lost and things go haywire. I can always be thankful that I'm alive and healthy.

DRIVING FORCE

To do everything in my power to help people face the terror and confusion of cancer diagnosis.

BUSINESS MAXIM

Prayer, persistence, and a positive attitude.

GREATEST REWARD FROM CAREER

The lives I have touched. Being featured in *Portraits of Hope,* along with cancer survivors Nancy Reagan, Betty Ford, Julia Child, and Bella Abzug.

WAYS OF DEALING WITH PRESSURE AND STRESS

In stressful times I use exercise and quiet talks with God. In these conversations I pray for the strength and grace to use wisely the gifts He has given me.

ADVICE TO ASPIRING BUSINESSWOMEN

Look carefully before you leap. If you make a decision to do it, jump off the cliff running.

i really didn't have any expertise in this field; I never even thought I would start a business. It was just a dream built out of passion.

Suzanne Locklear was thirty-one when she was jarred from her average life by breast cancer: "Before the diagnosis, I was going about my life in a very simple manner, raising my children and working every day. I wasn't much involved in the community." The last thing on her mind was selling the salad dressing she enjoyed preparing for her family. Today it's not only her livelihood, but a medium for Suzanne's message—eat right, be aware, intervene early.

Suzanne's first round with breast cancer changed everything. "My entire life dissolved at that point," she says. "My marriage fell apart, I lost my home because we didn't have medical insurance, I lost my job because I was having radiation treatments every day." When it was all over, as she recovered her health she found that although she had been living an average life, she was not an average person: "I rebuilt my life very quickly. I got an excellent job in sales the day after I finished my last radiation treatment. I met a wonderful man who would become my new husband." She shared the strength she discovered as a volunteer counselor with the American Cancer Society and found more rewards in life than she had known before.

This made the second diagnosis even more stunning. "It was really a thunderbolt," she says. "This was it, it was not a dress rehearsal. I knew then that I wanted to make more of a difference in the lives of others." This diagnosis was far more serious, but Suzanne continued counseling, exercising, and reading up on nutrition. "I learned what an important part eating right can play, so I began to hatch a plan as I was doing my walking of products that would promote eating vegetables. People won't sacrifice good taste for healthy eating." By the time she was well again, Suzanne had a small line of recipes to test, a mock-up of a label, and a batch to take to gourmet stores. "Everyone who tasted it said they would buy," she says.

Suzanne's Sensational Dressings—raspberry, garlic, and red wine vinaigrette, honey mustard, ginger teriyaki—have since been picked up by Albertsons, the nation's second-largest grocery store chain, and Suzanne is selling hundreds of thousands of bottles a year, "soon to be more than a million," she adds. A portion of proceeds from every sale goes to breast cancer causes, and each bottle carries a small pink ribbon. "It's a subliminal message," Suzanne explains. "Every time they use it, it's there to be a reminder that they need to think about a checkup."

The company got it's first big boost thirty days after its founding when a local paper picked up the story. She was at a grocery store doing a demonstration when a man approached her to meet the woman who "the fuss was all about." She says people had literally lined up for her product, and messages were piling up at home from stores asking for dressing or announcing that they had sold out. Suzanne couldn't have been more pleased: "I realized at that point that one little person could make a difference."

Suzanne is holding to "slow and consistent" growth to ensure that the quality of her products won't suffer, that she will still have time to work with cancer groups, and that she concentrates on "the most important job in life—being a mother." She still travels to California, where her dressing is now made and bottled, to oversee production. "I'm pretty particular about what goes in; I feel I have to watch over that end of it." It's still a cottage industry, she still takes help from her children, but the challenge these days is, she says, "knowing when to back off."

Support has come from every angle. The local college business courses put Suzanne on track, the local bank was behind her with a loan, and her husband has backed her all the way. But she knows that none of this would have happened if she'd never had to fight for her life. "I didn't know I had it in me," she says, "but I drew from a well of passion and desire that pushed me beyond anything I thought I was capable of doing before."

Francesca M. Maher, Esq.

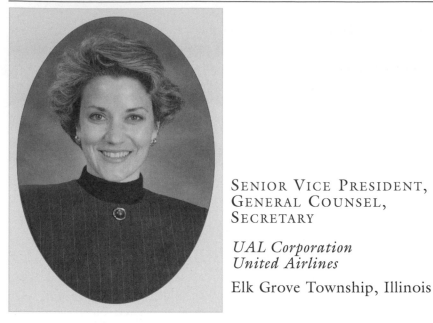

SENIOR VICE PRESIDENT,
GENERAL COUNSEL,
SECRETARY

UAL Corporation
United Airlines
Elk Grove Township, Illinois

WORK HISTORY

1981–1984   Associate, Mayer, Brown & Platt, Chicago, Illinois.

1984–1987   Director, Illinois Securities Department, Chicago and Springfield, Illinois.

1987–1988   Associate, Mayer, Brown & Platt, Chicago, Illinois.

1989–1993   Partner, Mayer, Brown & Platt, Chicago, Illinois.

1993–1997   Vice President, Law and Corporate Secretary, UAL Corporation.

1997–1998   Vice President, General Counsel, Secretary, UAL Corporation.

1998–present   Senior Vice President, General Counsel, Secretary, UAL Corporation.

EDUCATION

1978   B.A. (cum laude) in economics, Loyola University of Chicago.

1981   J.D. (cum laude), Loyola University of Chicago.

FIRST JOB

Working as a bagger in a grocery store.

ASSOCIATIONS AND NETWORKS

Ray Garrett, Jr., Corporate and Securities Law Institute, Northwestern University; Steering Committee, Senior Businesswomen's Forum; Chicago Bar Association, including Chairman (1991–1992) and Securities Law Committee; Governor's Task Force on Financial Securities (1985–1986); Advisory Committee on State Regulation to the Board of Directors, National Association of Securities Dealers, 1987–1993.

COMMUNITY SERVICE

Board of Directors, YMCA of Metropolitan Chicago; Board of Directors, United Center Community Economic Development Fund; Board of Directors and past President, Illinois Humane Society for Children.

AWARDS AND HONORS

"40 Under 40," Crain's *Chicago Business,* 1997.

FAMILY

Married, two children.

GREATEST OBSTACLE OVERCOME

My own insecurities.

PERSONAL GOALS

To make sure that I raise healthy, well-balanced, successful, and happy children. My kids are my first order of business. To have a happy marriage and be generally satisfied with life.

DEFINITION OF SUCCESS

Setting high objectives for yourself, achieving them, and being respected for it.

BUSINESS MAXIM

You don't know what you don't know.

WAYS OF DEALING WITH PRESSURE AND STRESS

Stress comes with the territory. Over time, you just have to learn to accept it and keep a cool head about it.

ADVICE TO ASPIRING BUSINESSWOMEN

Do the best you can. Look for opportunities to showcase yourself, think outside the box, and broaden your skills—don't keep yourself in a narrow niche. Keep a sense of humor.

*a*s long as I can remember, I wanted to be a corporate lawyer. I even remember my mother saying I would make a good corporate lawyer.

Francesca Maher hasn't been disappointed. An example of what deep-seated desire can achieve, she has moved on an arrow-straight career path, achieving positions and goals in short order, at an early age. Francesca is now in a corporate lawyer's dream job. Working for a Fortune 100 company, also the world's largest air carrier and the world's largest majority employee-owned company, the legal and business challenges are to be found nowhere else. But challenges of this magnitude have been part and parcel of Francesca's entire career.

Straight out of law school with honors, Francesca went to work for one of Chicago's largest law firms, Mayer, Brown & Platt, as an associate. As if the legal world was already looking for ways she could top herself, Francesca was, three years later, offered the directorship of the Illinois Securities Department. She was only twenty-six and of the opposite political party from those in power, but lack of confidence was not an issue. "At the time I took it on," she says, "I thought I knew everything. I quickly realized how little I knew. Between dealing with the press and the budget, it was a real wake-up call, and it did create some humility on my part." But her confidence allowed her to wade into the fray, and wasn't entirely out of order.

More central to her professional development, she says, was confronting the world outside of private practice. "Being a corporate lawyer in a big law firm is a somewhat rarefied experience," she explains. "At the Securities Department we participated in indictments, we saw suicides and disappearances. Since being at United, I've worked on transactions that resulted in the layoffs of thousands of people. You really feel it much more personally when you're in a job like this or at a job like the securities department as compared to a law firm job. I don't think I really appreciated the human side of what a lot of these jobs entail."

With three years of this trial by fire behind her, Francesca returned to Mayer, Brown & Platt, and applied her management experience to becoming the partner, which took only another two years, in charge of developing associates in corporate law. After thriving as partner for four years, she could claim knowledge or experience of how the law touches real estate, securities, environmental issues, labor, and a host of other areas. "Having that kind of background was a good basis for a generalist sort of management position," Francesca says. In other words, she was primed to become an in-house corporate counsel. And, she had been working with an airline at Mayer, Brown & Platt, so when a space opened at United, what choice was there?

Once again, Francesca emerged from private practice and into another complex post. United had just gone through layoffs of 10 percent company-wide, and had lost 40 percent of its legal department. "The two VPs in charge of legal functions had both retired and that job was combined into one and given to me," she recalls. With barely any time to adjust to her new surroundings, "it all hit the fan" and Francesca was in the middle of "the most complicated corporate transaction I'd ever seen," namely, the employee stock ownership program (ESOP) that would completely transform the company, leaving United Airlines 55 percent employee-owned, with a new management team, and embarking on uncharted waters.

The ESOP, Francesca says "turned our culture upside down." After four years under this agreement, she says she's pleased with the results: "The craziness has reached an equilibrium. We're in a dynamic of constant change, but at least it isn't with the same kind of frenzy we had coming out of the ESOP." The atmosphere of change is absolutely necessary—there has never been a company this large majority-owned by employees. It's a curious position for a lawyer, a profession where precedent so often carries the day. The upside, however, is that Francesca gets to have a hand in creating precedent out of thin air. "There is really no template out there for a lot of what we have to do. It's been a fascinating experience to try to make this work in an environment where you really don't have any predecessor you can look up to."

Since starting at United in 1993, Francesca has been promoted twice, most recently to Senior VP and General Counsel, just as she turned forty-one. Her great accomplishments in such a relatively short career draw plenty of praise, for which Francesca has a ready answer: "People have said to me, 'Look at how far you've come,' and my response to them on that is, 'Yes, but how far can I go?' I'm not belittling my accomplishments, but I don't ever want to sit on my laurels."

Barbara Berghoff

PRESIDENT AND CHIEF
EXECUTIVE OFFICER

*Professional Federal
Credit Union*

Fort Wayne, Indiana

WORK HISTORY

1968–1969   Office Clerk, Bookkeeper, Golden's Men's Wear, Fort
Wayne, Indiana.

1969–1978   Teller, Accounting Clerk, Loan Processor, Bookkeeper,
Loan Officer, Assistant Manger, Manager, F.W.C.S.
Federal Credit Union, Fort Wayne, Indiana.

1978–1987   Accountant for F.W.C.S. Federal Credit Union, N.A.V.L.
Federal Credit Union, and First Wayne Street U.M.
Church, Fort Wayne, Indiana.

1985–1986   Acting CEO, F.W.C.S. Federal Credit Union.

1987–1996   Vice President Operations, Senior Vice President /
Controller, Executive Vice President / Chief Operating
Officer, President / Chief Administrative Officer,
Professional Credit Union (formerly F.W.C.S.).

1996–present   President and CEO, Professional Federal Credit Union.

EDUCATION

1969   *Associate Degree*, International Business College, Fort Wayne, Indiana.

1990   NCUA Financial Management School, University of Colorado, Boulder.

FIRST JOB

Office clerk and bookkeeper for Golden Men's Wear in Fort Wayne.

ASSOCIATION AND NETWORKS

Credit Union Executive Society; Indiana Credit Union League Services Committee; Northeastern Indiana Credit Union Chapter Board of Directors; Board of Directors, NEI Leasing, Inc.; Board of Directors, Pro-Fed Financial Advisors, Inc.; Board of Directors, Pro-Fed Financial Services, Inc.; Education Credit Union Council; Director of Finance Committee at University of St. Francis; Supervisory Committee of Indiana Corporate Federal Credit Union; President's Association for Credit Unions over $100 Million; Board of Directors, YWCA; Board of Directors, Indiana Corporate Federal Credit Union.

COMMUNITY SERVICE

Past Volunteer, Parkview Memorial Hospital; past Member, Phi Theta Delta Sorority; Sponsor, Fort Wayne Philharmonic; active with 4-H Clubs.

AWARDS AND HONORS

Fort Wayne's Highest Ranking Female Banking Executive, *Business People Magazine,* 1997; Women of Achievement, YWCA, 1998; Nominated for Professional Achievement Award, Indiana Credit Union League, 1998.

FAMILY

Married, two children.

GREATEST OBSTACLES OVERCOME

Being considered for promotions as a female in the financial industry meant a lot of hard work and some personal sacrifices. At times, I needed to be more assertive so that I was not overlooked.

PERSONAL GOALS

To be a good mother, wife, and respected leader in my community.

DRIVING FORCE

My parents, who encouraged me to always go for the gold ring and never hold back have played a big role in my success. Their encouragement continued to influence me throughout my career and inspired me to always set high goals.

BUSINESS MAXIM

Surround yourself with strong, capable people.

GREATEST REWARD FROM CAREER

Since I became CEO the rewards have been very abundant. The credit union has not only grown bigger and stronger, but has become more efficient. The staff has continued to amaze me with their innovation and teamwork.

WAYS OF DEALING WITH PRESSURE AND STRESS

Trying to combine a career and family needs, and still find time for myself, has been very difficult at times. If I can balance all three, it helps to keep my stress level down.

ADVICE TO ASPIRING BUSINESSWOMEN

When obstacles come between you and your dream, don't quit! Keep striving to overcome the obstacle either directly or by finding another way around. Learn and grow from each experience and you will be a stronger leader. Remember that you are in charge of your own destiny.

i started when this credit union was still very small, became acquainted with our members on a personal basis, and was able to build a real rapport with them. I've seen so much growth and so many changes. It really became a part of me.

✻

For thirty years, in nearly every conceivable position—teller, loan officer, controller, COO—Barbara Berghoff has served Indiana's Professional Federal Credit Union. She watched her organization develop from a three-person, $700,000 operation to one that employs 120 and claims over $160 million in assets, a figure that places Professional in the top 4 percent of the nation's nearly twelve thousand credit unions. Under Barbara's leadership, Professional even continued to grow during a time when credit unions everywhere were prohibited by a Supreme Court ruling from gaining members outside their primary sponsor base. Professional played a vital role in organizing grassroots support for a bill that allowed them to return to doing business the way they had for years.

By the time she was selected as President/CEO by Professional's Board of Directors, Barbara knew she was well prepared. She had already served as acting CEO for three months, assisted the new CEO with the transition, then moved through a number of management positions until he retired. But Barbara's career path wasn't always so clear-cut; the first time the idea of becoming CEO was presented to her, she turned it down: "The board asked me if I was interested in 1985, but I told them it wasn't the right time for me to take on that responsibility." For the previous nine years, Barbara had been living a working mother's dream—working from home for Professional and, on a lesser scale, for another credit union as her children grew up: "I guess I was a little ahead of my time, working at home. I was able to stay involved with the credit union and go into the office once a week. I feel very fortunate that I was able to do that, and I wouldn't trade that time for anything."

But with the new CEO asking for her help, Barbara knew it was time to return to the office: "I decided my kids were old enough, and that it was time to get back on my career path. I had always planned to go back, and now the timing seemed right." Ten years later, she took the reins as CEO. It sounds easy, but Barbara acknowledges that "it wasn't a cakewalk. Until the succession plan was in black and white, I really didn't know for sure." There were times she felt tested, there were times she felt she had been given overwhelming tasks, and there were even times she felt that she was being held back because she was a woman. "But now, in retrospect, I feel that some of those ordeals I experienced made me a stronger leader."

Barbara's experiences with various positions within the credit union has made her a leader of a different stripe: "There has to be someone in charge, but there doesn't have to be a dictator." Barbara involves all her employees (85 percent female) in the decision-making process. Employees at all levels are encouraged to join committees where current plans are under discussion—a seat on committees is open to any employee who wants it. "It's so rewarding to hear all the ideas and see the staff being interactive voluntarily. And they get to see the results of their participation." The results of this policy are easy to see, Barbara says. "Trying to involve as much of the staff as possible makes them feel more responsible and supportive. The results also are reflected in our bottom line."

Professional requires that all employees serve at least some time in the teller booth, in order to get a sense of what happens on the front line of their operation, and regularly distributes "career intent forms" to employees to get them thinking about where they want to go, and to learn how management can help them get there. "We prefer to promote from within," Barbara says, "and we want to give our staff an opportunity to work in a different area if they have interest."

Having risen to the top in an organization that supported her growth, her decision to devote herself to family, and her ambition to lead, Barbara wants to return the favor: "I've taken a real interest in the careers of our staff—in their success and seeing them move up. It's very rewarding to see some of our staff reach different levels of their career goals. I strongly believe that our most important resource is our staff."

Monte Maupin Gerard

VICE PRESIDENT
MARKET MANAGER

*Susquehanna Radio
Corporation*
Indianapolis, Indiana

WORK HISTORY

1975–1976   Production and Copywriter, WLAC AM/FM Radio, Nashville, Tennessee.

1977–1978   Account Executive, WSIX AM/FM Radio, Nashville, Tennessee.

1978–1980   Account Executive, KLAK/KPPL and KHOW FM, Denver, Colorado.

1980–1986   Account Executive, WSB AM/FM Radio, Atlanta, Georgia.

1986–1989   General Sales Manager, WAPW FM Radio, Atlanta, Georgia.

1989   Joined Susquehanna Radio Corporation.

EDUCATION

1975   B.A. in Communications, University of Tennessee, Knoxville.

1976–1977   Attended M.B.A. program, University of Tennessee, Knoxville.

FIRST JOB

Copywriter, WLAC in Nashville, Tennessee.

ASSOCIATIONS AND NETWORKS

Board Member, Country Radio Broadcasters; Contributing Writer, *Indianapolis Business Journal* Corporate Opinion Board; Board Member, Indiana Sports Corporation.

COMMUNITY SERVICE

Board Chairman of Development, Indiana Literacy Foundation; Chairman, Community Leader Roundtable.

AWARDS AND HONORS

Country Music Association's Station of the Year, 1997; Country Music Nomination, Radio & Records Station of the Year, 1998.

FAMILY

Married, two children.

GREATEST OBSTACLES OVERCOME

Juggling my career and personal life. Learning to communicate with men.

DRIVING FORCE

A desire to do things differently, not necessarily the way they've been done.

BUSINESS MAXIM

Change is the only constant.

WAYS OF DEALING WITH PRESSURE AND STRESS

Exercise and delegation.

ADVICE TO ASPIRING BUSINESSWOMEN

Learn to communicate. Mentor others, especially women. Remember that you deserve the best.

i'm a big believer in teaching, training, and consensus building, which is a lot of hard work. Command-and-control type management is a lot easier, at least on the manager, but I don't think it builds a great and growing organization.

Running three radio stations with distinct formats in a competitive market would make the consensus-minded manager's job even more complex, but Monte Gerard is making it work. Monte is Vice President, General Manager, and "chief psychologist" for the Susquehanna Radio Corporation's Indianapolis stations, and during her seven-year tenure has seen and overseen risks and consolidations that demand a unified approach.

In 1997, Susquehanna, the nation's tenth-largest radio broadcast company with two country music stations in the Indianapolis market, bought a third low-frequency station, and Monte formulated a daring plan. The acquisition was given one of the country station's higher frequencies, allowing a new oldies station, WGLD, to break onto the scene with a competitive edge. These changes ran the risk of losing listeners all around, but the oldies station moved up the ratings with surprising speed, and proved to be a perfect match with the country stations. "The oldies audience and the country audience are pretty similar," Monte says. "There's a lot of cross-listening in those formats and so there's a lot of promotions we can do there."

But gathering listeners is only part of the job. Creating a single team from three stations was a task in itself. "In years past in our industry," Monte says, "you never had, for example, morning show people talking to other morning show people. They were huge competitors and would probably spit on each other in public. It was an internally competitive situation. Bringing them together was a whole new way of thinking." Getting them all in the same building was one huge step, something Monte had never seen in her twenty-three years in radio. Getting them to cooperate took even more creative solutions, one of which was the formation of the Susquehanna Family Foundation. "This is a way all three stations come together under our own cause," Monte explains. The foundation is committed to developing parenting skills, helping children by supporting parents. Employees of the various stations get to work together on a single project, and the community benefits. Monte says it's a perfect solution: "There's no reason you can't make money while doing good things."

In other little ways, Monte is making sure that her stations and employees aren't working against each other. Salespeople are paid a salary, rather than a commission, allowing them to take more risks and develop more relationships. Many procedural checks and redundancies have been eliminated: "When you're inspecting someone, you're saying they don't know how to do their job." Instead, Monte tries to facilitate a constant interdepartmental dialogue. "It never ceases to amaze me that communication sometimes doesn't happen when we are in the communication business. Shame on us." Monte's preferred mode of communication is plain to see: direct, forthright, and "everything on the table."

The rewards have been spectacular. Susquehanna station WFMS, which had been a regular in the Arbitron rating's number one spot for years, finally won the Country Music Association's Station of the Year Award in 1997 after being nominated twice. The group has launched a sales promotion company to help advertisers use other media, and plans are under way to purchase a fourth station in Indianapolis. But no matter how diverse the company becomes, Monte believes her tasks have a single goal: "My job here is just to get people on the same path, or at least the same interstate."

Somehow, in the middle of achieving the promotion to Vice President, Monte was able to turn her attention to her personal life as well, and became a mother. "Subconsciously, I'd been thinking that if I get to this level, then

I could have a family, when I have more time. I just kept going and going, and finally realized I was running out of time here." She had her son at age forty and her daughter two years later. "I guess I was a bit of a late bloomer on the personal side," she jokes, "and now I won't be in Florida until I'm in my sixties."

Debra J. Arrett

PRESIDENT

Northwood Dairy Sales Ltd.

Bettendorf, Iowa

WORK HISTORY

1970–1978   Various positions, including Waitress, Oil Filter Tester, Telephone Operator, retail positions for the Army/Air Force Exchange Service.

1978–1983   Started as Secretary, left as Sales Manager, Swiss Valley Farms Company, Davenport, Iowa.

1983–1984   Sales Representative, International Distributing, St. Louis, Missouri.

1984–present   President, Northwood Dairy Sales.

EDUCATION

Currently a senior at the University of Iowa, Iowa City.

ASSOCIATIONS AND NETWORKS

Member, American Dairy Products Institute.

COMMUNITY SERVICE

I work with various organizations but prefer to work anonymously.

AWARDS AND HONORS

Iowa Small Business Entrepreneurial Award, State of Iowa, 1989; Ranked 173rd in the *Working Woman* 500, 1998.

FAMILY

Two children.

GREATEST OBSTACLES OVERCOME

Being a woman in a male-dominated industry. However, I prefer to think of those obstacles as challenges, and I turned them into opportunities and advantages.

DRIVING FORCE

My children.

DEFINITION OF SUCCESS

Waking up in the morning excited by the new day.

BUSINESS MAXIM

If you dwell too long on your accomplishments, you will lose sight of your goals.

GREATEST REWARD FROM CAREER

The diverse cast of characters I have had the opportunity to work with and befriend.

GREATEST DOWNSIDE TO CAREER

Finding a new challenge after reaching all my goals.

WAYS OF DEALING WITH PRESSURE AND STRESS

I go upstairs, close the door to the basement (office), and get lost in a good book.

ADVICE TO ASPIRING BUSINESSWOMEN

If you go looking for discrimination, you will find it. Don't look for it; and don't use it as an excuse for failure.

*g*oing back to school gave me an outlet and new goals. I had some very distinct goals for myself back when I started my business, like becoming a millionaire by the time I was thirty-five. I met those goals, and when I was turning forty, I had to look at where I was.

Debra Arrett should have her degree by the year 2000, opening more doors and expanding her possibilities for whatever might come next. "I've thought of joining the foreign service and working with developing countries," she says, "of starting other businesses, of joining the Peace Corps. Who knows where I'm going to end up?" Having grown her basement-based dairy sales company into a $50 million enterprise in less than fifteen years, Debra still sees daily challenges, but they aren't what they once were.

Debra had worked on an assembly line, as a waitress, and as a cashier before finding a company she could grow with, a dairy co-op in Davenport, Iowa. "It was a great education," she recalls, "because co-ops are known for requiring their employees to wear several hats." But when she was expecting her second child, she realized that she'd worn as many hats as they had to offer, and "retired to motherhood." That plan lasted about a month. "I was stir-crazy," Debra explains, "desperate for something to do." She was contacted by a St. Louis dairy distributor she'd done business with before; they agreed to put her on a salary, and she says she started selling out of her home with her child by her side: "I would pray that she wouldn't scream at an inopportune moment. But it did happen, and boy, did my credibility go out the window. Or at least I thought."

Debra says this new plan lasted about six months: "I was not setting the world on fire. They primarily dealt with dry dairy products, but my true love was cheese." So many of the buyers she dealt with also worked with cheese products that Debra realized she could do better on her own. A little more than a year after leaving the co-op, Northwood Dairy Sales was born.

An extra push for her business came soon after, when Debra and her husband divorced. "Like a mother bird feathering its nest," she says, "I set out to provide and maintain security for my children." Within a couple of years, Debra moved from being a broker working on commissions to a trader buying and selling product. "By taking possession," she explains, "my contacts stopped thinking of me as a middleman."

When Debra talks about buying dairy, she's not talking about a quart of milk. Northwood sells diary for industrial applications—cheddar in five-hundred-pound barrels, sweet cream in forty-thousand-pound tankards, or lots of dry milk for export. With her name known throughout the industry, she says she can often have a dual relationship with a single contact, selling them one product and buying something else: "We can be at both doors and maximize that relationship, while my competitors specialize in one thing. That's one way we were different and still are."

Debra says her company is also unique in that it's woman-owned, but adds that this has clearly been a benefit: "I was the only woman in this industry, and maybe it did close some doors for me, but it probably opened many more because I was memorable. I was the only woman in a sea of men." Almost everyone in this business does everything by phone, Debra explains, and her voice was recognized and credible, and particularly valuable when she was running a start-up: "Back when I got started, everything was all based on trust, on the fact that I had an honest-sounding voice. You can do million-dollar transactions with someone all the time and never meet. It's all based on relationships. It's a very unusual business."

But those relationships have also eased Debra's transition into her newly forming life. "When I explained to my customers and suppliers that they're going to be hearing less from me, they knew pretty well by then who I was and what motivated me, and they accepted it." Northwood will be a part of Debra's life for the near future, but she knows that new goals are needed: "Once I had become established and had so much money that I didn't have to work another day in my life, that's when I no longer woke up looking forward to a new day. I hate that I lost that spirit, but that's where going back to school comes in. Now I can foresee all sorts of things down the road."

Mary A. O'Keefe

SENIOR VICE PRESIDENT

Principal Financial Group

Des Moines, Iowa

WORK HISTORY

1978–1983   Manager / Manpower Generalist, State of Iowa Job Training, Des Moines.

1983–1985   Associate Director, Job Training Partnership / Eastern Iowa Community College District, Des Moines.

1985–1988   Bureau Chief, State of Iowa, Des Moines.

1988–1990   Marketing Manager, State of Iowa, Des Moines.

1990–1993   Media Relations Manager, Principal Financial Group.

1993–1997   Officer—Corporate Relations, Principal Financial Group.

1998–present   Senior Vice President, Principal Financial Group.

EDUCATION

1978   B.S. in social work, Northern Illinois University, DeKalb.

1993   Accredited Public Relations, Public Relations Society of America.

FIRST JOB

Baby-sitting, working through high school as a clerk and cashier in a women's clothing store.

ASSOCIATIONS AND NETWORKS

Public Relations Committee, American Council of Life Insurance; Iowa Business Council; Public Relations Society of America; Arthur Page Society.

COMMUNITY SERVICE

Room Mom, Volunteer, St. Pius Elementary School; Board of Directors, Partnership for a Drug-Free Iowa; Marketing Advisory Council, Iowa Department of Economic Development; Downtown Partnership Board; MBA Board, University of Iowa; Downtown Coordinating Council.

AWARDS AND HONORS

Named an "Up and Comer," *Des Moines Register* 1993; Named one of "20 Women You Should Get to Know—Candidates for Your Board Opening," *Des Moines Business Record,* 1995.

FAMILY

Married, one son.

PERSONAL GOALS

To raise a strong, happy child; to strive to do the right thing and thus achieve success on my own terms; to have a good marriage.

PROFESSIONAL GOALS

To continue to succeed in work I enjoy and believe in.

DEFINITION OF SUCCESS

Succeeding at a job I enjoy. Finding balance between work and personal pursuits.

BUSINESS MAXIM

Plan ahead. Get ahead.

GREATEST REWARD FROM CAREER

Being named first female Senior Vice President in the company's 120-year history.

WAYS OF DEALING WITH PRESSURE AND STRESS

Having a twisted sense of humor helps.

ADVICE TO ASPIRING BUSINESSWOMEN

Each assignment offers the chance to show success (or failure), so look at every assignment as an opportunity to do your best. Have fun—if you're not succeeding, you're probably in the wrong job.

FAVORITE PART OF THE DAY

Hearing about my child's day.

i don't follow a specific path or outline narrow goals. I never thought I would do one thing or achieve a certain position by a certain age. I'm passionate about what I do, so recognition and advancement has followed naturally.

⚜

By keeping her goals generally defined, Mary O'Keefe has allowed herself to chart an unlikely career path from the front lines of social work to the Fortune 500. As the first female Senior VP in the 120-year history of the Principal Financial Group, Mary's background and flexibility allow her to bring advertising, public relations, employee communications, human resources, and Internet services under one banner as part of a massive redefinition of the Principal's corporate strategy. She's here today, she says, because she took advantage of "one of those accidental career changes" and made every experience from her previous jobs count.

The venerable Principal Financial Group, with more than $72 billion in assets and ten million customers, is learning some new tricks. Says Mary, "We're moving from a traditional mutual insurance company, which is very long term in its view, into a much faster-paced environment. We're becoming more aggressive, faster in our decisions, and gaining a higher risk tolerance." Mary came up in the Principal through the PR side, but the scope of the current restructuring calls for human resources to be in the hands of someone intimately involved with executing those changes. "Our growth strategy is going to require a lot from our people," Mary explains. "Our challenge is to provide employees with the right kinds of training and information so we can move faster. That's underpinning our entire strategy—developing people."

Mary's background fits into this strategy perfectly. The first step in her career change was working with job training programs for the State of Iowa, designed to help businesses grow and attract more business to the state. After working directly in these programs for ten years, she moved on to marketing state programs before she was asked to join Principal Financial Group as media relations manager. The introduction of human resources into her communications responsibilities in a sense brings her full circle. "It's really interesting to see the marriage of these different pieces of corporate strategy. It takes me back to job training, and allows me to figure out how to deal with both sides of my career."

Mary says the skills she needed for her current post were being developed long before she had any idea she would one day work in finance: "The ability to be flexible, and deal with different situations, came partly from doing social work. In college I worked on a suicide prevention hot line, and having to think on your feet was something I learned from that and used in public relations years later." Her first job in social work was in juvenile probation, so handling intense situations, motivating people, and listening to their concerns came naturally as Mary moved into the corporate world: "I found that figuring out how to represent the business to the public and the public back to the business requires a great deal of empathy and understanding. Changing careers worked out really well."

Mary's original commitment to her community continues today with her participation in the Iowa Department of Economic Development, where she helps market the state. "We're trying to break certain perceptions about the state. There are actually businesses in Iowa. There's technology in Iowa. There's no lack of culture in Iowa." Mary feels strongly about this point, and is working with other businesses in the state to develop an ad campaign with endorsements from Iowa businesses.

By remaining open to the possibilities, Mary has found that careers can just happen to those who are willing to work deliberately and quietly. "I've always felt that if I like what I'm doing, cared about it, and worked hard, it would work out," she says. "I wasn't looking to make a change when I was offered the job at the Principal, but I thought that if there was ever a time to make a jump from the public to the private sector, this would be the company to do it with."

Lynn Gardner Hinkle

PRESIDENT

Astra Enterprises, Inc.
Topeka, Kansas

Berton Photography

WORK HISTORY

1978–1980   Copywriter, Emerson-Franzke, Topeka, Kansas.

1980–1984   Account Executive, Emerson / Nichols / Bailey-Franzke,
               Topeka, Kansas.

1984   President, Midwest Division, Emerson / Nichols / Bailey-
               Franzke, Topeka, Kansas.

1985–1995   President, the Hinkle Agency, Topeka, Kansas.

1995–present President, Astra Enterprises.

EDUCATION

1979   B.A. in Journalism, University of Missouri, Columbia.

FIRST JOB

Assistant (receptionist, pill counter, filer) in my father's osteopathic medicine clinic at age thirteen.

COMMUNITY SERVICE

Founder, Women of the World, Inc.; International Women's Forum, Kansas; Central Exchange, Women in Politics Committee, Kansas City, Missouri; Georgia Neese Gray Lecture Series Board, Washburn University, Topeka, Kansas; Secretary of the Board, Kansas Surplus Exchange (business/civic recycling center).

AWARDS AND HONORS

Topeka Capital-Journal's Kansan of the Year, 1994 (with U.S. Senator Nancy Kassebaum); Pollie Awards from the American Association of Political Consultants, 1991, 1994; Silver Metal Lifetime Achievement Award, Topeka Advertising Federation, 1994; JCPenny Golden Rule Award, 1996; bronze medals in 1982, 1986, International TV & Film Festival, New York, NY; Telly Awards in 1983, 1987, 1988, 1991; Silver Microphone Award, 1986; Small Business of the Year, Greater Topeka Chamber of Commerce, 1986.

FAMILY

Four sons.

GREATEST OBSTACLES OVERCOME

Fear of failure—I conquer it over and over again, and it keeps coming back.

PERSONAL GOALS

Have a life. Laugh more, savor small moments, remember the best.

PROFESSIONAL GOALS

To integrate (or cross-pollinate) the essential parts of my life and achieve balance—as a woman, an entrepreneur, a mother, and a teacher.

DRIVING FORCE

I have a God-given desire to change the world for the better, and to use my gifts to the utmost of my ability.

DEFINITION OF SUCCESS

Getting back up again.

GREATEST REWARD FROM CAREER

To know I have encouraged another, either directly or indirectly by example, to pursue her dreams, reach for the stars.

GREATEST DOWNSIDE TO CAREER

There have been times when I felt that I had to be more like a man to succeed, and by doing so, I sacrificed something essential in myself.

ADVICE TO ASPIRING BUSINESSWOMEN

Remember, there's more time than you think. Pace yourself. Believe in yourself. Be true to your own life mission and success follows.

*I*t seemed like everything was happening so quickly—it was almost a blur. So many parts of my life were like that—I finished college in three years so I could get on with my career, and then my career moved at this incredible pace as well. But it all happened that way because I like that pace.

Five years after graduating from college, Lynn Hinkle was President of the Mid-West Division of Topeka's largest ad agency, Emerson / Nichols / Bailey-Franzke. Hers was a mercurial rise, from Copywriter to President of her division in six years. And she's proud to say that she rose playing by her own rules.

"I didn't play the corporate hierarchy—I skipped over layers to go straight to the top, much to my peril. I felt I was at the height of my achievement when I made President, but at the same time, it came with a lot of responsibility and required a lot more experience than most twenty-eight-year-olds are likely to have." But Lynn hardly had time to adjust to her new role before change brought another opportunity—her division was put up for sale. Lynn soon realized that it was her relationships with her clients that were on the block. "I was really put off by the idea of being sold, and that triggered my thinking. If someone's going to buy these relationships and make a profit, why shouldn't it be me?" So she bought the company.

Getting the bank loan was straightforward—the bank was a client and knew Lynn well—but disaster was right around the corner. Her largest account, worth over a million dollars, decided to do their ads in-house. It's an all-too-typical story in the high-risk world of advertising, but one Lynn is well equipped for: "Because I'm more of an optimist, I don't dwell on the fact that I've been knocked down. If there's anything I recognize in successful women, it's that ability to get back up again—that perseverance." Lynn took the hit, and got her business back up by focusing on graphic design, moving into the Internet, and taking on "any client that moved."

This included car dealerships and a funeral home, but the business that remains close to Lynn's heart is the political campaigns. Astra Enterprises, which Lynn formed after she closed the Hinkle Agency, has won two Pollie Awards—one for an ad produced for U.S. Representative Jim Slattery (D-KS), and one for U.S. Representative Harold Volkmer (D-MO). Lynn is particularly proud of a campaign that didn't result in victory, but got her client plenty of attention, including a televised spot during the Democratic National Convention. This was "Gloria vs. Goliath"—Gloria O'Dell's campaign against Senator Bob Dole.

Lynn enjoys working with politicians, but being on the receiving end of campaign funds is problematic for her: "I'm slightly cutting my own throat to say this, but campaign finance reform is essential. You can't continue to allow unlimited amounts of money to be raised and spent on political campaigns and expect to have a representative government." So while she works within the political process with Astra, she works with women outside the political process with her nonprofit organization, Women of the World (WOW).

In the face of the most dire political upheaval in Russia since 1917, Lynn and her group traveled to St. Petersburg in 1993 to help prepare women for political life. Since then, their program has trained more than 180 women and shipped $4 million in humanitarian aid. But the most dramatic result Lynn has seen was when her group formed a political party in a matter of months to upset the mayor of St. Petersburg in the 1995 election. Encouraged by this success, WOW is now taking what it learned from Russia to the women of the Native American nations. "WOW is more like having children," Lynn says. "While my career seems to be sort of a blur, when I'm thinking about WOW, I can see crystal-clear pictures and moments that I know I will never forget."

Turning forty was a blur for Lynn as well, but the following years have brought it into focus: "The moment of turning forty didn't feel significant at the time, but now I see that there's something to it. There's a certain amount of soul-searching, of finding your authentic self." It's also a time when confidence is at an all-time high: "I have less fear of failure in my forties than at any time in my life—now I make only new mistakes."

Janet Skees

PRESIDENT

Skees Engineering, Inc.

Louisville, Kentucky

WORK HISTORY

1979–1980   Civil Engineer, W.M.B. Engineers, Lexington, Kentucky.

1981–1986   Civil Engineer / Systems Analyst, U.S. Army Corps of
Engineers, Louisville, Kentucky.

1986–present   President, Skees Engineering.

EDUCATION

1978   B.S. in civil engineering technology, Western Kentucky University,
Bowling Green.

1979   M.S. in civil engineering, Purdue University, West Lafayette,
Indiana.

FIRST JOB

Reporter for a weekly neighborhood newspaper.

ASSOCIATIONS AND NETWORKS

Kentucky Society of Professional Engineers; National Society of Professional Engineers; Consulting Engineers Council of Kentucky, American Society of Civil Engineers.

COMMUNITY SERVICE

Mission work with Pinehaven Christian Children's Ranch, St. Ignatius, Montana; Coach for a Bible Bowl team of middle- and high-school children; Leader of a small Bible study group; regular judge at local science fairs.

AWARDS AND HONORS

Woman Business Owner of the Year (one of three), National Association of Women Business Owners, Louisville, Kentucky Chapter, 1998; New Principal of the Year, Consulting Engineers Council of Kentucky, 1988.

FAMILY

One child.

GREATEST OBSTACLES OVERCOME

Overcoming my lack of knowledge about running a business and learning how to develop business relationships in a male-dominated field.

DRIVING FORCE

The desire to keep my commitments and to take the extra steps to be the best at whatever challenges come my way.

DEFINITION OF SUCCESS

Knowing what you really want to do in life and having the opportunity to do that, while helping others achieve their goals for success as well. Success has nothing to do with how the world views you, but with how you view yourself in line with your personal goals. I believe I am successful, not because of what I have achieved at Skees Engineering, but because I have found peace and contentment in where I am in my personal relationship with the Lord.

BUSINESS MAXIM

Work hard, prioritize your goals, and delegate to capable people. Always keep your commitments.

GREATEST REWARD FROM CAREER

Seeing Skees Engineering become a team of top-notch engineers and technicians that really work together as a team and care about what they are doing and about each other.

GREATEST DOWNSIDE TO CAREER

The amount of paperwork and administrative duties that have pulled me away from the technical side of engineering.

ADVICE TO ASPIRING BUSINESSWOMEN

Make sure you are going after what you really want in life. Women are torn between family and career, and we can't always have it all. We are seeing more women who have achieved status in major corporations step down and admit that they have other priorities at that time in their lives. Don't assume that there will be bias just because you are a woman. Just do your job, go the extra step, and people will take notice.

*S*kills like attention to detail and organization that are typical of engineers are great for running a business, but we also tend to be very introverted. I really had to change that. I had to come out of my shell, get out there and meet people.

⚜

Janet Skees was happy working for the Army Corps of Engineers in Louisville, Kentucky, and had only thought occasionally of starting her own company or working as a consultant. There are still times when she misses those days: "My life's a lot more complicated now," she says. But she won't be going back. Skees Engineering has beaten the odds, winning high-profile contracts in direct competition against established firms, taking in over $2 million a year in fees, and employing twenty-five people, including seven licensed civil engineers.

Janet says that the first time she seriously considered starting her own company was when the director of engineering at the Louisville Metropolitan Sewer District told her she could make it work. The MSD had decided to award 3 percent of its contracts to women and minority-owned firms, but was having trouble finding companies that fit their needs. "There were clear opportunities for young start-up firms to participate in a small part of a very big project," Janet remembers. "The director knew my abilities and mentioned that now would be a good time to start a business."

Janet thought the timing was right as well: "My son was one year old, and I thought this might give me an opportunity to stay at home more. That was pretty naive." She soon found herself in a flurry of activity, as she attended business courses at night and tried to drum up work during the day. "I didn't want to survive just on one client's goals for women-owned businesses. I felt I was good enough at what I did that I'd be able to get work on my merits. That was pretty naive too. I just didn't have the network. Working for the federal government, I'd never really gotten out of my cubicle."

So Janet was not only taking on the old boy network, but her own personality. She even says that she left her original calling, journalism, because it didn't fit with her introverted nature: "When I was in journalism at Western Kentucky University, I'd feel sick from being so nosy." Joining engineering associations helped, but making the extra effort was sheer will: "I just had to push myself to make the calls, and really push myself to make the appointments. Later I found out that other engineers also lack communication skills, so we were all out there doing the same thing."

Within a year, she landed a contract that allowed her to hire an employee, and she began the process of learning to become a manager. "One thing I was not good at at this point," she recalls, "was offering constructive criticism. I was always afraid that I'd hurt someone's feelings or they'd get mad and quit." As she brought in higher-level employees, the learning process continued: "Everybody approaches work differently, and I had to learn when it was just a style or when it was something that needed to be changed. It was hard for me because I'm not a confrontational person."

Living from one contract to another, Janet was in for plenty of lean times as she grew her company. But the key to pulling through both her own self-doubt and the occasional financial tangle was her faith. "There were times," Janet says, "when our credit limit was at the max, our credit cards were at the max, and payroll was coming due. My bookkeeper and I would get together and pray over the incoming mail." Janet adds that not only did they never miss payroll, but even when she was at her busiest, she never missed church. "I think that when you are in the deepest trouble or worst difficulty, that's when you have the best awareness of God, and how he is seeing you through," Janet claims.

From her first job, "baby-sitting" a global positioning system, Skees Engineering has gone on to build an impressive list of projects, including work on the Louisville Waterfront Park, the 4,200-car Louisville International Airport parking complex, the Louisville Zoological Gardens, and several major highway projects. Business doubled in just the past three years, and the days of seventy-hour work weeks and self-doubt are truly over. Janet now devotes herself to generating business, leaving technical execution to her four team leaders, each professional engineers with over fifteen years experience. She's found this suits her well—freeing her up for more time with her family, work with her church, and time for herself. As she explains, "Civil engineering is what I do. It's not who I am."

Phyllis Jordan

FOUNDER AND DIRECTOR
OF MARKETING

PJ's Coffee and Tea, Inc.
New Orleans, Louisiana

WORK HISTORY

Social Worker involved with runaways, drug abuse, drop-outs. Then a Manager for a record store.

EDUCATION

1971 B.A. in sociology, University of Missouri, St. Louis.

FIRST JOB

Playground supervisor.

ASSOCIATIONS AND NETWORKS

Former Board Member and President, Specialty Coffee Association of America.

COMMUNITY SERVICE

Advisory Board, Coffee Kids (industry group seeking to improve quality of life in coffee-growing areas); President of the Board, WRBH, Radio for the Blind and Print Handicapped.

AWARDS AND HONORS

Role Model Award, Young Leadership Council, 1995; Business Hall of Fame, Junior Achievement, 1996; Entrepreneur in Residence, University of New Orleans, 1995.

FAMILY

Married, one son.

GREATEST OBSTACLES OVERCOME

Learning to see myself as someone capable.

PROFESSIONAL GOALS

One day I would like to stop dealing with daily activities. I've done this for twenty years.

DRIVING FORCE

A need to be seen as successful in the community, both the local community and the coffee-selling community.

BUSINESS MAXIM

Being stubborn is highly underrated.

GREATEST REWARD FROM CAREER

Being an integral part of the communities where we have stores. The neighborhood coffee house is an integral part of the lives of our customers, and being part of the community comes with the territory.

WAYS OF DEALING WITH PRESSURE AND STRESS

I have a great husband who is completely supportive. I've also learned over the years that worrying about things doesn't get them done. Getting up and doing things is the only way to solve problems.

ADVICE TO ASPIRING BUSINESSWOMEN

Find something you truly love, something that will allow you to get up in the morning and do the work. Visualize where you want to be.

i found I really liked the black-and-white nature of retail business. At the end of the day, you count your receipts and you know whether you had a good day or not.

Phyllis Jordan has had quite a few good days, and now, twenty years after she started her specialty coffee shop near Tulane University in New Orleans, she's roasting six thousand pounds of coffee a week for twenty-three stores in four states, with new franchises slated to open as far away as Jacksonville, Florida. Getting here took several adaptations and a process of slow, managed growth, but the result was a business that was already established when coffee shops caught on in a big way in the early nineties.

"In 1978, specialty coffee was hardly a household word," Phyllis points out. "Sitcoms didn't take place in coffee bars. It was a real struggle in those early years." Phyllis's first six-hundred-square-foot foray into business ownership was strictly retail, offering whole bean coffees, loose teas, grinders, brewers, and associated products. It held its own, but wasn't a wild success. It was a year and a half before Phyllis decided to put out a table and chairs. "I never really intended to be in the food service business," she recalls. "But the location, which was a neighborhood shopping area, was better suited for that sort of thing." What she found was that customers who bought by the cup were hardly ever the same ones who bought by the bag, and she had greatly expanded her market.

She also discovered that she liked it. "Greeting customers, making them feel welcome, giving them a place to sit was all really enjoyable. Now, we've had customers who have been coming in for twenty years, who've changed and grown, gotten married and had children. We're really a part of the community." The next step was taking control of manufacturing. Phyllis bought a large roaster from a defunct coffee shop and made herself learn how to bring out the best in a raw coffee bean. "It was really a way to manage quality and cost. It seems logical now, but at the time it was a big risk. Luckily, it was in my nature to take risks." Soon she was shipping her fresh-roasted coffee to a second location in New Orleans.

Up to that point, Phyllis had done nearly everything herself, comfortable with keeping total control over her start-up, even though she now admits it was time to start letting some responsibilities go. "That happened due to a strange kind of luck," she says. "I got mono, which forced me to turn responsibility over to other people. It wasn't easy, but I had no choice. I learned that the world does not cave in just because you're away." Somehow the timing was right—PJ's Coffee was about to expand beyond Phyllis's immediate influence through franchising.

Many of PJ's franchises are owned by former employees or former customers, people with a sensitivity to the product and environment, which makes the founder very pleased. Beyond the contractual arrangement that makes franchising work, Phyllis says, "This sort of relationship works best when there's a lot of trust on both sides, and that trust is properly earned. They trust us to support them and maintain the brand name, and we have to trust them to execute our system in the way that maintains the brand name." The success of the franchises so far has opened opportunities to continue throughout the southeast, and has created a need for a larger base of operations in Louisiana. The roasting operation now rests in larger facilities at the foot of Bayou St. John in New Orleans. As the franchises took off, Phyllis was also serving as the first woman president of the Specialty Coffee Association of America. Now she's hired a CEO, allowing her to concentrate on her original loves: good coffee and good customers.

In 1998, New Orleans was finally visited by coffee giant Starbucks, which opened two doors down from one of Phyllis's company-owned stores. Phyllis, however, is completely fearless: "I think Starbucks has been very good for all of us in this business. They've gotten the word out. This new store has not affected us at all. Our customers, who heard so much about Starbucks, now have a chance to try it and discover that they've had a very good coffee shop over the last twenty years." Besides, Phyllis isn't out to become another Starbucks. "I don't have unlimited ambition. I like having parameters on how my business grows."

Barbara Tome Schneider

VICE PRESIDENT OF MARKETING

Remstar International Inc.
Westbrook, Maine

WORK HISTORY

1976   District Sales Manager, *McCall's* magazine, Cleveland, Ohio.

1977–1983   Started as Bank Coordinator, left as New Business Development Officer, Bank Systems Association, Cleveland, Ohio.

1989   Started as Marketing Coordinator, Remstar International.

1996–present Vice President of Marketing, Remstar International Inc.

EDUCATION

1976   B.A. in speech and communications, University of Delaware, Newark.

1988   B.S. in data processing, Westbrook College, Westbrook, Maine.

ASSOCIATIONS AND NETWORKS

Education Committee, Material Handling Institute; Women's Maine Network; Advisory Committee, North American Warehouse Distribution Education Council.

COMMUNITY SERVICE

Board of Directors Funding Committee, PR and Marketing Chairperson, Maine Conservation School; past Chairperson (1992–1996) Gorham Community Services, co-host of local television program "Around Town."

FAMILY

Married, one son.

PERSONAL GOALS

To create a more acceptable balance for women with careers and a home life while forging ahead. To be the best that I can be.

PROFESSIONAL GOALS

To bring our marketing department into the year 2000 and achieve our company's five-year plan.

DRIVING FORCE

Myself, my family, my mentor and President of Remstar, Gary Gould, and my peer group.

DEFINITION OF SUCCESS

Achieving our goals and objectives while maintaining a balance of work, stress, and personal achievement by enjoying work every day.

BUSINESS MAXIM

If I can't enjoy my work and the people I do business with, it's time to move on. Laugh.

WAYS OF DEALING WITH PRESSURE AND STRESS

By always looking at the glass as half full—always. Exercise, good nutrition, meditation in the early part of the day. Celebrating each moment with my husband and son.

ADVICE TO ASPIRING BUSINESSWOMEN

Stay focused. Always be proactive, willing to listen. Communicate honestly—always.

*r*eentering the workforce after five years was a rude awakening. Having been away and being a mom had a lot of negative baggage attached to it. I found out I was going to have to start at the bottom of the ladder and work my way up again.

Barbara Schneider was an officer in a credit card verification company, a position she achieved at a young age through deliberate work, when she and her husband relocated and she opted to take time off with her child. Her rude awakening came as he was entering school and she was ready to pick up where she had left off. "It was a humiliating time, those first interviews," she recalls, "going from a position where I was an officer, feeling confident in my abilities and my credibility, knowing what I had to offer and not being given the opportunity to show it." But she can now look back on this time without bitterness—her opportunity came and her perseverance paid off.

Barbara wasn't sitting on her hands while she was taking time with her child. She pursued a second bachelor's degree, taught aerobics, and got involved in her new community. But she discovered during interviews that she had a "lethal combination" in being a woman, being a mother, and having been away: "It didn't matter that I had this experience and two degrees. I was out of the workforce loop, the business network. I've come to understand that it's crucial to have that connection." She took a job she knew she was overqualified for, took up networking, and made it work. Then a friend guided her to Remstar, where she found a job, a mentor, and a future.

Remstar manufactures storage solutions—vertical and horizontal carousels, tool dispensing systems—for industry, food service, records management, and warehousing. These high-tech storage units are fully automated and packaged with Remstar's own software, and used by companies as diverse as Motorola, Ford, Boeing, Eli Lilly, Gillette, Hewlitt Packard, and L.L. Bean. "What we manufacture is like closets," Barbara says, "customers can't get enough of them." Remstar employs just over sixty, but is setting its sights high; its five-year plan is to grow sales to $70 million in five years. Barbara's role is to "be the glue that holds the manufacturing divisions together, to give them strength and forward movement, and to be the communications link to the outside world."

Even though her first "post-child" job was starting to offer rewards, Barbara felt it wasn't a good fit. The opportunity at Remstar came like a breath of fresh air. Never mind the fact that the materials handling industry is, according to Barbara, "a field mostly made up of men." At least now she had the chance to prove herself within an organization. Barbara was Marketing Manager a year after she started, Marketing Director five years in, and Vice President two years later. Next to her own hard work, Barbara credits Remstar's President, Gary Gould, for guiding her forward: "He's one of those exceptional individuals with a clear vision of where he wants the company to be, and he's guided me to achieve my potential as well. He's my boss, but we communicate as peers, and he provides a guiding light."

One of the keys to moving the company forward, Barbara says, is educating customers about what the materials handling industry can offer. Barbara's work on Remstar's website was one small step; opening the lines of communication with Remstar's competitors was a big one. After an investment of "six to eight years," every one of Remstar's competitors will work with Barbara to develop a workshop at the Materials Handling Institute's annual convention. "We're finally talking and meeting and exchanging information," she says. "It's a humongous move for our industry."

Looking back on the retooling of her career, Barbara says what was most important was to avoid developing an attitude. "You could in this situation go off and have a pity party or carry a chip on your shoulder, or you can say, 'Fine, I'll just go after it anyway.' That's the attitude I've had throughout my life, and I haven't been disappointed."

Mary Kay Spencer

OWNER

The Potter's House
Winthrop, Maine

WORK HISTORY

1979–1983   Senior Psychiatric Technician, The Institute of Living, Hartford, Connecticut.

1982–1986   Self-employed potter, Chaplin, Connecticut.

1986–1989   Potter, Georgetown Pottery, Georgetown, Maine.

1989–present   Owner, The Potter's House.

EDUCATION

1980   B.A. in psychology, University of Connecticut.

FIRST JOB

Baby-sitting and housecleaning at age thirteen–fourteen.

ASSOCIATIONS AND NETWORKS

Maine Crafts Association.

COMMUNITY SERVICE

Chairman, Winthrop Mural Project.

FAMILY

Married, one daughter.

PERSONAL GOALS

To keep my independence.

PROFESSIONAL GOALS

To pass on traditions and encourage someone else to make pots. To develop my artwork on pottery or paper.

DRIVING FORCE

Faith in God and thankfulness for the gifts I've been given. Faith in my husband, who has always been supportive and fun to work with.

DEFINITION OF SUCCESS

To be able to achieve a comfortable living pursuing and developing talents and gifts.

BUSINESS MAXIM

Be honest and ethical.

WAYS OF DEALING WITH PRESSURE AND STRESS

Praying, talking things out with my husband, taking walks. I've learned that I need to take care of myself so that I can create.

ADVICE TO ASPIRING BUSINESSWOMEN

Believe in yourself and your ideas. Search out help from others. Always be honest in your endeavors.

i was at a crossroads where I had to decide whether we were going to be a factory or whether we were going to be more hands on. We're actually going to do the latter. We're going to step back and try to nurture that creative aspect of the business.

After years of watching her pottery business grow—sometimes by as much as 40 percent in a year—Mary Kay Spencer came to the conclusion that there were more important things than money. First, there was the need to retain the magic that she felt in her connection to the brightly painted pots, bowls, lamps, mugs, and even birdfeeders that she crafts by hand. Second, there was a connection to her family that was too important to lose. "Once our daughter's grown up," Mary Kay says, "she's gone. If we can beef up production, we'll do it then, but right now I think that we can do it right and figure out a way to maintain our lifestyle without having to kill ourselves doing it."

Mary Kay was moving forward in a psychology career when she began to question where that career was taking her. At the time, she had a small potter's wheel and a studio near her Connecticut home where she would spend long hours contemplating her position. "The more I questioned my career, the more I was hanging out in the studio working with clay," she remembers. Then her decision came to a head when she was injured by a patient at the hospital where she worked. "It wasn't a serious injury," she says, "but it was enough to really make me wonder what I was doing."

By this time, Mary Kay knew that throwing pots was something she enjoyed enough to do full time, so she worked her way toward that goal. Trade shows and arts and crafts fairs were a first step, and she found enough interested students to start teaching on the side. Finally, she was ready to quit her job. "It was a big risk," she reflects. "I was comfortable with the money I was making. But it was a risk I needed to take."

After moving to Maine with her husband and working with an established potter to develop her style, Mary Kay founded The Potter's House and things really took off. Most of their business these days is wholesale, and Mary Kay's sales reps place her designs in gift stores "up and down the East Coast." Many of her products sell through the L.L. Bean stores, but she's shied away from being included in their catalog—doing that kind of volume would irrevocably change the nature of her business, she says. Their reach is also broadened through a website, now being improved and developed by a local webmaster who takes pots as payment.

The Potter's House has chosen to stay small, but there's still enough to keep Mary Kay busy. While she still throws many of her thirty to forty different products by hand, keeping up with demand has required that she create molds for the most popular items, and hire painters to duplicate her designs. This small-scale production line sends four to five hundred pieces into the kiln each week, and the demand for more is there if she wants it—and that's why she became torn about growing this business.

"I hired a few women to decorate the pots, and found that their influences change the designs," Mary Kay says. "Not that that's always bad, but it's hard to control. In that aspect we were starting to lose a little quality control here. We had to rethink our growth, and I got back into design, which I'd missed." The Potter's House is scaling back growth, with Mary Kay hoping that a 10 percent annual increase will be manageable, but, she adds, "I might want to back off even further." While there may not be as much pottery coming out of her kiln, what does make it to the shelves will be products that this business owner and artisan will be proud of.

Laura Henderson

PRESIDENT AND CHIEF
EXECUTIVE OFFICER

Prospect Associates
Rockville, Maryland

WORK HISTORY

1976–1979   Vice President, SysteMetrics, Bethesda, Maryland.

1979–present   President and CEO, Prospect Associates.

EDUCATION

1966   A.A. in Business, King's College, Charlotte, North Carolina.

FIRST JOB

At Duke University, research on a Ford Foundation grant looking at the impact of intervention on breaking the cycle of poverty.

COMMUNITY SERVICE

Chair Emeritus, National Foundation for Women Business Owners; Chair, Montgomery County Economic Advisory Council; Board of Directors, Maryland High Technology Council; Board of Trustees, National Small Business United; Advisory Board, Office of Technology Development,

Maryland Department of Economic and Employment Development; Member, former Member, Board of Directors, Former Vice Chair, and Executive Committee, Professional Services Council; Delegate, White House Conference on Small Business; Co-director, Youth Leadership Montgomery; Board of Trustees, Pfeiffer College, North Carolina; Board of Visitors and Advisory Council, Graduate School of Management and Technology, University College, University of Maryland; Secretary and Board of Trustees, Lab School, Washington, D.C.

AWARDS AND HONORS

Executive of the Year, Montgomery Gazette Newspapers, 1998; National Woman Business Owner of the Year, National Association of Women Business Owners, 1995; Board of Directors Award, National Foundation for Women Business Owners, 1995; Best Small Companies to Work for in America, *Inc.*, magazine, 1993; Social Responsibility Award, School of Business and Public Management, George Washington University, 1993; Washington Area Women in Business Advocate of the Year, U.S. Small Business; Arthur Young's Entrepreneur of the Year in the category of women-owned businesses in the Washington Area; Distinguished Lecturer, Georgetown University School of Business Administration; Mother of the Year, March of Dimes, 1998; Free Enterprise Award, Montgomery Chamber of Commerce, 1999.

FAMILY

Two children.

GREATEST OBSTACLES OVERCOME

The same obstacle many women have—being taken seriously.

PERSONAL GOALS

To raise my three children—my company and my two boys—to be independent, strong, and successful without my being a directive part of their lives.

PROFESSIONAL GOALS

To be someone who makes a difference and makes the world a fairer place.

DEFINITION OF SUCCESS

I think I'd define success as contentment, the ability to feel that you control your own destiny, that you've made a difference, and that you've always been true to who you were and what your values are. And to have fun, joy, and love in your life.

WAYS OF DEALING WITH PRESSURE AND STRESS

Having children helps because they certainly don't let you take yourself seriously. I also read trash novels, cook, and spend time being introspective.

ADVICE TO ASPIRING BUSINESSWOMEN

Dream big dreams, then put the elbow grease behind it to make it happen. Women often limit their dreams when there's no reason to. It's not easy to have everything in life—children, family, community, career—but if you believe you don't have to be traditional in these roles, it can be done.

*M*ost entrepreneurs are schizophrenic when they start their organizations. The fear of failure is great, but at the same time, we're almost cocky, so sure its going to work. I can look back twenty years with some amusement over how I would swing from this ultimate sense of confidence to ultimate terror.

It would be impossible to put a figure on how many people have benefited from Laura Henderson's entrepreneurial bravado. Since 1979, Prospect Associates has provided health science research, communication outreach, and project development for government agencies, health care companies, foundations, nonprofit organizations, and industries. The simple idea is to adapt scientific research for mass media. But the passion that saw Laura through the terror of going out on her own was the knowledge that she was changing, improving, and saving lives.

When a company has a product or a government agency has a program, Prospect takes it to the streets. "We do television, radio, work with the community, create materials," Laura says. "We can honestly feel that we're touching people's lives." They've helped state agencies with tobacco control programs; one of their studies was instrumental in getting smoking banned from domestic flights. They've designed web pages for issues ranging from women's health to heart disease. They've worked on a national campaign to explain the importance of people with diabetes getting flu shots. The range is nearly limitless, but Laura says they won't be taking any contracts from the tobacco industry. "We also won't touch projects we feel don't have a strong scientific basis, as it relates to health," she continues, "or anything we don't believe would be in the interest of the audience it's targeted to."

Laura started the company, which now employs over 160 and earns over $17 million a year, with $35,000 in personal savings after, she explains, "I perceived that it was very difficult to run a business the way I wanted to unless I was the CEO. In the male-dominated organization I was in, I found it difficult to have them understand that their management approaches worked for them, but wouldn't work for me. It wouldn't be consistent from the inside out." She says she wanted a "barrier-free" company that would accept different styles, career paths, and even mistakes. "My mother always told me I was at my most innovative and creative when I was in trouble," she says. "Our mistakes bring us a tremendous amount of innovation."

Laura points to two very different times in her company's history when she was in trouble. After it had done $1.2 million in the first ten months in business, there was a recession, and Prospect's revenues dipped for the next three years. "This was the most important stage we ever went through. We learned how to be a focused business." Laura also learned that she had a good reason to keep her doors open: "We got a lot of encouragement from our clients, who told us they really needed us to stay in business for them. That was a big help."

Further refinement came when the opposite happened and the company grew too rapidly: "We faced having to do business with all of our systems broken. They couldn't tolerate the increased load. That was the most difficult time for me as a leader because it made me focus on the systems and policy manuals that entrepreneurs don't find a lot of fun." Clients were wondering if the company that brought them individualized service would grow out of control, while Laura fabricated a new team from new and long-standing employees. "Bottom line was the team effort," she says, "as everyone came to grips with how growth doesn't just bring good things. In the end, it brought amazing challenges."

Looking back on her own experiences as a woman business owner inspired Laura to help establish the National Foundation of Women Business Owners (NFWBO), which has stunned corporate America with its studies on the impact of entrepreneurial women—one out of four hires in America are in women-owned businesses, which in total employ more in this country than the Fortune 500 does worldwide. NFWBO's research is not only changing perceptions but encouraging women to push those numbers even higher.

But while Laura's life is dedicated to disseminating information, she can joke about being ambivalent toward giving the full story behind starting a business: "We shouldn't teach entrepreneurs too much or they would never start their company. We have to find a balance of providing information and tools and not let them know the real downside. The truth can be too scary."

C. Dianne Sloan

COSMETIC CREATOR AND OWNER

Color Investment Cosmetics
Boston, Massachusetts

WORK HISTORY

1969–1980   A variety of jobs in Europe and Asia—hotel worker, au pair, assistant to designers and photographers.

1980–present   Owner, Color Investment Cosmetics.

EDUCATION

1969   B.A., Indiana University, Bloomington.

1991   Broadcasting Certificate, Northeast Broadcasting College (now Massachusetts Communication College), Boston, Massachusetts. Valedictorian of fall 1991 class.

FIRST JOB

Sales clerk in a fashion store, helping father with his photography business.

COMMUNITY SERVICE

1991 Mt. Everest Marathon—raised $6,000 for Dana Farber Cancer Research.

AWARDS AND HONORS

"Crème de la Crème" awards, 1997 and 1998 *Boston Best Guide* for "Best Cosmetic Colors" and "Best Skin Care."

FAMILY

My soul mate, confidant, and inspiration to keep on striving, Paul Bolden. He backs all my off-the-wall ideas 200 percent.

GREATEST OBSTACLES OVERCOME

Being one small cosmetics company against the giants.

PERSONAL GOALS

To laugh and have fun—I can't take it all so seriously!

DRIVING FORCE

I've always wanted to see more, do more, go further. I was first aware of this when I was five years old.

DEFINITION OF SUCCESS

It's an inner peace within yourself, deep within the soul. It's very elusive, but successes, whether the small daily ones or the ones that get attention on a larger scale, are presents you give yourself. They are deep satisfactions which don't come very often, and don't stay very long.

BUSINESS MAXIM

Please yourself and you will please others.

GREATEST REWARD FROM CAREER

To see the finished product of something I actually created, with my name on it, and have women use it, come back, and tell me, "This is the best product I've ever used."

ADVICE TO ASPIRING BUSINESSWOMEN

There are no limits. There are no ceilings. Do what you want to do. Whether you are a success or not, you can lean back, relax, and say to yourself, "I did it." At least you didn't let your life go by and say "I wish I had . . ."

*t*here's always this point after the initial rush of deciding to do something where I wonder "Why did I do this?" In my business right now, I'm wondering why I keep banging myself over the head. But I always manage to come out on the other side and say "Wow. That was unbelievable."

For Dianne Sloan, running a business isn't so different from jumping out of a plane, riding a motorcycle from Boston to Alaska solo, or running a marathon at the 17,500-foot-high base of Mount Everest, all of which she has done. "As an entrepreneur, you really have to go for broke," she says. "You're out on a limb and you never know what's coming up next." This is, however, the only way Dianne knows how to live.

After growing up and attending university in Indiana, Dianne decided to expand her horizons and, like many recent graduates, headed for Europe on a work abroad program. Unlike other young wanderers, however, she was bitten by the travel bug so hard that her short stay became a ten-year odyssey through thirty countries in Europe and Asia. Along the way, she took a variety of odd jobs, rough accommodations, and various modes of transportation to keep moving. She was also becoming inspired in a way that she never suspected.

"Starting a cosmetics company wasn't something I planned on. I thought I would be going to law school," Dianne says. When her wander-lust finally ebbed, Dianne discovered Boston, "Where I felt at home for the first time in all my travels." Inspired by having seen the faces and dress of so many different cultures, and drawing on her background in design and photography, she became a fashion consultant. It wasn't long before she discovered that her clients were having trouble finding makeup that matched colors recommended by Dianne, so she started mixing her own foundations and lipstick. "People kept talking about my cosmetics," Dianne says, "and one thing led to another. I felt perfectly content, and it seemed I had a gift for color."

Finally, after much urging by her clients, Dianne opened a small shop in 1995 amid the posh stores of Boston's Newbury Street and established a full line of cosmetics. While her theories about color have grown more elaborate, she still takes inspiration from her travels: "My entire line was influenced by seeing firsthand all those different skin tones and colors and how culture influenced women's cosmetics choices. Not everyone is lily white with pink tones, so I have a full range of cosmetics for every skin type." She also has colors influenced by the world's scenery: "Sun Rising," a lipstick color inspired by the sunrise in Hong Kong; "Eastern Spice," reminiscent of the spices she tasted on the Trans-Siberian Railway; or "Arctic Ice," from the ice formations she saw while riding through Alaska.

The entire concept behind the business is also driven by a negative experience close to home. "When I was a teenager and sat for the first time at the cosmetics counter, I left in tears," she says. "I looked like a streetwalker. I couldn't wait to wash it off." Her customers, she vowed, would always get personal attention, and their look, however colorful, would be based on who they are. "My customers always leave looking natural, and they've brightened their own look naturally. They're satisfied with who they are, confident about their own beauty."

After three years of strong growth, a burst of attention by local print and TV news, and a steady clientele, Dianne is poised to go national. Her catalog has caught the eyes of several major distributors, her products were "well received" at a Hong Kong trade show, and her website will allow customers to experiment with color combinations online. But word of mouth is still driving this business, as customers from around the world walk into her shop on the recommendation of a friend.

Dianne says she's amazed at how her business has taken on a life of its own; she can always look to the satisfaction of her customers to guide her through a difficult stretch. Women come to her for a new look, a small boost, a life change, or even to help them face serious illness, and Dianne feels privileged to help in this small way. "My customers are not models walking down runways. They're just normal people walking down the street. But when they tell me that they feel more confident and better about themselves because they are wearing my products, that's the biggest compliment I can receive."

Jodi F. Solomon

PRESIDENT

Jodi F. Solomon Speakers Bureau, Inc.

Boston, Massachusetts

WORK HISTORY

1977   Assistant, L. K. Simsarian Artist Management Firm, New York, New York.

1978   Interviewer, Senior Citizen "EasyRide" Program, Vera Institute of Justice, New York, New York.

1979   Assistant, Yellow Springs Chiropractic Clinic, Yellow Springs, Ohio.

1980–1982   Applications Engineer, Tapco Pump Company, Dedham, Ohio.

1982–1990   Vice President, K&S Speakers, Cambridge, Massachusetts.

1990–present   President, Jodi Solomon Speakers Bureau.

EDUCATION

1980   *B.A.* in social work and women's studies, Antioch College, Yellow Springs, Ohio.

FIRST JOB

Working for the family business during the summer as an administrative assistant.

ASSOCIATIONS AND NETWORKS

Women's Center for Enterprise; Young Entrepreneurs Association; The Commonwealth Institute; women on Wheels; Yankee Beemers.

COMMUNITY SERVICE

Advisory board, *Teen Voices,* a progressive magazine by and for teenage girls; various local community and neighborhood associations.

GREATEST OBSTACLES OVERCOME

The greatest challenge for me in my business has been managing people, both speakers and office staff. I didn't come into this business with management skills; it's something I've been working on, through classes and networking with other business owners.

PROFESSIONAL GOALS

To remain a very strong, focused, and concentrated small company with an excellent reputation. I've been doing this for eighteen years now, and it's been a road I paved myself, without many potholes. For that I feel extraordinarily proud and grateful for all the people who have supported me.

DRIVING FORCE

To find a place for myself in the workforce where I've created a great non-traditional environment.

DEFINITION OF SUCCESS

Happiness and finding balance.

WAYS OF DEALING WITH PRESSURE AND STRESS

Motorcycling and martial arts—my saving graces.

ADVICE TO ASPIRING BUSINESSWOMEN

Take the chance. Never look back and say I wish I had. Close your eyes, take a big step, and go forward. Surround yourself with as much as support as possible. Put your fears aside, learn that flexibility is your greatest gift, and go forward.

i feel that I need to take a stance in what I do with my life—that I can actually walk my talk—and know that my politics are represented by the work that I do, both in my business and in the community.

Jodi Solomon takes a stance by putting her clients behind lecture stands. Her agency, Jodi F. Solomon Speakers Bureau, places hundreds of clients at colleges and conferences around the country, but getting them in the door isn't Jodi's sole purpose. She's also very concerned with what they have to say. Her authors—academics, celebrities, activists—all reflect Jodi's own political beliefs—progressive, liberal, egalitarian—and getting them into the spotlight means that the issues this entrepreneur believes in are getting the attention she thinks they deserve.

"Every time there is an issue out," Jodi explains, "from computer hacking to what's going on in Bosnia, there is a need to gather information and disseminate it to the public. Thirty-second news blips are not satisfying to most people." With a client roster of experts from a vast range of disciplines, and a staff of seven who share her beliefs and commitments, Jodi can meet almost any issue head on. But some topics are particularly important to advance: "I really try to promote debates on the topics of abortion, gun control, genetic engineering, and euthanasia, these really tough issues people are facing, so they can be educated by experts."

Experts don't necessarily have to be trained, Jodi believes. Besides high-profile leaders and luminaries such as Spike Lee, Patricia Ireland, and the founders of Greenpeace and Amnesty International, Jodi has placed Holocaust survivors and entrepreneurs, speakers who rely on personal experience, "so they can share their stories and teach others that they have the power within them to make a difference in their lives, their communities, and hopefully their world." But Jodi thinks her clients, famous or obscure, are benefiting from her political commitment and her bureau's relatively small size: "I think they understand that they've been handpicked by the forces that move my staff. I also think they're very happy that I'm not representing people who they might have real political differences with."

After graduating from Antioch College with a degree in social work and women's studies, Jodi joined with an association and founded a lecture bureau that focused on programs for colleges and universities. "I thought that by opening a bureau that had represented nontraditional, nonconservative speakers," she recalls, "I would help open the minds of students who I feel have become very apathetic and conservative in their thinking." Eight years later, she went out on her own, founding her company with a small client base and a blend of personal savings, family support, and a line of credit. There was no doubt in her mind that she was ready, but she admits that she could have been better prepared for what lay ahead: "I wish someone had sat me down and mapped out what my life would look like when I started this business—how much time it would take, how much energy it would take. Everyone encouraged me to go ahead and do it, but no one told me the negative side of things."

Jodi now tries to make sure that other women in business understand what they're in for. Mentoring three women through the Center for Women in Enterprise, she draws the road map she was never given. However, the map doesn't only chart the obstacles; her own experience points to the entrepreneur's greatest reward. "One of the most amazing things I've discovered is my own inner strength and how empowering it is to realize, when you're looking back on everything, 'Wow. I've accomplished so much.' "

It's a feeling not unlike what Jodi describes she experienced when she sees her client Adam Werbach, the former president of the Sierra Club, speak to college audiences not much younger than himself. "He's just a regular guy," Jodi says, "but one who was able to focus all his talents and make a difference. I really feel that even for a moment, the audience can be taken someplace where they feel an empowerment they've never felt before." At times like these, according to Jodi, the difficulty of entrepreneurship can clearly be lessened through commitment to a higher purpose: "We all have to work for a living, but what we're doing here makes it very worthwhile to me. It's helped me keep perspective through some very challenging times."

Beverly F. Erickson

VICE PRESIDENT, REAL
ESTATE DEVELOPMENT

Peter D. Cummings &
Associates/The Fisher Group

Detroit, Michigan

Glenn Triest Photographic

WORK HISTORY

1974–1988   Various positions including Accounting Clerk and
Assistant Administrator, Henry Ford Health System,
Detroit, Michigan.

1988–1996   Assistant to the Executive Vice president, then Vice
President, Business Development, Detroit Medical Center,
Detroit, Michigan.

1996–present   Vice President, Real Estate Development, Peter D.
Cummings & Associates.

EDUCATION

1985   B.S. (honors) in management, Oakland University, Rochester,
Michigan.

1989   M.B.A., Wayne State University, Detroit, Michigan.

FIRST JOB

Microfilm technician while in high school.

ASSOCIATIONS AND NETWORKS

Advisory Board, Women's Economic Club; Associate Member, Urban Land Institute; Board Member, Haven.

COMMUNITY SERVICE

Oakland University Alumni Association; past Member, United Way Allocations Committee; Volunteer, Special Olympics.

AWARDS AND HONORS

Crain's "40 Under 40," 1996; Detroit's Most Influential Women, February, 1990.

FAMILY

One child.

GREATEST CHALLENGE OVERCOME

Career change after twenty years in the health care industry.

DRIVING FORCE

Wanting always to learn more.

DEFINITION OF SUCCESS

Meeting my objectives and goals, and to be respected for what I do.

BUSINESS MAXIM

Truly know what you are talking about when you open your mouth.

WAYS OF DEALING WITH PRESSURE AND STRESS

Don't take it too seriously.

ADVICE TO ASPIRING BUSINESSWOMEN

Integrity to yourself, first and always.

I'm not saying that I spent twenty years in the wrong career, but maybe when we get into our forties, we become a little bit more insightful and introspective.

Some career changes are spurred by a midlife crisis, some are brought on by downsizing, but Beverly Erickson's move from the health care industry to real estate development was started because she finally had time to think. Beverly had entered health care at nineteen as a clerk, and worked her way up to corporate Vice President while getting two degrees and raising her daughter. It took all her determination and drive, of which she had plenty, but that desire to get the job done overshadowed the possibility of doing something else. "I was busy doing other things," she explains, "so I wasn't really introspective about why I was in health care. I kept getting promotions, so why would I want to do something else?"

Some doubts came to the surface after she had her M.B.A and her daughter was in high school: "It became increasingly clear to me that some of the characteristics that made me successful also made me a bit controversial. I had a strong sense of vision and the ability to drive pretty hard to bring it about, and in a bureaucratic system, they want that, but they also don't want it. They want it if it doesn't disrupt anybody or change anything." She enjoyed most of the people she had worked with, the things they had accomplished together, and the opportunities the job provided, but the structure of the health care system in general seemed to conflict with the progress she felt she had to make: "When you work in a big health care system, what you're working on takes years to implement. I need to know there's an ending point, that I can move on." She told her boss, who supported her decision, allowing her to continue work while researching her new career choice. When an offer came from one of Detroit's top developers, Peter D. Cummings & Associates, she was ready.

While Beverly and her employer found that many of her skills translated easily into her new job, there was still a period of adjustment, to be expected after two decades in the same field: "After twenty years, you're used to opening your mouth, having an opinion, getting people to listen to you, and do what you suggest. All of the sudden I was in a new field, and not talking very much."

But she made a great match for this firm with her experience with community boards and organizations, gained while working in nonprofit health care. Peter D. Cummings & Associates, Beverly says, is a firm "very committed to the community." She continues: "Detroit is desperately attempting to become a viable urban community, and it was dormant for many, many years. We have to promote the concept and be the cheerleaders, we have to show that we have a social commitment, knowledge, and direction." In the process, they have to make a profit, and in urban renewal, that means staying with an idea until it works. "We don't just walk away," Beverly explains, "we invest in what we build." This commitment, along with the clout and respect that the firm has locally, made her transition much easier than it could have been, and made the decision to take that risk fairly straightforward: "I don't think I would have gone to work for just any developer."

It took a long time for Beverly's path to wind up at this point, but she remarkably holds few regrets and plenty of fond memories. Attending night school while climbing the corporate ladder, she built a support network around her of family and friends to help raise her child, something far more significant to her than the twists and turns of her career: "Jobs come and go," she says, "but the part we play in nurturing a child into adulthood is the greatest gift of all."

Being deeply involved in health care developed her community spirit, and working while attending school allowed her to apply right away what she'd learned. Beverly recently compared her career trajectory to that of a friend who had gone the traditional route, and realized that although they had taken widely different paths, the result was the same. "I just took a different route to get there." But still, she says, "It wasn't easy. I wouldn't recommend it to anybody."

Tommi A. White

EXECUTIVE VICE PRESIDENT,
QUALITY, SERVICE DELIVERY
AND INFORMATION
TECHNOLOGY

Kelly Services, Inc.
Troy, Michigan

WORK HISTORY

1972–1981   Various positions, including Assistant Vice President;
Regional Banking Division, National Bank of Detroit.

1981–1986   Various positions, including Director, Systems and
Programming, Ryder Financial Communications Services.

1986–1988   Vice President, Systems and Operations, American
Express.

1988–1990   Director, Systems, Ryder System, Insurance Division.

1990–1991   CIO, Vice President–MIS; Skandia Direct Operations
Corporation (formerly Ryder System Insurance Division).

1991–1992   Division Vice President, Client Services and Operations,
ADP.

1993–present   Vice President, Service; then Senior Vice President, Service and Quality; now Executive Vice President, Quality, Service Delivery and Information Technology, Kelly Services, Inc.

EDUCATION

1971   B.A., Oakland University, Rochester, Michigan.

FIRST JOB

Management trainee, National Bank of Detroit.

ASSOCIATIONS AND NETWORKS

National Association for Temporary and Staffing Services.

COMMUNITY SERVICE

Leadership Committee, Brother Rice High School.

AWARDS AND HONORS

Featured as one of Detroit's Most Influential Women by *Crain's Detroit Business,* 1997.

FAMILY

Married, one son.

GREATEST OBSTACLES OVERCOME

Information technology has been, and still is, a male-dominated area. As a woman in such an area, I'm automatically not taken seriously. I've had to prove my competencies first. Making the decisions needed to balance work life and home life, so they both work and are both successful.

DRIVING FORCE

I live for the challenge of the project, to fill in the steps toward a goal or vision, to see something come together and be successfully completed, and then to look forward to the next bigger, more complex set of achievements. Like starting with a blank canvas and creating a wonderful painting.

DEFINITION OF SUCCESS

To do what I love and be paid for it.

BUSINESS MAXIM

There is nothing more valuable than your reputation and your credibility.

GREATEST REWARD FROM CAREER

Working with very competent people who have respected me enough to be willing to move across the country to work for me again.

WAYS OF DEALING WITH PRESSURE AND STRESS

I married my best friend. There has always been somebody there to talk to. He's also in a technology business and understands me.

ADVICE TO ASPIRING BUSINESSWOMEN

First, never doubt yourself. Second, understand that life is a compromise and you can't "have it all." You will have to find a balance between home and work that works for you. Finally, go to work for a company and for people who reward based on performance. Avoid companies that have programs to help women succeed. Look for people who say that as long as you perform, we will reward you—period.

*O*nce people see me, or see any woman perform, they forget you're a woman and accept you for the fact that you're the best at what you do.

Tommi White always wanted to be the best at what she does. Now, by overseeing quality and information systems for Kelly Services, she's in a position that allows her to help 750,000 temporary workers be the best at what they do. Twenty years ago, Tommi says she never suspected that she would be the chief technology officer of a Fortune 500 company, but her unusual path to working in information technology has now led to a perfect home.

"From my perspective, information technology is a lot less about the writing of the code; information technology is the science of behavior," explains Tommi. This is how a psychology major grew to love the computer systems that not only keep businesses running, but determine how businesses will be run. When your business is staffing, when your product is people, understanding behavior becomes all important. "Fifty years ago, when Kelly was a new company, the supervisor in the field on the front line with our customer did it all in their head—what were the techniques they used for matching the right person to the right job and the right person to the right company? Now we are using technology to do the same thing and reduce the work demands on the branch staff."

Tommi was at the National Bank of Detroit when her boss, Jim Bartlett, encouraged her to explore the technology side of business (he later recommended her to Kelly), even if it meant that she would have to trade salary for training. She found the opportunity at Ryder, but that also meant that she would be one of a small number of women at a trucking company, working in a field where clients and co-workers didn't expect to find a woman. She was not dissuaded: "I had to prove my competencies first. This has been true all my life, from playing goalie in hockey (with a helmet on at the start of practice so my teammates didn't know, at first, that I was a girl), to proving my skills in some very tough corporate environments."

When she started with Kelly services, she had the opportunity to find another skill—quality management. "Quality management is an area of expertise I have today," says Tommi, "but when I started with Kelly I was really a novice as far as what a quality system could mean, what it could bring to an organization, and the impact it could have on a corporate culture. The experience of building a methodology—the Kelly Quality Management System—was one of the best things for the growth of my career." She might have thought of herself as a novice, but with her understanding of behavior coupled with her expertise in technology, she was able to hit the ground running. Under her direction, Kelly met the rigorous standards of Ford's Q1 certification, as well as those of Xerox—two of Kelly's major clients.

Tommi has also worked to meet the needs of the temporary workers themselves, who she refers to as customers: "We view them as a customer of our processes, just as we view the end client as a customer of our processes." This view has resulted in improved payment systems, the PinPoint software package, and a hot line that temps can call if they need technical assistance while on assignment. "Any improvements we make to the quality system throughout the corporation have an impact on our ability to help them build their career path," Tommi explains. "People are starting to choose this type of work as a career, and we need to help them continue to improve their careers, just as if they were full-time employees."

For Tommi, all the work with quality management systems and information technologies leads to one thing—people. The peak of her career didn't have to do with the mastering of a piece of hardware or the implementation of a successful quality program, but with her employees. When she was with American Express, she moved a data processing operation from Nashville to Denver and made job offers to thirteen employees she had worked with over the years. "All thirteen of those people packed their bags and moved to Denver, knowing they would have to work for me when they got there. The best day of my career was the day the thirteenth person said 'Sure, I'll move and work for you again.' "

Mary P. McConnell, Esq.

SENIOR VICE PRESIDENT, SECRETARY, AND GENERAL COUNSEL

Genmar Holdings, Inc.
Minneapolis, Minnesota

WORK HISTORY

1979–1984   Wetlands Ecologist, U.S. Corps of Engineers, St. Paul, Minnesota.

1985–1988   Assistant County Attorney, Dakota County, Hastings, Minnesota.

1988–1994   Partner, Lindquist & Vennum, Minneapolis, Minnesota.

1995–present   Senior Vice President, Secretary, and General Counsel, Genmar Holdings, Inc.

EDUCATION

1978   B.S. in Wildlife Biology, University of Minnesota, St. Paul.

1984   J.D., William Mitchell College of Law, St. Paul, Minnesota.

FIRST JOB

Waitress at the Minnesota State Fair, at age fifteen.

ASSOCIATIONS AND NETWORKS

Minnesota State Bar Association.

COMMUNITY SERVICE

Big Brothers and Sisters Program.

PROFESSIONAL GOALS

To continue to be challenged intellectually and to attain a position where I can make a real difference in the direction of an organization and its people.

DRIVING FORCE

Intellectual curiosity and the ability to turn adversity or problems into a positive learning experience.

DEFINITION OF SUCCESS

A life rich in varied experiences, both personal and professional, and one that has achieved the proper balance between career, home, and personal relationships.

BUSINESS MAXIM

Do the best you can with integrity, treat people fairly and with respect.

WAYS OF DEALING WITH PRESSURE AND STRESS

I live in a peaceful place where at the beginning and end of the day I can enjoy and reflect on simple, tangible things: a garden, the woods, birds, a river, playing the piano.

Mary P. McConnell, Esq.

ADVICE TO ASPIRING BUSINESSWOMEN

Welcome every opportunity for new experiences and challenges whether or not you are fearful to make a change or concerned you do not have the background or experience. If you have a history of success in a variety of roles you will almost always land on your feet whatever you choose. Always think ahead on how to take advantage of opportunities in your current position. Actively seek the advice of others you respect. It can save you a lot of learning time.

i like choices. I like options. I don't like to have doors shut. Going to law school expanded the universe of choices I knew I would have when I got out.

It was an exciting time for biologists when Mary McConnell took a job with the U.S. Corps of Engineers. The Clean Water Act had recently been passed, and this organization, formerly associated with less than environmentally friendly projects, was given the task of assessing environmental impacts on America's wetlands and waterways. But it took only a few years before she felt she had hit the wall as a scientist with the government: "The government has a very rigid system of career advancement which can impede personal and professional growth," Mary says. "I'd already gotten to a high level in a short time, and realized I would be constrained from reaching my potential if I didn't make a change."

Adding a law degree to her degree in biology turned out to be a powerful combination, and it took Mary on a course from the county attorney's office to private practice, and finally to general counsel and corporate secretary for the largest independent boat manufacturer in the world. She's fully exercised the options the law degree gave her, and they've given her more than a career: "I've seen my career from so many different sides. In law, the only thing I haven't seen is the judicial side. It's taught me that nothing is black and white. When I was at the Corps of Engineers, I was in a black-and-white world. Law school was a great educational tool for breaking down those barriers."

After enforcing environmental regulations for the county attorney's office, Mary switched teams, or so she thought when she initially moved to private practice and began representing corporations. Mary explains, "I'd worn the white hat, so to speak, and I was afraid at first of putting on the 'black hat.' But my sense of right was never tested. I found that my clients wanted to do the right thing. This was an eye-opening experience."

One of her clients was recreational power boat manufacturer Genmar, and she was recruited by the President after a number of successful cases. Although Mary's energies are now focused on one corporation, she says, "There are always challenges, if you are willing to take the initiative." Genmar employs five thousand and has eight plants in five states and one in Canada, all of which are subject to environmental regulations. There's plenty more to do in the areas of contracts, employment law, finance, banking, and legislative affairs: "There's a huge variety. I'm never bored."

In a career path that's so varied, and yet so seamless, it's almost surprising to find a few bumps along the way. Starting work in a male-dominated field, Mary experienced being treated as a novelty or a threat: "Some men wanted to work with me because I was a woman, which isn't good, or they didn't want to work with me because I was a woman. At times it seemed as if there was no right place to be." It became easier after law school, but getting through law school while working full time took its own toll. "It was tough," she says. "You forget who you are—you have to—for that period of time."

These have been minor glitches as far as she can tell. "I've been pretty lucky. It has been pretty smooth for me. For some reason, at the point at which I've been ready to move on, or I've gotten bored or started looking for new challenges, these great opportunities have come before me." If she didn't get everything she always wanted, Mary's not planning on regretting anything: "It's hard to do, but at a certain time in your life, you have to modify what your goals are and what's going to make you happy. Who you want to be at twenty-five isn't always who you're going to be at forty-five. In many ways that's good."

Bernadette S. McCormick

REGIONAL MANAGER

Business Wire, Inc.

Minneapolis, Minnesota

WORK HISTORY

1982–1983   Teaching Associate, University of Minnesota, St. Paul.

1983–1984   Account Executive, Media Loft, Inc., Minneapolis, Minnesota.

1985–1986   Sales Consultant, Northway Fabricators, St. Paul, Minnesota.

1986–1990   Account Representative, Dayton's Commercial Interiors, Minneapolis, Minnesota.

1990–1992   Director of Sales and Marketing, A&M Business Interior Services, Inc., Minneapolis, Minnesota.

1993–present   Regional Manager, Business Wire, Inc.

EDUCATION

1981   *B.A.* in art, minor in economics and journalism Macalester College, St. Paul, Minnesota.

1983   *M.A.* in general design, journalism minor, University of Minnesota, St. Paul.

FIRST JOB

Teaching Associate, University of Minnesota.

ASSOCIATIONS AND NETWORKS

Vice President of Programs, National Investor Relations Institute, Twin Cities Chapter; Macalester Alumni.

COMMUNITY SERVICE

Counseling Macalester College "students of color" for career opportunities; Mentor for University of Minnesota undergraduates on careers in design.

FAMILY

One son.

GREATEST OBSTACLES OVERCOME

Language barriers, understanding corporate cultures.

PERSONAL GOALS

To ensure my son has everything necessary to build his future. Take care of my parents. Continue to grow spiritually.

PROFESSIONAL GOALS

To contribute at an upper-management level. To own a business in the leisure industry.

DEFINITION OF SUCCESS

A combination of accomplishments and achievements: health, happiness, peace, and contributing to family and community.

BUSINESS MAXIM

Businesspeople are people, first.

WAYS OF DEALING WITH PRESSURE AND STRESS

I think of my childhood days, dodging bullets or rough living conditions, overseas, and the perspective seems to adjust what I consider to be "stress."

ADVICE TO ASPIRING BUSINESSWOMEN

Learn to "make the difference." Learn to pick your battles. Truly dedicate to putting your energy only where it counts.

i still think of myself as an internationalist. I don't think it will ever go away. It's me, a part of who I am.

After having lived in nine countries before she turned nineteen, Bernadette McCormick joined her siblings in Minnesota for college and soon made the Twin Cities her home. Today, she lends her global perspective to the Minneapolis branch of media-relations wire service Business Wire, a branch she was recruited to establish. Even though taking the job meant leaving an established and profitable career in sales, and required her to totally change fields, the word "risk" never entered her mind: "The company has thirty offices nationally, and I was charged with opening the local branch here in the Twin Cities, starting it from ground zero. But I don't see things as risks. I saw it as a huge challenge. I guess when you grow up dodging bullets overseas, nothing's that scary here."

Those bullets were a constant part of life for Bernadette and her family from the time they left Thailand when she was six. Her father, a United Nations Officer, moved the family from one peacekeeping mission to the next: "Wherever there was trouble, we soon were there," Bernadette says, "and stayed until there was a crisis, until they were no longer 'family missions,' but just war zones." Bernadette was in Lebanon after the eruption of civil war, and recalls a close shave when she was stuck in a crossfire on her way home from play rehearsal. "We were always somehow stuck in crossfires, but typically in a moving vehicle or in a building. Here it was just myself, alone. It was the scariest experience I've ever had."

With the real danger behind her, Bernadette established Business Wire's Minneapolis branch with flair. In five years, starting from scratch, this branch has captured 30 percent of the market in their five-state region, including top-name clients such as Honeywell and General Mills. All this has been accomplished with a staff of only six. "It's pretty good," says Bernadette. "We run lean and mean, and everybody carries more than their fair share." Although Business Wire runs an international operation, Bernadette's branch operates with a certain degree of autonomy, and for the branch manager, she says, "It's like running your own business."

This is a perfect fit for someone like Bernadette. Being in charge has allowed her to escape strident corporate culture clashes she might have experienced somewhere else: "Sometimes I like to march to my own drumbeat and might not be so process-oriented or politically correct, because I believe there are certain things I won't compromise." She's firm on this point, but other adjustments she had to make for the corporation she can look back on with humor. "My English was not always this good," she says. "We were very good students and attended American schools, but in terms of business, something like 'ASAP,' which can't be found in any dictionary, would get me. Things like 'Don't short-change yourself' I'd say as 'Don't short-sheet yourself.' You could have a heyday with some of the things I said."

Now much of the adjustment appears to have been completed. Prior to joining Business Wire, she was regularly selling over a million dollars in commercial office furniture per year. From knowing "nothing" about investor relations when she started with Business Wire, Bernadette now is a regional Vice President of the National Investor Relations Institute. In 1995, she was given Business Wire's Gold Brush Award for making off with competitors' clients. And, she adds, she's never had to compromise.

Not all her overseas experiences were terrifying, and it's the good memories that make Bernadette want to live abroad again. Someday, when she's done all she can in the U.S. business world, she wants to retire with a business of her own: "I picture being up in the Swiss Alps somewhere in a small shop, cooking and stuff like that. Maybe a resort, where I would be serving people on vacation who just want to be happy. It's just a little aspiration."

Lisa Daniel McAdams

Gil Ford Photography

VICE PRESIDENT
CORPORATE DEVELOPMENT

WorldCom, Inc.
Jackson, Mississippi

WORK HISTORY

1973–1975   Credit Card Verification, Bank Americard (part time), Jackson, Mississippi.

1975–1981   Claims Department Clerk, Secretary, Allstate Insurance Company, Jackson, Mississippi.

1981–1984   Customer Service Rep and Trainer, Telecom Plus, Jackson, Mississippi.

1984–1986   Manager of Sales Engineering, Southeastern Telecom, Nashville, Tennessee.

1986–1988   Telecommunications Consultant, Callahan & Associates, Fairhope, Alabama.

1988–present   Started as Traffic Engineer, WorldCom, Inc., Jackson, Mississippi.

EDUCATION

1975   *A.A.* in secretarial science, Hinds Jr. College, Raymond, Mississippi.

FIRST JOB

Working in a local department store, gift-wrapping during Christmas holidays. Also modeled and worked as a high school representative for a line of cosmetics marketed toward teenagers.

COMMUNITY SERVICE

Board of Directors, Willowood Developmental Center (for developmentally disabled children); Board of Directors, Mississippi Children's Home Society; Volunteer, Habitat for Humanity.

AWARDS AND HONORS

Employee of the Year, Southeastern Telecom, 1986.

FAMILY

Married, one child.

GREATEST OBSTACLES OVERCOME

Getting to the point where I was taken seriously and respected by my male peers. At first, there was a lot of resentment. It took years before I was accepted.

DRIVING FORCE

To make a difference in whatever I attempt. Being a perfectionist sometimes is a strong motivator.

DEFINITION OF SUCCESS

Personal fulfillment in what you do each day. A satisfaction with your accomplishments.

BUSINESS MAXIM

First and foremost, treat others as you expect to be treated and respect everyone as an equal. Never ask someone to do something you wouldn't do yourself.

WAYS OF DEALING WITH PRESSURE AND STRESS

Enjoying my family, friends, and hobbies takes my mind off work. I'm also trying to work from the house more often—with a computer, fax, and copy machine, I'm just as functional there as I am in the office.

ADVICE TO ASPIRING BUSINESSWOMEN

Find a career you really enjoy. Set your goals. Find out what you need to accomplish in your current position to go to the next level. Always keep a positive "can do" attitude, and be willing to do whatever it takes to get the job accomplished. Do not openly complain.

*I*t's so phenomenal to have been involved in a company like this from a very, very early stage. When it was announced that we were going to be merging with MCI, it was like seeing your child grow up to become President. It almost seemed unreal.

Lisa McAdams joined WorldCom when it was a minor player in the telecommunications industry with around $12 million in revenue, and has helped see it through countless acquisitions and changes as it grew to become the fourth-largest long-distance carrier in the United States. The merger with MCI in 1998 makes it second only to AT&T. It's an outrageous success story, not unlike Lisa's own.

In 1981, Lisa found herself at a dead end. Without a college degree, opportunities for advancement at her insurance company were limited. Despite having no training in telecommunications, she took a "huge" pay cut and became a trainer for a small telecom company. The company was on such a tight budget, however, that she was soon required to join technicians in the field to get the job done: "I'd pull my hair up at night," Lisa recalls, "put a baseball cap on, and pull cable. I'd come back the next day dressed to meet with and train customers. Very few people realized I was the same person." In the process, Lisa found her calling: "I was very intrigued by the programming of the phone systems, and found I had a knack for it—I could understand the manuals, and find new ways to make things work. It just grew from there."

At this point, all her training was on the job or self-taught, requiring late nights at an installation site or hours at home with a technical manual. One thing, Lisa says, drove her forward during this time:"I don't like anything to beat me, so I can't give up. I'll sit at a computer for twenty-four hours or more before I'll let it win." Her perseverance paid off, gaining her the respect not only of her employers, but of the predominantly male technicians she worked with in the field. But there was still more to learn—when the call came from WorldCom, asking if she'd like to work as a traffic engineer, her first reaction was "what's that?"

She soon found out (the very "very broad" position involved reading traffic reports, ordering circuits, and working on installations), and also found herself in on the ground floor of a rapidly expanding company with plenty of room for initiative. When Lisa first got to WorldCom, she says, it was a phone company without a network—so she and three others built one: "It was largely done by trial and error. It was not smooth as silk," Lisa says. "It got really quite comical at times."

Lisa's move into management was sudden and partly due to someone else's error. The man who hired her was scheduled to go on a due diligence trip to Kansas City to check on a company WorldCom was considering buying. Instead, he called her at six in the morning the day of his flight: "He'd shot himself in the foot—literally. He called me from the hospital and told me I had to get on the plane." Due diligence trips are now a major part of Lisa's job in a company that's known for its deal making.

The theme of Lisa's forties appears to be satisfaction. She has achieved the goals she set for herself back when she started, and now hopes to broaden her focus outside work; "There came a time in my life when I realized that my whole life has been work. I had *no* personal life. I missed several of my son's early years. I wasn't taking care of myself; I'd run myself into the ground and had to undergo major surgery. But still it was very hard for me to step back." These days, she devotes time to her family, to two local charities, and to her horses. She no longer feels that she has to be on call twenty-four hours a day, seven days a week: "I don't have to live like that anymore. When I leave the office—most days—I really leave. My work doesn't have to come with me. Working forty to fifty hours a week is like a dream come true."

Melody K. Bradley

EXECUTIVE DIRECTOR

Jackson County Port Authority
Pascagoula, Mississippi

WORK HISTORY

1980–1984   Senior Rate Auditor, Delta Steamship Lines, Inc., New Orleans, Louisiana.

1984–1986   Senior Rate Analyst, Lykes Lines, Inc., New Orleans, Louisiana.

1986–1987   Manager, Accounts Receivable, Southern Steamship Agency, Inc., Mobile, Alabama.

1987–1993   Manager, Sales and Public Relations, Port of Pascagoula.

1993–1998   Port Director, Port of Pascagoula.

1998–present   Executive Director, Jackson County Port Authority.

EDUCATION

Attended Jackson County Junior College and University of New Orleans.

FIRST JOB

Working in parents' jewelry store at age fifteen.

ASSOCIATIONS AND NETWORKS

Past or present Board Member of: American Association of Port Authorities, Gulf Seaports Marine Terminal Conference, Mississippi Water Resources Association, Jackson County Area Chamber of Commerce, Jackson County Economic Development Foundation; Executive Committee, Strategic Planning Process for the city of Pascagoula; Gulf Ports Association; Mississippi District Export Council; Southeast Regional Dredging Team; National Dredging Caucus.

COMMUNITY SERVICE

Service for United Way of Jackson and George Counties: Vice President of Campaign and General Campaign Chairman, 1996–1997; Member, Board of Directors; Member, Executive Committee; Member, Hickory Club.

AWARDS AND HONORS

Gulf Coast Achievement Award, Mississippi Gulf Coast Community College, 1997; Mississippi's 50 Leading Business Women, *Mississippi Business Journal,* 1997, 1998; recognized by the Pascagoula Moss Point Business and Professional Women Club for Outstanding Achievements in the Business and Professional Community, 1997.

FAMILY

Two daughters, three grandchildren.

GREATEST OBSTACLES OVERCOME

My age. I was fairly young for the position when appointed Port Director. Also, political climate and influences.

DRIVING FORCE

For a long time, financial security for my family. I have been a single parent since my children were very young. More recently, it has been to see this port achieve its full potential.

DEFINITION OF SUCCESS

When, through your work to achieve goals and successes, you have also gained the respect of your colleagues, peers, and family. When you have managed to stand firm through adversity and still maintain a high work ethic.

BUSINESS MAXIM

Actually there are two—both given to me by my father. Ask not what your company can do for you, but what you can do for your company. And never back up to the pay window.

WAYS OF DEALING WITH PRESSURE AND STRESS

I rely heavily on my faith to restore balance and serenity and to provide grace. Exercise, when I can fit it in.

ADVICE TO ASPIRING BUSINESSWOMEN

Be yourself, but refine that into a business/professional self. Pick your fights carefully, both in your personal and professional life. Most of them are not worth your time and energy. Save your "cards" for the ones that are truly worth using them on.

i loved turning forty. It was like getting to the top of the hill and realizing that I could say no, and that I'd proven myself. I could step back and take a look at what I've done.

The view is pretty broad from where Melody Bradley is now sitting. After an impressive career in the shipping industry, she returned to her hometown and developed the previously nonexistent marketing and PR departments for the port where she first discovered her love for the water and the ships that travel across it. In six years, while she was still in her thirties, Melody was selected by the Jackson County Board of Commissioners to be the new Port Director. This appointment made her one of only four female port directors in the United States, and the only female who rose to the job through the private sector.

The Port of Pascagoula is the nation's sixteenth largest port, in terms of cargo tonnage, and is visited by large vessels more than six hundred times a year. It's the single most important piece of infrastructure in Jackson County, the most industrialized county in the state, and the port has a clear-cut economic impact throughout Mississippi—25,800 jobs, $925 million in personal income, and $52 million in tax revenue are dependent on the port. Melody recently demonstrated the importance of the port to the Mississippi State Legislature, and was so convincing that her proposed grant of $20 million dollars for improvements, channel deepening and widening, and cleanup programs passed with 100 percent of the vote in both houses.

The state should see a quick return on its investment. Melody is making certain that aside from these large-scale improvements, the Port of Pascagoula will be a self-supporting part of the community. She points with pride to the negotiation of a lease for a new shipyard that will bring in three thousand jobs, and has plans to further introduce the global economy into Mississippi by attracting ships from Russia and Latin America. For Melody, her business is community service: "This is my hometown, where all of my family live—parents, children, grandchildren, siblings. So it is much more than a job or position for me."

Surprisingly for a business so associated with masculinity, Melody has never felt held back because of her gender, but she picked up some subtle tactics early on: "I never wore pants to the office. In the early years of women coming into this industry, and the business world in general, it was important to let men know that I wasn't trying to be a man—that I just wanted to be an equal in business." Melody admits she will always appreciate men opening doors for her, both literally and figuratively: "My primary biggest supporters and mentors have been, for the most part, male. They definitely gave me more opportunity than problems. And I've been really impressed with the fact that Jackson County, Mississippi, put a woman in this position." More of a problem early on was her age: "I've always thought I was older than I was. I'm sure my young age had some people a little concerned when I became Port Director, but they've become comfortable with it." And besides, she jokes, with the vast responsibility she holds, "This position's aged me. I don't have that problem with being too young any more."

Knowing people are depending on her isn't a novelty, however. Melody was for twenty-three years a single mother of two children while she worked and sometimes attended school. But to hear her tell it, she might not have made it without them: "They were my biggest supporters and my biggest critics. They went to work with me sometimes, and sometimes I brought work home, but they were very supportive in realizing that I was trying to make a better life for them. They were always encouraging and loving children. I was very lucky—and I still am."

Everything seemed to have fallen into place by the time Melody was forty, and the chance this milestone offered for reflection was welcome, but not overwhelming: "It doesn't mean I have to quit working hard, but I finally felt comfortable with myself," she explains. "But I don't know how I feel about turning fifty!"

Susan L. Anderson

DIRECTOR AND OWNER

MIDWESTOCK

Kansas City, Missouri

WORK HISTORY

1980–1982   Associate Editor, *Impressions Magazine,* Windsor
                Publications; Dallas, Texas.

1984–1991   Editor, *Lawn & Garden Marketing Magazine,* Intertec
                Publishing; Overland Park, Kansas.

1991–present Owner, MIDWESTOCK.

EDUCATION

1980   Bachelor of Journalism degree, University of Missouri at
                Columbia.

FIRST JOB

Counterperson at a Burger Chef in Nebraska. It was a terrible place to work,
but I learned a lot about serving the public. We should all be forced to work
a service job at sometime in our career.

ASSOCIATIONS AND NETWORKS

Member, Picture Agency Council of America. Service for the National Association of Women Business Owners includes: Secretary of Kansas City Chapter, 1995–1996; President of Kansas City Chapter 1996–1997; Representative and National Council Director, Corporate and Economic Development Council, 1998–1999; Member, Website Development Committee.

COMMUNITY SERVICE

Kansas City sponsorship committee member, NAWBO liaison, Take Your Daughter to Work Day Initiative of the Girl Scouts of America.

FAMILY

Married, two children, one golden retriever.

DRIVING FORCE

The real force behind me is knowing that my family, staff, and business associates have such incredible confidence in me. They believe in me and what I've built. How could I fail with all that energy behind me?

DEFINITION OF SUCCESS

Life balance. I don't work sixty hours a week to achieve my business success, and I don't have this incredibly immaculate home with a kitchen floor you can eat off! I try to maintain some sense of balance in both my personal and business life by keeping my expectations of success realistic. It keeps me— and everyone around me—sane.

BUSINESS MAXIM

Find a balance and you can find success—even if it isn't financial success.

ADVICE TO ASPIRING BUSINESSWOMEN

No detail is too small or insignificant to demand your attention. I hang in my office a photo reminder of a day that I was too busy to check a detail that nearly cost me a trusted business friend. It was a humbling experience and I look at that photo every day to remind me of it.

*I*t doesn't matter whether we have 2,500 square feet or 25,000 square feet. All that matters is that we have the personnel and the technology to resolve the needs of our clients. It really doesn't matter how big you are.

Founded by Susan Anderson in 1991, MIDWESTOCK has carved a comfortable and profitable niche in areas neglected by the powerful international stock photo houses with only four full-time employees and Susan's technological savvy. Niche markets, in this case images of America's heartland, often have limited growth potential, but Susan says they haven't yet seen where that limit might be.

MIDWESTOCK represents fifty photographers and holds around 250,000 images that are licensed to advertising agencies, book and magazine publishers, and corporate marketing departments. While a quarter million images may seem enormous, Susan calls her company a midsize agency, and says that its size gives them a significant advantage in the area of customer service: "I've actually had clients tell me that sometimes they call up big stock houses, who act like they're doing them a big favor by taking their call. It's not like that here."

Despite their spectacular growth—50 percent for the first six years—and their continual technological improvements, Susan still depends on a low-tech method for serving requests: "I still look at every single photo that comes through here. I have an incredible memory for knowing whether I have something on file or not." From this personal database and her electronic databases, Susan can take a request, give the caller an individual, one-time website address, and have scanned photos online in a matter of hours for the client's review. She says her clients are always amazed, especially those who have had experience with the big stock houses: "I don't know if they'd ever thought of doing those kinds of things," she says. "There seems to be too much red tape."

Electronic media is a great leveler for MIDWESTOCK. Instead of spending $240,000 on a full-color catalog, as the big houses do at least once a year, Susan put down about $25,000 on the website, and spends maybe an additional $15,000 per year keeping it up to date. In 1997, for the first time, MIDWESTOCK released a CD-ROM catalog, but Susan says this format had a distinct advantage over print: "All the scanning, programming, and coding was done here. We simply learned how to write CDs, and just sent the master off to be replicated." MIDWESTOCK's next technological advance will be a keyword-searchable online database of their images, which will, Susan says, "put us into a much bigger international spotlight."

Susan had been trained as a journalist and worked as a magazine editor most of her professional life, gaining skills she still uses daily, namely the "ability to pool creative resources." She'd worked with stock houses, and her husband is a photographer, so she saw clearly the need for an agency "just west of New York, slightly east of L.A." Starting with seven photographers and a small bank of images, she spent a year on her own before hiring clerical help. "It seemed like forever. Just the pulling and refiling of images could be overwhelming," she remembers. "Now my staff won't even let me in that department. I'm not allowed to file anything without their help."

Assistance has also come from the local chapter of the National Association of Women Business Owners. Susan was surprised when she first attended their meetings at how much she shared with women in completely different industries: "You find that no one understands what you are going through like other women business owners, even if you have nothing in common but what you deal with on a daily basis. It's important to have people like that at your side." In return, Susan has served on several governing boards and helped develop a billboard campaign for the NAWBO chapter, a campaign now repackaged for use by other chapters across the U.S.

She was also active in the local NAWBO's version of Take Your Daughter to Work Day, where entrepreneurs took other people's daughters to work. Susan knows firsthand the value of taking her daughter to work—she did it for years and business is now in the young girl's blood. One year for her daughter's birthday, they had a tea party—the girls wore dressy outfits and big hats, "and as the tea was being served," Susan recalls, "my daughter leaned over to her friend and asks, 'Well, how's your business?' Not 'How are the kids,' or that kind of make believe, but she actually asked, 'How's your business.' I was so proud that she could think that way."

Sandra M. Stash

VICE PRESIDENT
ENVIRONMENTAL SERVICES

Atlantic Richfield Company
Anaconda, Montana

WORK HISTORY

1979–1980 Production and drilling roustabout, pumper and welder,
Union Oil Company of California, various locations.

1980–1981 Offshore drilling engineer, Marathon Oil Company,
Louisiana and Texas.

1981–present Atlantic Richfield Company, Anaconda, Montana.

EDUCATION

1981 B.S. in Petroleum Engineering (honors).

FIRST JOB

Farm worker, Red Hook, New York.

ASSOCIATIONS AND NETWORKS

Member of U.S. Federal Reserve Bank Board of Directors (Minneapolis branch); Clean Air Act Advisory Committee, FACA for Ozone, PM, Regional Haze, Washington, D.C.; National Association of Manufacturers Environment, Health and Safety Committee; American Petroleum Institute Health, Safety, Environment and General Committee; National Mining Association Water Quality and Solid Waste Committees, NACEPT Committee—Superfund Reform.

COMMUNITY SERVICE

Montana Ambassador; Board of Directors, Butte YMCA; Vice President, Butte–Silver Bow Chamber of Commerce; Board of Directors, Butte Junior Achievement; Vice President and Board of Directors, Montana Tech Foundation; Appointed by Montana Governor to Commission on Reinventing Government; Volunteer, Expanding Your Horizons (program that appeals to fifth- and sixth-grade girls to study math and science).

AWARDS AND HONORS

Engineer of the Year, Montana Society of Professional Engineers, 1993.

PERSONAL GOALS

I would like to *have* a personal life.

PROFESSIONAL GOALS

To continue to stay in a high-profile job, either in government or industry.

DEFINITION OF SUCCESS

Be happy with what you are doing. It's not money, it's not titles. It's just wanting to go to work every morning and enjoying every minute of the day.

BUSINESS MAXIM

1. Take risks and don't be too hard on yourself if you fail.
2. Always take the high road. Nobody ever faults you for taking the high road.

WAYS OF DEALING WITH PRESSURE AND STRESS

I feel fortunate in that I have the type of personality that I can confront the issue, deal with it, and then move on. I do not dwell on things. I do not worry things to death or second-guess decisions. I think that's kept me mentally healthy.

ADVICE TO ASPIRING BUSINESSWOMEN

First, you have to have a top-notch education. Second, you have to get in the field. The fact that I spent seven years in the field—on a drilling rig, on construction sites—gives me a level of credibility I wouldn't have had if I'd never left the office. You need to get out and do the real work. Third, there's nothing wrong with being nice. I think in particular women develop bad reputations, more so than men, for being confrontational or ugly with people.

i have so many older women who come up to me in the grocery store and say, "It's so great to see a woman in your position." That's very gratifying.

When Sandy Stash was sent by her employer, the Atlantic Richfield Company, to a town some visitors, due to pollution, have called the worst place on Earth—Butte, Montana—she was handed what might have seemed an impossible task: manage the cleanup of the nation's largest Superfund site, reduce ARCO's massive liability, and, in general, make everyone happy. Nine years later, Sandy can look back at a long list of achievements squeezed out of this patch of unforgiving ground. "I came up to Montana kind of naively,"

she admits. "I didn't realize just how controversial the job was going to be. But I feel I was able to rise to the occasion."

When ARCO bought Anaconda Mining in 1977, they had no idea what they were in for. Three years later they closed the copper mining operation in Butte, laying off thousands, and a year later they were looking at a massive bill for the cleanup of Anaconda's old sites. The EPA was determined to make ARCO pay for everything, while the town, still stinging from the layoffs, was determined to preserve its heritage, even though much of that heritage had been labeled toxic waste.

Sandy may have come up naively, but not unprepared: "Natural resources issues are by definition controversial in the West," she explains. But having negotiated this environment from the age of nineteen as the only woman on various drilling sites and offshore oil rigs, she has acquired a gift for finding common ground. Sandy, however, attributes this gift as much to her gender as to her experience: "I think this is something in general that women tend to be good at. We leave our egos at the door more often than not. I think we are more focused on the end point rather than who won. In these sorts of negotiations, nobody wins. You just try to come up with something everyone can live with."

Her approach, backed up with years of hands-on experience, has yielded some incredible results. For her company, she has helped reduce the liability from over $2 billion to under $1 billion over the years, and recently completed the final settlement, mapping out the last stages of the cleanup. In Anaconda, Montana, she recently attended the opening of a Jack Nicklaus–designed golf course that serves as a cap over an old dumping site—a cap that contains the waste while generating the funds needed to pay for its maintenance. This "crazy idea" originated with the townspeople, and Sandy saw the possibilities right away, but the hard work came when it was time to convince the government agencies and lawyers that this could work. "Superfund is such that anyone who is in the chain of title can be held liable, so people don't usually want to redevelop these sites," she explained. Nevertheless, the one-of-a-kind golf course/cap was constructed, and 3,500 people turned up for its opening.

Along with the love she feels for her job, Sandy has come to love the rough-and-ready town of Butte as well, and supports the local effort to preserve historical parts of the town that some would consider an eyesore: "We sit here and judge things people did one hundred years ago, totally forgetting that we wouldn't have electricity in this country if it weren't for Butte, Montana, just because of the sheer amount of copper produced here. I think we ought to celebrate that history. If we can incorporate that into our cleanups, I think its good for everybody."

There's still plenty of work to do in Butte, which suits Sandy fine: "I get to do what I love doing in a place that I love living in. It really doesn't get much better than that."

Margaret Maronick Sample

PRESIDENT

MTB Management, Inc.
Missoula, Montana

WORK HISTORY

1971–1974   Classroom Teacher, New Mexico.

1986–1988   Accountant, Atlanta, Georgia.

1989–present President, MTB Management.

EDUCATION

1971   B.A. in Education, University of New Mexico, Albuquerque.

1986   B.S. (honors) in Business Administration, University of Montana, Missoula.

FIRST JOB

Baby-sitting for a family of seven children.

ASSOCIATIONS AND NETWORKS

Past President, Missoula Area Chamber of Commerce; Member, Business Advisory Council, School of Business Administration, University of Montana; Member, Advisory Council Community Medical Center; Member, Montana Society of Certified Public Accountants; Member, American Institute of Public Accountants; Executive Board Member, Missoula Area Economic Development Corporation; Executive Board Member, Missoula Convention and Visitors Bureau; Member, Rotary Club; Member, Montana Women's Forum; Member, Ambassadors of the Governor of the State of Montana; Charter Member, Northwest Operators Franchise Association; past President, Missoula Chapter of Young Audiences.

AWARDS AND HONORS

Paul Harris Fellow, Rotary Foundation, 1996; YMCA Outstanding Business Woman of the Year, 1997; Co-recipient of the Outstanding Senior in Accounting, University of Montana, 1986.

FAMILY

Two children.

GREATEST OBSTACLES OVERCOME

Learning to recognize my own strengths and weaknesses and respond to that knowledge.

PERSONAL GOALS

To provide my children with the tools to develop into good citizens—sensitive to those around them and appreciative of the gifts God has given them. For myself, I hope to leave this world having known true friendship.

DRIVING FORCE

The values I learned growing up. Curiosity about the world around me and seeking constant challenge.

BUSINESS MAXIM

Be fair, be firm, be consistent.

WAYS OF DEALING WITH PRESSURE AND STRESS

Humor and exercise.

ADVICE TO ASPIRING BUSINESSWOMEN

Develop your own style regardless of societal preconceptions. Women who accept themselves, their knowledge, and their talents overcome the barriers that exist in today's still male-dominated business world. Develop your strengths and surround yourself with people whose strength lies in areas where you are weak. Be passionate about what you do and have fun.

i used accounting as a stepping-stone, not as an end in itself. I felt that it was necessary to understand that side of business, but my strengths have always been people. And yet I knew that if I wanted to succeed, I had to understand the numbers.

With two children to support, former school teacher Margaret Sample knew she couldn't go back to the classroom: "I felt I wouldn't have the emotional depth to give to kids all day, and then give my kids what I thought they deserved. So I decided on a different field." Margaret attended business school, where she received high honors, and then started a career in accounting. But it wasn't until she formed a business alliance with a partner that things really took off. "I was much more people-oriented," she says, "and he was much more creative, so we made a dynamite team."

The two formed MTB Management and built or purchased sixteen Taco Bell franchises in three states that employ more than five hundred people. Since then, she and her partner have separated their business interests, with each taking eight restaurants. Growing steadily in this niche, Margaret has been recognized for her quiet achievements by the Missoula Chamber of Commerce, who elected her President, and the Governor's office, who made her an ambassador for the state of Montana. It's all been very surprising to Margaret, whose humility seems to prohibit self-congratulation. "I didn't think being elected President was ever possible," she says. "It's a very public position, and I don't care for that. I prefer to be in the background, and prefer to acknowledge others who do tremendous work. But I took it because I thought I could grow, and grow I did."

Margaret describes herself as a "small-step person," and grew the business in line with this trait. After the first restaurant was built, the second was two years in the making, as was the third. After that, with an SBA loan cleared and traditional funding sources no longer reluctant, MTB Management grew "exponentially," becoming, in Margaret's words, "A process of opportunity and innovation." The path was relatively clear and smooth, with challenges coming as a result of growth rather than standing in the way of the next expansion.

Margaret says working with construction crews not accustomed to seeing a woman on the site proved difficult in the beginning: "It was interesting for my partner and me at the time," Margaret recalls, "because they would automatically defer those questions to him and he'd look quite blank and say, "You'll have to ask my partner.' " Margaret made a point of visiting construction sites and making her presence felt, allowing the contractors to just "get used to" her being there. Finally, she discovered, there wasn't really any underlying prejudice standing in the way: "Ultimately, what I found was that all most people really want to know is who is going to make the decision. As long as you are willing to make a decision and stand by it, you have the ability to succeed in any environment."

Employing five hundred in a fast-food franchise requires a special management approach; many of Margaret's employees are teenagers in their first job. Managing their work habits requires striking a balance between shielding them from unpleasantness, and preparing them for greater responsibilities. "The first thing I want to do is protect them," she explains. "Protect them physically, of course, but also protect them from the increasingly angry atmosphere that we all face. There are lots of times a customer will come in, see a sixteen-year-old employee, and just unload on them." That's why, she says, her home phone number is posted in every restaurant, and that's why she occasionally gets the late-night call from a panicked employee or an irate customer.

Having grown into an entrepreneur, and from there into a community leader, Margaret is grateful for the opportunities: "I've had the chance to do things I'd never dreamed of doing. I've had opportunities to meet people I never thought I would meet." And yet, she's chosen a path of humility, and succeeded without ever calling it a success: "I'm not too sure if I see myself as successful. Perhaps my perception is very different from other people's. I just have a passion for doing things right."

Pamela Watanabe-Gerdes

PRESIDENT

Tender Heart Treasures, Ltd.

Omaha, Nebraska

WORK HISTORY

To 1987   Worked in various aspects of managing the family business, Oriental Trading Company, Inc., Omaha, Nebraska.

1987–present   Founder and President, Tender Heart Treasures, Ltd.

EDUCATION

Attended University of Hawaii, Honolulu, Hawaii, majoring in environmental studies.

ASSOCIATION AND NETWORKS

Junior League of Omaha; ICAN (Institute for Career Advancement Needs, Inc.); JACL (Japanese American Citizens League); Beta Beta Gamma Society; Advisory Director of the Methodist Hospital Foundation.

COMMUNITY SERVICE

Junior League of Omaha fundraiser committee; Sunday school teacher.

AWARDS AND HONORS

Number 240 in the "Working Woman 500"; recognized by the *Midlands Business Journal* as the largest women-owned business in Omaha; selected in 1998 to take part in an "influence class" sponsored by ICAN.

FAMILY

Married, two daughters and a son.

PERSONAL GOALS

To continue to have a positive influence on my children, to give more time to community service.

PROFESSIONAL GOALS

To maintain and continue to build a very stable and successful business.

DRIVING FORCE

From the very beginning I welcomed the challenge of running my own business wholeheartedly. I wanted to prove to myself I could succeed despite the challenges I would face along the way. Now I'm continually driven by a desire to perform a service for customers, to help other people develop professionally, and to give back to God and the community.

DEFINITION OF SUCCESS

The satisfaction of achieving goals and peace of mind.

GREATEST REWARD FROM CAREER

I've had the opportunity to enjoy many rewards and successes throughout my career and who knows, the best may be yet to come. Ask me again in twenty years.

GREATEST DOWNSIDE TO CAREER

The inherent time constraints and the challenge of maintaining the balance to build and nurture personal relationships.

WAYS OF DEALING WITH PRESSURE AND STRESS

Personally, I try to maintain a positive and objective attitude. In a business sense what helps is empowering my employees to make good decisions. My husband helps—he can be very objective and practical when dealing with sensitive issues.

ADVICE TO ASPIRING BUSINESSWOMEN

Relentlessly pursue all possibilities, keeping in mind the journey will bring enjoyment and satisfaction. Embrace your challenges and remain highly driven; you will survive adversity.

FAVORITE PART OF THE DAY

Morning, when I have the most energy.

i started in the family business labeling merchandise, stocking shelves, and cashiering for customers when I was five. By the time I was nine, I was typing invoices. By the time I was eleven, I was doing bookkeeping. At fourteen or fifteen, I was handling all the merchandise documentation. That was how I learned about managing a business.

Pamela Watanabe-Gerdes was fairly comfortable at Oriental Trading Company, a business founded by her father, Harry Watanabe, in 1932. At that time Oriental Trading was a wholesale company dealing mostly in carnival merchandise. She'd been there her entire life, first working for her father, and then working with her elder brother. But at the age of twenty-nine, a series of discussions with her brother planted the seed for a new venture of Pam's own making. "I thought I was going to stay at Oriental Trading forever," Pam remembers, "but my brother and I came up with this idea for a giftware catalog."

More than ten years later, Tender Heart Treasures is a $40 million business with a catalog mailing of 17 million. Pam started the company with thirteen associates and now employs approximately three hundred. Tender Heart Treasures exclusively designs and distributes unique giftware and home decor products. Sourcing and producing merchandise overseas allows Tender Heart to keep its treasures priced to sell, and sales continue to look up, with 20 to 25 percent growth expected over the next few years.

Although she worked a variety of jobs at Oriental Trading, Pam admits it wasn't in the realm of her responsibility to see the company as a whole. "I wasn't involved in the big picture. Instead I was mainly responsible for marketing and merchandising. All of a sudden I was out on my own and accountable for everything that could have an impact on my business. Then everything came full circle, the pieces all fit together, and I knew what it would take to make my company successful."

Pam started her venture with the understanding that merchandise would bring strength to the company. The first order of business was to define exactly what Tender Heart would sell. This "process of elimination" resulted in a broad and varied catalog that would allow Pamela to test the waters. As she remembers, "We had everything from plush toys and jewelry to stationery and collectibles. At that time, country-themed products represented only about 20 percent of the catalog. But they really caught on and were the most profitable line I sold." So began a love affair with country giftware products, the cornerstone of Tender Heart's business.

The company grew steadily the first year thanks to a highly focused and popular country product line. Pam's formula for success: offer the right merchandise to the right audience at the right prices, with exceptional quality and timely delivery. With the encouragement and support of her husband, Kyle, working by her side, Pam was able to stay focused on her goal of building a very profitable business. Since then she has continued to grow her company, emphasizing stability over rapid growth and risk. "I'm not the kind of person who tries to bite off more than she can chew," Pam says. "Everything is tightly managed and I've always been able to stay relatively debt-free. I'm not a big risk-taker and that's probably why I've not grown as quickly as I could. I just want to be able to sleep at night."

Pam's business hit the $40 million mark at about the same time she and her husband started a family. With the country giftware business firmly in place, she has been looking for other ways to expand. Her next venture centers around Victorian and traditional giftware, and she continues to develop new avenues to fill her customer's needs. Now, with three children, she's looking forward to letting go of some of the day-to-day details and decision making, freeing up more time to spend with her family. With that end in mind, she created two new key positions, Chief Operating Officer and Director of Merchandise, and filled them with highly experienced and passionate individuals who would help her fulfill her mission and vision for Tender Heart Treasures. She says it's an exciting time: "My whole goal in life right now is to maintain an even balance between my personal and professional life, and with the help I'm receiving, I really think I can have it all."

Sheri Idelman

PRESIDENT
PTM, Inc.
Omaha, Nebraska

WORK HISTORY

1973–1975   Assistant, Dempster Animal Hospital, Skokie, Illinois.

1975–1976   Assistant, Jericho Animal Hospital, Syosset, New York.

1979–1981   Camp Counselor, Teacher, School Bus Driver, Kelly's Day
Camp, Halfday, Illinois.

1981–1986   Co-founder, Vice President, Operations, Wats Marketing
Outbound, Omaha, Nebraska.

1986–1995   Founder and COO, ITI Marketing Services, Omaha,
Nebraska.

1995–present   Co-founder and President, Product & Technology
Management, Inc.

EDUCATION

1968–1972   Studied art education at Southern Illinois University, Carbondale, and Kendall College, Evanston, Illinois.

FIRST JOB

Filing job at age sixteen.

COMMUNITY SERVICE

Private Industry Council for the City of Omaha; Department of Economic Development Commission for the State of Nebraska; past Chair, Diet Pepsi/University of Nebraska at Omaha Women's Walk; past Chair, Combined Health Agencies Drive.

AWARDS AND HONORS

Business Excellence Achievement Award, University of Nebraska–Lincoln College of Business Administration Alumni Association, 1994; Mallory Kountze Award for Entrepreneurial Achievement, 1993; Outstanding Woman of Distinction (entrepreneur category), YWCA, 1996.

FAMILY

Married twenty-five years, one daughter.

GREATEST OBSTACLES OVERCOME

Being able to speak to a crowd, speaking to employees, even picking up the telephone to get what I want. But that's what the job called for, so I learned how to do it.

DRIVING FORCE

I'm competitive. I like to win.

BUSINESS MAXIM

Make something happen.

WAYS OF DEALING WITH PRESSURE AND STRESS

Putting things down on paper, working out, forging ahead.

ADVICE TO ASPIRING BUSINESSWOMEN

Believe in yourself. Set short-term goals so you can see your accomplishments.

*W*e had so much business, and it moved at such an incredibly fast pace, that there were only a few times when I could stand back and see what we had accomplished. When I did take those moments in, it was extremely rewarding.

Sheri Idelman might have been a vet, or might have pursued a career in teaching, or might have gone back to school to finish her degree. But when her husband, Steve, was asked to move to Omaha, Nebraska, to establish an outbound telemarketing company, which became an affiliate of American Express, Sheri got a taste for entrepreneurship that never left her. The Idelmans are now on their third successful start-up, and with the intensity of the first two behind them, Sheri is now adapting to a more manageable pace.

After five years of helping Steve build his division, after watching it grow from one hundred employees to over fifteen hundred, Sheri realized new opportunities were limited under her husband's arrangement with the parent company. Once she made a decision to leave, she moved at a pace that would define her company for the next nine years. "Two of my friends, my husband, and I left on a Friday," she remembers, "and on Monday, my two friends and I incorporated ITI Marketing Services. My husband had to comply with a six-month non-compete clause in his employment contract." The new venture started simply with outbound telemarketing, but satisfied clients asked for more, and ITI bought an inbound services company and an

Hispanic telemarketing firm to add services. From fourteen employees when it was founded, ITI grew to eight thousand employees in twenty-three locations and had revenues of $125 million. "I'm lucky to have high energy," Sheri says of that time. "I was there at seven-thirty in the morning, and wouldn't go home until seven o'clock at night. I worked long, fast, fun, and smart."

If there's any accomplishment that stands out for Sheri from those days, it was being able to provide thousands of jobs. The responsibility of running such a large staff is one that she handles well: "My leadership skills are my best asset," she says. "I learned to relate to people, listen to them, observe them, and help them achieve success." Even as founder and COO, Sheri says that during her entire time at ITI, she kept her feet on the ground: "I felt like an employee, and treated myself like an employee of the company rather than an owner. I wiped off the bathroom counters like everyone else. I wouldn't ask someone do to something I could easily do myself. You have to lead by example."

With ITI secure as a leader in the industry, Sheri began to attempt to live a personal life: "My daughter was competing with my business, and I sometimes thought about retirement, but every time I would try to slow down, we would expand again. It just never seemed to happen." When a private equity firm knocked on their door with an offer to buy the company, Sheri and her husband saw the benefit right away. "It was time," she says.

Sheri could now turn at least part of her attention to the community and her causes. Since 1995, she has been Chair of the Diet Pepsi / University of Nebraska at Omaha Women's Walk, devoted to raising money for the women's athletic department, and has exceeded the financial goals each year. She also sits on two committees for the university's men's athletics department. Two government volunteer organizations have also called on her expertise—the local Private Industry Council and the State Department of Economic Development. Then there's a new business to look after, Product and Technology Management, Inc.

"PTM will never be another ITI," Sheri says. "It will be done with maybe five people, and will always be a really small thing." PTM develops promotions and new business opportunities in the local area. They are already looking to acquire another company, and have developed a promotions subsidiary to bring big-name entertainment to Omaha. Having made her mark, Sheri says this company is a way to enjoy the benefits. "Hopefully we'll make some money," she adds, "but we're not looking to become billionaires from this endeavor. PTM is just a way for us to give back to our community, give a few people good jobs, and have some fun along the way."

Patricia Gallup

CHAIRMAN AND CHIEF
EXECUTIVE OFFICER

PC Connection, Inc.
Milford, New Hampshire

WORK HISTORY

1978–1980   Field Archaeologist, Public Archaeology Survey Team, Inc., Storrs, Connecticut.

1980–1982   Project Manager, Audio Accessories, Marlow, New Hampshire.

1982–present   Chairman and CEO, PC Connection, Inc.

EDUCATION

1979   *B.A.* in Education, University of Connecticut, Storrs.

FIRST JOB

Baby-sitter.

ASSOCIATIONS AND NETWORKS

Member, Board of Directors, Markem Corporation; Chairman, Board of Directors, PCTV, Inc.; Chairman, Board of Directors, En Technology Corporation; Member, New Hampshire Partners (a group of New Hampshire CEOs); Member, Swift Water Girl Scout Council; Member, Lake Sunapee Protective Association.

COMMUNITY SERVICE

Governor's Commission on Child Care and Early Education; Advisory Board, Forbes Executive Women's Summit; Advisory Board, Apple Hill Center for Chamber Music; Volunteer, Guatemala Eye Care Clinic.

AWARDS AND HONORS

Working Woman top 50 Women Business Owners, each year from 1993–1998; Entrepreneur of the Year Award, New England Region, Ernst & Young, LLP, 1998; Ten Most Powerful Women in New Hampshire Award, *New Hampshire Editions,* each year from 1995–1998; inducted into Leading Women Entrepreneurs of the World, 1997; #1 Retailer, 100 Most Influential Companies in the Computer Industry, *PC Magazine,* 1997 and 1998; *PC World* World Class Award, each year from 1990–1997.

FAMILY

Married.

GREATEST OBSTACLES OVERCOME

When we started the company, we had a goal to change the way people thought about how they purchased computer products—or any type of product for that matter. We wanted to convince them, through our efforts, that buying direct was the best way to go. Being named as the top retailer in the computer industry was verification that we'd reached this goal.

DRIVING FORCE

A desire to exceed customer expectations—and by "customer" I mean our vendors and employees as well.

BUSINESS MAXIM

Work smart and hard.

GREATEST REWARD FROM CAREER

Receiving the highest rating of any retailer on the first-ever list of the 100 Most Influential Companies in the computer industry.

GREATEST DOWNSIDE TO CAREER

I find my work so exciting and so rewarding, I often lose track of the time. Late nights in my household are common.

WAYS OF DEALING WITH PRESSURE AND STRESS

Stress is generally caused by the inability to make a decision or take action. But at my company, decision making is easy—we always do what's best for the customer.

ADVICE TO ASPIRING BUSINESSWOMEN

Stay focused. This is easy to do if you choose a business you love.

*C*ommunicate, communicate, communicate. You can't communicate enough.

☀

Key to Patricia Gallup's success with PC Connection has been this mantra, one she sees as particularly vital in the fast-changing computer industry. It's served her well; through streamlined communication networks, she pioneered many of the services computer shoppers now expect and demand, including on-demand customer support, overnight shipping, and custom-built systems. These innovations have been repeated and copied by major industry players and start-ups alike.

But this competition hasn't stopped PC Connection from becoming a $550 million company (in 1997) with outstanding potential for growth. In the next several years, Patricia says, she hopes to take the company over the billion-dollar mark. It's an ambitious goal, but one made possible by again offering more—two sophisticated web-based programs, system selector and memory selector, now help shoppers easily determine their needs online.

All this has sprung from an unusual background. Patricia was trained in archaeology and anthropology, but has always felt these disciplines gave her an edge in business: "Working in archaeology requires detail-orientation, and that's always been a part of my personality," Patricia says. "I'm a 'needs-to-know' person, and I dig until I find the answer. I'm also very solution- and results-oriented, and that too comes from my archaeology background. Anthropology is an excellent background to have for business. It gives you a great foundation to build on by understanding people—what makes them tick—and understanding how organizations develop."

Patricia was working for PC Connection co-founder David Hall's family business when the idea for the venture was formed. The company needed new computers, but the closest store was more than two hours away and wasn't customer-focused. So Patricia and David pooled $8,000 to start a mail-order business, placed an ad in *Byte,* and before long were watching orders for peripherals and software pour in. In just five years, PC Connection was named the second-fastest growing private company in the U.S. by *Inc.* magazine. In 1990, it received its first World Class award from readers of *PC World,* who went on to vote them to the top seven times.

According to Patricia, this explosive growth has been due as much to her training programs for employees as it has been to customer loyalty. "Right away we give employees a very high level of autonomy," she explains. "The best way to make people feel they're making a difference and having an impact is to give them a job that allows them to make decisions and act upon the decisions they make. We have a great training program for our sales and customer service people, and once they successfully go through the program, they're generally ready to be in a decision-making role." Patricia completely side-stepped the moment that causes so many entrepreneurs to stumble—the moment when growth means that you can't do it all yourself: "I was never hesitant to bring in someone who knew more than I did. I've always been a good delegator."

But training and delegating is only half the picture. Patricia is the mediator of a series of constant dialogues—between departments, customers, and vendors. "We have a very good system for sharing information. The people on the front lines dealing with customers on a daily basis have many ways to communicate what they've learned to those who make larger policy decisions. Communication is the key." The conversation continues with PC Connection's vendors: "We think of our vendors as customers as well. We're a critical link in the flow of information between people who use products and the people who manufacture them. Both sides depend on us."

PC Connection employees get the customer service treatment as well. PC Connection offers continuous training, and was one of the pioneering companies that offered family leave long before it became a national issue. These efforts have been noticed by the Clinton administration—Patricia was an invited participant in the 1992 Clinton-Gore economic summit—and on a local level by the Governor of New Hampshire. Participating in the Governor's Commission on Education brings Patricia's educational and business background to focus on this vital issue. "Through my background in anthropology, I bring an understanding of the family unit and then try to come up with proposals that make sense from a business perspective. The name of the game is trying to figure out what role business should play in developing our children."

With so much going on, it's not surprising that turning forty was almost completely lost on Patricia: "I didn't skip a beat," she says.

Veronica Ann Williams

PRINCIPAL AND
MANAGING DIRECTOR

ACT, Inc.

South Orange, New Jersey

WORK HISTORY

1979–1982	Account Executive, Systems Marketing Representative, Chicago, Illinois.
1982–1988	Product Manager, Data Account Manager, Staff Manager, AT&T Corporation, New Jersey and New York.
1988–1989	District Sales Manager, UniSoft Corporation, New York City.
1990–1991	Director of Business Development, Software Corporation of America, Stamford, Connecticut.
1991–1993	Northeast District Account Manager, Fujitsu, Inc., Mountain Lakes, New Jersey.
1986–present	Principal and Managing Director, ACT, Inc.

EDUCATION

1977   B.A. (honors) in economics, Brandeis University.

1979   M.B.A., Kellogg School of Management, Northwestern University.

FIRST JOB

Piano teacher for other children in the neighborhood. At age fifteen, I began working as a summer intern at the U.S. Department of Agriculture.

ASSOCIATIONS AND NETWORKS

Telecommunications Industry Association; National Black MBA Association; Advisory Board Member, COMDEX conferences; New Jersey Technology Council; Advisory Board Member, Consumer Electronics Show; Advisory Board Member, ExpoComm.

COMMUNITY SERVICE

Founder, Manager, computer training program at St. Paul Baptist Church; Member, South Orange Citizens Budget Advisory Committee, 1983–1986; former Member, South Orange Planning Board.

AWARDS AND HONORS

Top sales awards at Control Data, AT&T, and Fujitsu; 1996 Woman of the Year, St. Paul Baptist Church, Montclair, New Jersey; Outstanding Young Woman of America, 1979; Journée Française d'Économie et de Finance Conference Participant, 1978.

GREATEST OBSTACLES OVERCOME

Lack of money when starting business, lack of minority and female role models. Learning the "rules of the game," the structure, and the culture of corporations, which was difficult in the beginning.

DRIVING FORCE

The need to destroy barriers, the need to show those who say I can't that I can, and the need to be in control of my own destiny.

DEFINITION OF SUCCESS

Seeing someone else benefit from my efforts.

BUSINESS MAXIM

1. Identify a need, create win-win solutions, and then deliver.
2. Some succeed because they're destined to, others succeed because they're determined to.
3. Entrepreneurs need the four F's: Focus, Financing, Fortitude, and Faith.

WAYS OF DEALING WITH PRESSURE AND STRESS

My belief in God, the love and support of my family, swimming and scuba diving, travel.

ADVICE TO ASPIRING BUSINESSWOMEN

1. Decide what you want to achieve or what position you want to be in, understand what it takes to get there, find someone to give you the *real* answers, determine if you are willing and able to make the sacrifices, then fish or cut bait!
2. You have to learn what comes from racism or sexism and what comes from the normal corporate culture. Look at what the white males have to go through to get where they are—you have to be able to discern what's just part of the game and what's due to something else.

*t*here are no words to describe what I went through. I did whatever was necessary and legal to support myself as I went out to look for business.

In 1993, Veronica Williams finally took the leap. For seven years, she had dreamed of establishing her own consulting firm, but offers kept rolling in; offers that promised growth and stock options that never materialized. The funds she had expected from these positions were supposed to pull her through the early lean years of making it on her own. Instead, she rented out rooms in her house, took temp work, and worked on a book that, if successful, would establish her as a premier authority in her field. She had put off her dream long enough—it was time to start, with or without capital.

It was hardly the position Veronica would have foreseen for herself. She had two prestigious degrees and fourteen years of experience at some of the biggest names in information technology. But she had never chosen the easiest route: upon graduating from business school, while her classmates were taking high-profile and high-paying jobs, she opted for a sales position: "In sales you get to see everything. I realized it probably wasn't the most prestigious job, but it got me onto the ground floor of the industry of my choice, and it gave me the opportunity to learn a lot more in less time." Back then, Veronica says, a salesperson in IT wasn't just devoted to selling: "If you take the position I held then, it would be split among ten people today. Twenty years ago, we did it all." She sold, but also designed systems, trained clients, and offered support, gaining on the job the overview and skills she had been seeking.

It wasn't many years after her first job, however, that Veronica realized she wanted to be out on her own. "The glass ceiling is there," Veronica realized. "There's a glass ceiling for women, and for minorities. Depending on how you work, there's a glass ceiling for white males as well. I began looking around and saw that my ambition wasn't going to be realized in a major corporation. I didn't want to wait to be given a chance to do all the things I knew I could do." After her position was closed at her last company, Veronica decided she was ready.

"Most people start a business without enough money," Veronica says. "I started with none." For three years, she used her only asset—"every waking moment"—to build a reputation and a client base. The turning point came in the third year, when Veronica finished her book, *The Wireless Computing Primer,* which helped her get speaking engagements and a position as an Advisory Board Member for COMDEX, the mother of all IT conferences. It was then that she realized it was nothing more than faith that had kept her going: "I reaffirmed my religious beliefs after I finished my book—I handed the manuscript over to the publisher and went to church. I couldn't believe I had made it through this, and I had to thank God."

Now the rewards come in both small and large forms. "It was such a little thing," she says, but when a young African-American boy, no more than fourteen, approached Veronica after a speaking engagement to say how much he admired her, "I wanted to cry. It was a private engagement and I don't know how he and his mother got in, but I gave up the schmoozing of the cocktail hour to talk to him. He made all of my sacrifices worthwhile."

With her business secure and new business ventures—such as a high-tech training course licensed by Motorola—in the works, Veronica is now in a position to turn work away in favor of clients and projects she really wants. With seventeen consultants on call, Veronica has time to devote to a basic computer skills training program at her church, one that she hopes will eventually branch out to include financial training. But Veronica also sees her professional life as a way to make a difference. There are still those who dwell on her race and gender rather than what she has to say, there are still those who walk out of her seminars assuming they have nothing to learn from an African-American woman. Veronica is, however, unfazed by these slights: "I got that in high school, I got that in college, but I look at it as an opportunity to prove people wrong. I'm proud of my heritage. I'll play with the hand that I'm dealt, and I'll win."

Linda Andrulis Berthoin

OWNER

Route 66 Clothing Company
Albuquerque, New Mexico

WORK HISTORY

1977–1978   Designer, Fiorucci, Paris, France.

1980–1991   Owner, Caprice Boutique, Inc., Ormond Beach, Florida

1991–1998   Owner, Route 66 Clothing Company.

EDUCATION

1976   B.F.A. in Graphic design, University of Idaho, Moscow, Idaho.

1978   Foreign student course in French, Sorbonne, Paris.

FIRST JOB

Graphic artist for a paper-packing company.

ASSOCIATIONS AND NETWORKS

Hispano Chamber of Commerce, Albuquerque, New Mexico.

COMMUNITY SERVICE

Assisting with seminars for Landmark Education.

FAMILY

One daughter.

GREATEST OBSTACLES OVERCOME

Losing my parents at a young age (and therefore not having their support and wisdom), but still starting a business on my own.

PERSONAL GOALS

Raising my child to be a positive, powerful human being and having a great relationship (even though it's getting late in life).

DRIVING FORCE

Financial survival. Creativity and self-expression of my artistic background. My daughter and the thought that I'm building something for her.

DEFINITION OF SUCCESS

Being able to use your gifts. Earning from them is a fringe benefit.

WAYS OF DEALING WITH PRESSURE AND STRESS

Acupuncture to help with physical stress, the support of dear friends for emotional support.

ADVICE TO ASPIRING BUSINESSWOMEN

When you find a field you love, stick to it and build one step at a time with integrity; everything is possible.

i wonder for how many people life winds up being the sum of everything they've learned, like a puzzle you put together. That's the way it happened for me.

✳

There's an almost eerie symmetry to Linda Berthoin's life; there is almost nothing she learned or did that hasn't become useful or provided guidance. Following her fortuitous path, this native of Queens, New York, has found herself as an entrepreneur clothing designer and manufacturer in Albuquerque, New Mexico, doing well thanks to her history of good choices and hard work.

Linda was working a graphic designer's dream job in Paris when her father passed away. At age twenty-three, she was thrown into the retail world by having to liquidate his furniture store business. "It was right after college, and it was like going from one school to another," she remembers. "From that experience I learned general business practice—taxes, employees, just the basics." From there, with a small inheritance and a developing business sense, she opened a boutique in Ormond Beach, Florida, and went to work. "I grew that shop like a seed," she says. After nine years, when it was becoming "too much of a routine," she sold the small store for seven times what she had put into it. "I was doing well, but it wasn't very creative for me anymore. I needed to 'graduate' to something more creative," she explains.

That's when Linda came full circle, back to her training in design, but now armed with years of business experience and capital to start a creative, winning venture. After she selected a new location, Albuquerque, New Mexico, and took a course on pattern making, she stepped into high gear. "In four months," she says, "I bought a shop, renovated it, and had my business up and running. It was unbelievable." On a sadder note, she adds, "I went through a divorce. It was all in one shot. I was like superwoman for four months." There was essentially no downtime once she had the capacity for production: "I got orders right away, from the minute I made my samples, I was off."

Linda says her designs are a "combination of Southwestern inspiration and city or contemporary style, a mix between New York City and Santa Fe." She says she'd learned from the French how to have fun with color, form, and shape, and added this sensibility to the increasingly popular Southwest-style skirts. "They're like a cocktail of my life in a way," Linda says. They've proven to be more than the flavor of the month: through a variety of outlets, Linda and her four employees are producing on average four hundred cut-to-order pieces each month. But even as her business grows, Linda remains committed to the value of staying small, at least in spirit. "Everybody's in the Gap, and everybody dresses the same, coast to coast. It's vitally important for the smaller guys to keep up some kind of creativity and for boutiques to survive or we will all look like robots."

While she's incredibly busy, Linda says she's never fallen into the entrepreneurial trap where original passion is sacrificed to keeping up with the daily grind. "I always make time to design," she says. "The inspiration can come at any time, sometimes at two-thirty in the morning. So I keep a notebook. If I see a form or shape that reminds me of something, I sketch it down and collect these shapes. When its time for a new design, I can draw my ideas right onto the pattern." Linda also credits her employees for helping her keep her plate clear for designing new products. "My seamstresses are truly excellent; one I've had for seven years. Sometimes I tease them about their salaries—I pay them really well—by saying that in L.A. manufacturers knock this stuff out cheap. But since I pay well, I can probably beat some of those places in terms of quality and production."

While some events in her past that led her to this place seem like chance, Linda resists calling herself lucky: "It's not luck at all, because I work very hard. I'm not afraid of work, of rolling up my sleeves, pushing boxes around, or staying up late. You cannot be a prima donna in this business."

Margaret E. Wyrwas

SENIOR MANAGING
DIRECTOR, HEAD OF
NEW YORK FINANCIAL
COMMUNICATIONS GROUP

Hill & Knowlton, Inc.
New York

WORK HISTORY

1981–1985 Joined as Datacenter Conversion Team Leader, left as
Assistant Vice President, Corporate Banking, Mellon
Bank, Pittsburgh and Boston.

1989–1998 Joined as Credit Manager, left as Vice President,
Corporate Communications and Investor Relations, Ames
Department Stores, Rocky Hill, Connecticut.

1998–present Senior Managing Director, Head of New York Financial
Communications Group, Hill & Knowlton.

EDUCATION

1980 B.A. in liberal arts, Simmons College, Boston.

FIRST JOB

Student Tour Guide, Admissions Office, Simmons College.

ASSOCIATIONS AND NETWORKS

Officer and Board Member, National Investor Relations Institute, Fairfield/Westchester Chapter; Case Instructor, University of Connecticut at Stamford Investor Relations Certificate Program, Simmons College Leadership Council.

COMMUNITY SERVICE

Simmons College Leadership Council; Junior League of Eastern Fairfield County; former President, Ames Charitable Foundation.

AWARDS AND HONORS

One of three nominated for "1998 Investor Relations Professional of the year," *Investor Relations Business.*

GREATEST OBSTACLES OVERCOME

Massive downsizing at my former employer, Ames Department Stores.

DRIVING FORCE

Fear of failure.

DEFINITION OF SUCCESS

Health, happy moments, periods of growth, and well-being.

WAYS OF DEALING WITH PRESSURE AND STRESS

Hobbies, horseback riding, playing with my dog.

ADVICE TO ASPIRING BUSINESSWOMEN

Be yourself, treat people fairly, work hard, and have a sense of humor.

$g$oing through Ames's Chapter Eleven and laying people off forced me to reevaluate everything. I never knew what was going to happen next. I learned through this process how not to take myself or my job too seriously and still do what had to be done.

Margaret Wyrwas is now on solid ground at Hill & Knowlton, one of the world's largest and oldest communications firms, but for nine years prior, she had been on a wild ride with Ames Department Stores as the company dipped and then dramatically recovered. The experience, Margaret says, changed her forever. As Vice President of Corporate Communications and Investor Relations, she not only had to break the bad news to analysts, investors, and the media, but internally as well. "I then had to lay off members of my own staff, since the downsizing was company-wide. These were people I had worked with for years," she says.

There was a cost, but restructuring brought the company around, and Margaret played a major part. She had joined at the peak of Ames's expansion, when it was a darling of Wall Street with a newly acquired company, 55,000 employees, and over $5 billion in revenue. Only a few years later it was in Chapter 11 and down to 22,000 employees. Margaret had shot from Credit Manager to Vice President in three years after saving the company millions through restructuring of vendor credit programs, and was placed in the investor relations seat as things looked darkest.

Attempting to regain the confidence of investors was a daunting task, especially as the top management posts changed four times during Margaret's tenure. One of the best items she had to sell, however, was the company's past. "I was always trying to find a common theme, so the company could keep its reputation. Just because a new CEO takes over doesn't mean that the culture of a company changes. So we'd try to leverage points of the company's history to attract certain investors," she explains. Her broadview approach, along with countless cold calls and monthly filings to the SEC helped restore a reputation, and Margaret watched Ames's stock go from $1.12 a share in January 1997 to $25 dollars a share when she left in May 1998.

"Not a lot of people get to see that sort of evolution," Margaret says. "In nine years, I had seen the entire life cycle of a corporation." When she was approached about rebuilding a New York Financial Communications Group for Hill & Knowlton, the idea of leaving a company she had helped save was difficult, but she knew it was time: "I had gone through so many changes with Ames, but at the same time I knew leaving was right because I had been through everything—a management change, Chapter Eleven, five years of restructuring, and another management change." The opportunity also gave her a chance to practice what she really loves, namely, "marrying finance, marketing, and the law, and crafting from that a story that makes sense."

The story isn't just for investors and analysts. Margaret often finds herself in the position of counseling companies on issues such as their stock price, their plans for an IPO, or the timing of a merger. Her staff takes regular "temperature checks" on Wall Street about its views of a company's strategy versus management's assumptions. The two are sometimes very divergent: "Wall Street values companies on a minute-by-minute basis," Margaret explains, "and corporations don't look at their own results like that. So I'll have to explain to management the whims of the market, counsel how they should think about the market in terms of their communicating strategy." Although she's outside the corporations she serves, Margaret says her "whole series of trials and tribulations" at her former employer gives her a close understanding of what a company in crisis is going through. "I'm more personally removed from the turmoil, but those experiences at Ames have made me a better counselor. I've been there."

Margaret says she never embraced deliberate career planning, but opportunities have always come to her as she stood by the companies she worked for. The first time she tried, she says, she learned how futile planning can be. At Mellon Bank, she was convinced that the only way she could become a corporate lending officer was to get an M.B.A.: "I felt my liberal arts degree was holding me back," she explains. Her supervisor had other plans—after he had learned that she would hear from Harvard Business School in four weeks, he offered her a spot in the credit training program if she gave him an answer in two weeks. "He knew I would keep my word," she says. "It was clearly a test of my commitment." She took her chances with the credit training program. "Four weeks later I found out I didn't get into Harvard, so fortunately I had made the right decision. Mellon treated me really well, and staying with them paid off."

Rose Marie Bravo

CHIEF EXECUTIVE

Burberrys Ltd.
New York
and London

WORK HISTORY

1974–1987   Various positions at Macy's, promoted to Senior Vice President and General Merchandise Manager of Cosmetics/Accessories and Fine Jewelry in 1985, New York, New York.

1987–1992   Chairman and CEO, I. Magnin, San Francisco, California.

1992–1997   President, Saks Fifth Avenue and Board Member, Saks Holdings, New York, New York.

1997–present   Chief Executive, Burberrys Ltd.

EDUCATION

1971   B.A. in English, Fordham University, New York.

FIRST JOB

Abraham & Straus—started in Executive Training, then became Department Manager.

ASSOCIATIONS AND NETWORKS

National Italian American Foundation; Cosmetic Executive Women; Board of Directors, Tiffany & Co.; Board Member, Fashion Institute of Technology; Board Member, Fashion Group International; Trustee, Marymount University.

COMMUNITY SERVICE

Board Member, Fashion Institute of Technology; Board Member, Fashion Group International; Trustee, Marymount University.

AWARDS AND HONORS

Honored for excellence in retailing by the national Italian American Foundation, the March of Dimes, City of Hope, Fashion Group International, and Marymount University.

FAMILY

Married, two grown stepchildren.

GREATEST OBSTACLES OVERCOME

Convincing myself that I was ready to embark on a new aspect of my career in a foreign country and continent after twenty-six years in U.S. retailing.

DRIVING FORCE

My husband and my father, who both believe I can do anything I set my mind to.

DEFINITION OF SUCCESS

Being able to look myself in the mirror and know that I have done something good today and tried to help someone else along the way.

BUSINESS MAXIM

Never, ever, ever give up. Make a decision and move on.

WAYS OF DEALING WITH PRESSURE AND STRESS

Prayer, family, exercise.

ADVICE TO ASPIRING BUSINESSWOMEN

Try to achieve a balance early on in your career and your personal life, when you are setting up your work habits for life.

i have always been very focused on my career and tremendously enjoy my work. I was so intensely involved in the current project at hand that I didn't give much thought to the next promotion. I tried to give my all to my current assignment.

This steadfastness and purpose hasn't meant that Rose Marie Bravo never got noticed. While staying with the job at hand, she had been rewarded, sometimes to her surprise, throughout her career by one great offer after another. The last was an offer to run Burberrys London, a global apparel and accessories company that demanded new energy and direction—and all she would have to do is leave behind a prestigious post at Saks Fifth Avenue along with the team she had built, and further complicate her life with regular travel between New York and London.

There was a point after she got this offer at which Rose Marie had to convince herself that she was ready for this colossal move, and the new challenge. "But," she says, "there's a point when you have to take a leap of faith.

I loved the people I was working with, but I realized that if I was going to do something different in my life, I'd better do it now—I may be less resilient as time goes by."

Resilience is an important character trait for this particular job. Burberry London, a division of the $3.5 billion Great Universal Stores Plc., has held firmly close to classic British styling since its founding in 1865, and had become less important in the global luxury market. Changes at Great Universal finally required Burberry to move forward, and Rose Marie was seen as the key to this transformation: "We're really trying to modernize the company in every aspect—to give it more of an edge and make it more relevant and fashion-influenced."

While it was clearly hoped that Rose Marie's American sensibilities could help revitalize the firm, she is also taking lessons from the experience: "I'd been in U.S. retail for twenty-six years; however, to live abroad and run a global company that is a retailer as well as a wholesale company, and has a major worldwide licensing network, made me aware of a whole other aspect of the business." Her role may have expanded, but Rose Marie is familiar with the process of turning a company around from her first days at Macy's: "Those were extraordinary years. In 1974, before Ed Finkelstein, Macy's New York was dismal. It was dark and musty—no one shopped there. Beginning as an associate buyer, I was part of that resurgence of trying to take something that has the potential to be great, and making it great."

Rose Marie was in cosmetics, and fortunately, cosmetics was a focal point for the restructuring of the store through purchasing of esteemed brand names that would have seemed completely out of place in the old Macy's. From cosmetics, she was trained in apparel and accessories, all of which led to her being asked to take over Macy's newly acquired specialty store, I. Magnin. She was so busy she hadn't even seen the promotion coming: "I was surprised when Ed Finkelstein tapped me on the shoulder and said, 'We want you to run I. Magnin.' I hesitated for a moment because it meant relocation. But my husband asked, 'Why did you work so hard if you didn't want to be the head of a store? What were you doing all these years?' "

Rose Marie holds a deep gratitude toward her husband for his support as her career developed and became more demanding. Taking charge at I. Magnin meant moving to San Francisco; being CEO of Burberrys London means she's overseas most of the month. Rose Marie sees this spousal support as essential in many professional women's lives: "In almost every case, successful women have a supportive, understanding husband who is truly cooperative and proud of her accomplishments. The spouse is very important in this whole picture."

Rose Marie finds this support not only in her husband, but in her parents, stepchildren, and nephews. Inspiration also comes from watching her employees strike that balance for themselves: "So many women are trying, and succeeding, in juggling family, children, and career. I just hope I can do it as well."

Diane M. Dutton

CHIEF FINANCIAL OFFICER

Allstate Rental and Car Sales

Las Vegas, Nevada

WORK HISTORY

1980–1984   Senior Accountant, Fox & Company CPAs, Las Vegas, Nevada.

1984–1985   Controller, International Teldata Corp, Las Vegas, Nevada.

1985–1986   Controller, INFA, Inc., Las Vegas, Nevada.

1986–1990   Electronic Data Technologies, Las Vegas, Nevada.

1990–1992   Corporate Controller, ATI Medical, Inc., Las Vegas, Nevada.

1992–1998   Chief Financial Officer, Equinox International, Las Vegas, Nevada.

1998–present   Chief Financial Officer, Allstate Rental and Car Sales.

EDUCATION

1977   B.B.A., Pace University, New York, New York.

1979   M.B.A., Pace University.

FIRST JOB

Staff Accountant, KPMG Peat Marwick, New York, New York.

ASSOCIATIONS AND NETWORKS

State Society of CPAs, CFO/Controllers Roundtable, CPA Club.

COMMUNITY SERVICE

Former Financial Vice President, St. Viator Church; former President, Soroptomist International; Creative Las Vegans.

FAMILY

Married, two children.

DRIVING FORCE

Myself.

BUSINESS MAXIM

Integrity comes first.

WAYS OF DEALING WITH PRESSURE AND STRESS

Singing at church.

ADVICE TO ASPIRING BUSINESSWOMEN

Don't take no for an answer. Learn to absorb everything you can and then pick your time to break out from the crowd. Look to your inner ability to judge right from wrong.

i refused to wait in line for my turn. I spoke out, and managed to stand apart by being assertive, not obedient.

⁂

Ever since she was a child following her father to his public accounting firm, Diane Dutton has cultivated a love for the numbers behind business. Her broad view, combined with her assertive stance, has allowed her to move from accounting to technology, health care, and finally into the automotive industry. But even as she serves as CFO for one of Las Vegas's largest group of companies, she dreams of taking her experience out on her own as a management consultant. "I can see this very clearly," she says, "becoming a mentor to businesses. It's not accounting, and it's not systems consulting. Some people might call it business process reengineering, but I think that's too stuffy."

Diane got her start at one of the nation's largest accounting firms at a time when new technologies were transforming the workplace. It was her first chance to refuse to wait in line. "Only managers were going to be taught how to use this new software," she remembers, "but I asked to sit in, and used my free time to learn it on my own. They didn't have a problem with that." Her insights into how this technology could be used led to her becoming the business plan developer for that office, and became her first big stepping stone: "I found myself developing skills that no one else wanted to take the time to develop, but what I was developing was an inroad to future jobs."

It was also a lesson in continuing education—the only thing Diane says can keep her job interesting. "You will become just a bean counter if you don't make something out of what you learn," she claims. "You have to look beyond the numbers." Through accounting, Diane has worked in telecommunications, baby products, gaming technologies, and health care. "I'm a sponge. I listen, ask questions, go into warehouses, talk to people working on the line, and go after customers. When I was working for a medical equipment company for example, I learned all I could about IV pumps, heart machines, and the length of hospital stays. I try to sponge up everything I can about an industry."

As she's moved forward, Diane says that there's no doubt that her drive wasn't always appreciated. "Especially in my early career, men were considered assertive, but women were aggressive. My standing up wasn't always appreciated. I've been razzed and teased, but I've refused to back down, and I think it's made me a stronger person." She describes her current post as one typically reserved for the male Harvard M.B.A., but says that's changing. "People are realizing that the good old boy's network doesn't work. I still have to stand up for myself, but people are more willing to put these things aside and get down to business."

Her current job has allowed her plenty of opportunity to get down to business. The automotive rental and dealership network brings her into contact with manufacturers and their diverse systems, and she has been charged with updating the system at home. "Like many dealerships, it's somewhat antiquated. We're just now getting progressive with our computer systems and utilizing some of the technologies other industries have." All this feeds into an overall business strategy that will fuel the company's expansion.

Meanwhile, Diane continues to network and develop a strategy, and business, of her own. Executive Solutions, she hopes, will be the area's premier small business consulting company, integrating web design, financials, troubleshooting, and quality management. This doesn't leave Diane much free time, but she says she's learned to savor what little time she has: "When I look out my window and feel a sense of comfort and contentment, then I know that I have been successful."

Jocelyn D. Dienst

MANAGING PARTNER

Dienst Custom Homes, LLC
Cornelius, North Carolina

WORK HISTORY

1969–1982   Consultant, R. B. Dienst & Co., Dover, Massachusetts,
and Charlotte, North Carolina.

1982–1985   Founder, Coordinator, Adult Basic Literacy Program at
Central Piedmont Community College, Charlotte, North
Carolina.

1985–present Custom homebuilder, Dienst Custom Homes (formerly
DeMars Enterprises).

EDUCATION

1967   B.A. in French, Mount Ida College, Newton, Massachusetts.

FIRST JOB

Working in the lingerie department at G. Fox & Co. in Connecticut.

ASSOCIATIONS AND NETWORKS

Builder 20 Club; Charlotte Home Builders Association; National Home Builders Association; Charlotte Chamber of Commerce; Lake Norman Homebuilders Association; Charlotte Women Business Owners Association.

AWARDS AND HONORS

People's Choice Award at HomeArama, 1997; Women in Business Achievement Award, the *Business Journal,* Charlotte, North Carolina, 1998.

FAMILY

Married, two children.

GREATEST OBSTACLES OVERCOME

Initially, the biggest hurdle was capturing the respect of the contractors, and then gaining customer confidence to build the biggest investment of their lives.

DEFINITION OF SUCCESS

Success is multifaceted. Personal success encompasses family, faith, and stability. Career success involves financial independence, reputation, honesty, integrity, and productive working relationships with employees, subcontractors, and clients.

WAYS OF DEALING WITH PRESSURE AND STRESS

By enjoying what I do. Most of the time I am working with good people, and nothing is better than seeing the look on a customer's face when I hand them the keys to their new home.

ADVICE TO ASPIRING BUSINESSWOMEN

Don't limit yourself in career options. Do what you like, do not do what society dictates as "proper." If you enjoy your work, you will automatically be that much better at it.

*E*very situation in custom home building is unique. Every situation and every plan is different. So basically, we feel our strengths are communication and organization—getting the clients to verbalize what their vision for their dream home is. Everybody comes to the process with their own perceptions.

⁂

In her corner of the country, Jocelyn Dienst's Dienst Custom Homes is poised to become the area's largest custom home builder, with fifteen to twenty new homes a year priced from $400,000 to over $2 million. But what's really impressive about these numbers is that each house, instead of dropping from a prefabricated blueprint onto an empty lot, is built to her client's needs and expectations. Sometimes, she says, they don't even fully realize what those needs are when they first walk through her doors.

It's a long and involved process, with outside help from designers and dozens of subcontractors. The rewards, however, are unique to Jocelyn's business. "When we're dealing at this level," she says, "anything flies. The opportunity is there, on the high-end, to do exciting new things every time." If the client can afford it, Jocelyn will never say no. She even arranged for plumbing fixtures to be flown in from all over Europe for an authentic French country home. If the client can't afford it, Jocelyn will still never say no—she'll just find another way. "Anything's possible—you just have to look at it. It might come down to cutting square footage or some features, but we can find a way. That flexibility and communication is what they're looking for."

Flexibility is a requirement for this line of work. Jocelyn recalls two occasions when final plans were drafted, grading was done, and foundations were laid, only to have the client change his mind. On one occasion the changes were drastic—the client decided a stone house rather than brick was in order. Nothing a bulldozer and a redesign can't fix. The important thing is that the finished house is what the client wanted. "They're more than just structures," Jocelyn proclaims. "They're people's homes, and every home needs to serve functions and suit a particular client's lifestyle. It also has to be something, from a design standpoint, that we can be proud of."

Jocelyn started her business in 1985 under her maiden name, DeMars, but had been in and around the construction industry since the late sixties, when she and her husband built a home in the Boston area. When he left his law firm to start a building company, Jocelyn joined him as a consultant. After they moved to North Carolina, Jocelyn concentrated on volunteer work, setting up an adult literacy program at the community college—a program that involved up to 250 volunteers. Today, fifteen years later, it's still going strong. "That was probably the most rewarding experience I've ever had in the community," Jocelyn says.

But with her children starting college soon, Jocelyn felt it was time to earn. Custom home building was the best option for her schedule. "It was a good, manageable opportunity for me to control my time, be there for the children, and still be in a situation where I could control it." For years, Jocelyn ran the business out of her home, and ran it on her own: "I did everything. I hired, fired, estimated, purchased. I did it all, and was still able to keep afternoons free for my children."

The opportunity to move the business to a new level came when she was selected to design a house for a golf course community north of Charlotte. Jocelyn quickly hired staff, moved into an office space, and shifted her focus to high-end luxury homes. She immediately got the work to support her expansion, and next found support in her own family.

Her son, Ryan, graduated from college at a critical time: "I knew I had to hire somebody, whether it was Ryan or somebody else. I couldn't continue to do it all myself—I was working just incredible hours." Jocelyn says her son has flourished in the business, and adds that the process finally came "full circle" when her daughter also joined the company's ten employees. "We're a family business," Jocelyn says, "but all our employees would be part of that family."

The end result of her company's gradual growth struck Jocelyn four years ago: "I think what's become so exciting is that I've realized this is something that I can pass on to my children, so they can provide a good living for themselves and a service to clients." It's given the company a new goal, and a new life: "We've taken on a much broader perspective, and we want it to be as professional as it possibly can, so we can make sure that it will continue into the future."

Darlene Jackson-Hanson

PRESIDENT AND CHIEF
EXECUTIVE OFFICER

*Fisher Flying Products Inc.,
and Jackson Manufacturing Co.*

Edgeley, North Dakota

WORK HISTORY

1965–1987   Bookkeeper, Jackson Family Farm, Edgeley, North
Dakota.

1966–1976   Secretary/Bookkeeper, Jackson Manufacturing Co.,
Agricultural Division.

1982–1984   Secretary/Bookkeeper, E&R Hobbies, Edgeley, North
Dakota.

1987–present   President and CEO, Jackson Manufacturing Co.

1989–present   President and CEO, Fisher Flying Products.

1992–present   Co-Manager, Fisher-Hanson Enterprises, Edgeley Super 8
Motel.

EDUCATION

1962   High school diploma, Edgeley High School.

FIRST JOB

Waitress during high school years, then farm wife and mother. I did the bookkeeping and hauled grain from the fields.

ASSOCIATIONS AND NETWORKS

Chairperson of the Board of Directors and Supervisory Committee, Dakota Plains Credit Union; Board of Governors, Dakota Aero.

COMMUNITY SERVICE

North Dakota Women's Business Leadership Council; President, Edgeley Business Association; President, Music Booster Club; President, REA Homemakers Club; Chairperson, County Homemakers Day; 4-H Leader; Sunday school teacher.

AWARDS AND HONORS

North Dakota Entrepreneur of the Year, Center of Innovation and Business Development—Rural Technology Center, University of North Dakota, 1994; North Dakota Women in Business Advocate of the Year, North Dakota U.S. Small Business Association, 1997.

FAMILY

Married, two sons, one grandson, two stepdaughters, five stepgrandchildren.

GREATEST OBSTACLES OVERCOME

Taking over after the death of my husband, Erv. Earning the respect of my peers in a male-dominated business.

DEFINITION OF SUCCESS

Being the best person you can be in any walk of life.

BUSINESS MAXIM

Treat others as you want to be treated.

WAYS OF DEALING WITH PRESSURE AND STRESS

Through prayer and the support of my family and friends.

ADVICE TO ASPIRING BUSINESSWOMEN

Have a positive attitude, never lose sight of your goal. Find someone you can confide in to help you through the rough times ahead.

*S*ome new customers are still surprised to find a woman in this business, but I've been here twelve years. Just surviving that long has earned their respect.

In the small town of Edgeley, North Dakota, population six hundred, Darlene Jackson-Hanson is flying high. Darlene manufactures airplanes—or more exactly, she manufactures the kits that dedicated flyers use to build their own aircraft. Darlene took on more than her share of difficulty to get this operation off the ground. Five days after opening, she lost her husband to cancer.

"It was his dream," Darlene says. "He asked me if I would try to finish what he had started. He felt he owed at least that much to the community." Her husband, Ervan Jackson, had run a successful family farm with Darlene ever since they married—one month after she graduated from high school. Darlene did bookkeeping, got meals to the crew, and ran errands to save time during harvests. When he started his farm manufacturing company, Jackson Manufacturing, she was by his side there as well. But Erv's mechanical tinkering took to the skies with an interest in model aircraft, and soon went full scale with a kit from Fisher Flying Products, then based in Ohio. He and Darlene decided to become manufacturer's representatives for the company. But Edgeley needed jobs, and the Jacksons had a product they thought they could sell. Darlene says this led them to break ground for a manufacturing plant in town in 1986. Erv's cancer was diagnosed three months later. Three months after that, Darlene was on her own.

The first year Darlene worked with three employees to make her late husband's dream a reality. For Darlene the struggles were immense. "I had to learn what a stabilizer was, what a rudder did, plus everything that's involved in this business. I'm still learning every day," she says. "I had no previous desire to be a pilot, build an aircraft, or anything like that." When she still found the company struggling after a year, she temporarily shut it down. "We didn't know where to go with it. It was time to stop and reorganize," she remembers. An unexpected option then dropped from the blue. Fisher Flying Products was up for sale, and they approached Darlene about taking over.

Darlene found a partner in Eddie Fischer, a native of Edgeley now in business in California. "It was a tough time and a tough decision, but we knew what we had to do to survive. Something just told us it was right," Darlene says. In 1989 the purchase was made and Fisher Flying Products became based in Edgeley. The acquisition brought the company rights to seven new designs, but each one got a complete update by her engineers, making them "Dakota dependable" and up to date.

Just over a year later, with Darlene still adapting the new line to her facility, she heard terrifyingly familiar news. "I was diagnosed with cancer in May 1990," she says, "the year my youngest son, Ryan, was graduating from high school." Aggressive treatment was prescribed: she went through surgery, extensive radiation treatments, and chemotherapy. Still, she went to work every day, driving 140 miles to Fargo every afternoon and back again, usually with her son. "It was hard, but I managed to stay focused on the positive. I lived each day to the fullest. I stopped putting off telling people what I had to tell them. You don't procrastinate in a situation like that. During one of the trips to Fargo for treatment, Ryan said, 'I guess this is what they call quality time.' We both laughed. He was eighteen at the time and we both had to keep an upbeat attitude."

Darlene pulled through, and as she was recovering she found support from an employee, Gene Hanson, who later became her second husband. Fisher Flying Products now sells over two hundred kits a year and continues to expand its line through development and acquisition. Governor Edward Schafer commended Darlene for her company's international reputation and contribution to state industry. Darlene also got to see the successful launch of a very personally important plane—the Dakota Hawk, a high-wing side-by-side two-seater. "This is the plane my late husband designed as a model. He always said he wanted to make a full-scale version later in life," Darlene says. The stylish plane is, she adds, one of their best sellers.

Sue Lan Ma

CHAIRMAN,
PRESIDENT, AND CHIEF
EXECUTIVE OFFICER

Elwell-Parker Ltd.
Cleveland, Ohio

WORK HISTORY

1973–1985   Development Engineer, then Senior Quality Engineer,
Union Carbide Corporation, Cleveland, Ohio.

1985–1986   Manager, Quality Engineering, T.R.W., Cleveland, Ohio.

1986–1994   Joined as Corporate Vice President–Quality, ultimately
Corporate Vice President–Business Development, Invacare
Corporation, Elyria, Ohio, and subsidiary locations.

1994–1995   President, Blue Dawn Corporation, Cleveland, Ohio.

1995–present   Chairman, President, and CEO, Elwell-Parker Ltd.,
Cleveland, Ohio.

EDUCATION

1971   B.S. in electronics engineering, Chung Yang University, Taipei,
Taiwan.

1973   *M.S.* in physics, Southern Illinois University, Carbondale, Illinois.

1984   *M.B.A.,* Baldwin Wallace College, Berea, Ohio.

FIRST JOB

Research assistant, Southern Illinois University.

ASSOCIATIONS AND NETWORKS

Ohio Venture Association; Pacific Trade Association.

COMMUNITY SERVICE

Board Trustee, Enterprise Development, Inc.; Board Trustee, Great Lakes Science Center; Board of Directors, Society for the Prevention of Violence.

AWARDS AND HONORS

Entrepreneur of the Year, Cleveland Regional Minority Purchasing Council, 1996.

FAMILY

Two sons.

GREATEST OBSTACLES OVERCOME

To raise enough money to buy the business I wanted to buy.

DRIVING FORCE

A midlife crisis.

DEFINITION OF SUCCESS

Simply to be the best.

GREATEST REWARD FROM CAREER

To see people blossom.

WAYS OF DEALING WITH PRESSURE AND STRESS

I'm always in control. If I can't do it not many people can, so I don't worry about it.

ADVICE TO ASPIRING BUSINESSWOMEN

Have fun and love what you do, so that every day it feels like you're playing.

i hit a pretty big crisis in my life. My oldest son left for college, and my youngest son started driving and had a girlfriend. Suddenly, I woke up one day thinking nobody needs me anymore. I needed excitement. Maybe owning my own business would be good excitement.

This decision turned out to be more exciting, and often times more gut-wrenching, than Sue Lan Ma could have predicted. Sue was responsible for fifteen hundred employees in six locations, mostly in plants she had dramatically brought back from the brink of a shutdown. She had been rewarded with a six-figure salary, ever-increasing responsibility, and the admiration of her staff. "If you go through that kind of turnaround," Sue explains, "the bond with your staff is different. When I said good-bye to the Mexico operation, I don't think there was a dry eye." There were also nay-sayers: "My boss thought I had lost it. He told me I should see an industrial psychologist."

But the best therapy for Sue has always been change. She first came to America from Taiwan to escape an arranged marriage. She then thought she would leave the workforce after her first child was born, only to find that she was "bored to tears." After getting her M.B.A. and succeeding in a growing international company, however, the only way to keep boredom at bay was to risk everything. If anything, Sue was overconfident. In four years, she says she had not just saved six plants, but made them thrive, growing sales from $110 million to $210 million and pretax profits from 3 percent to 12 percent while cutting lead time by three quarters and reducing inventory by one half. Buying a company and turning it around seemed like "no big deal" after success like this: "I heard it took two to three years to buy a company, and I said, 'Those people are working slow—they don't know me, I'll do it in six months. In six months I'll be home free.' How wrong I was."

When she first set up a holding company and invested, few people took her seriously. Getting a downtown office changed that, and she looked at fifteen hundred companies over two years, investigating forty of them closely. She made offers on a dozen, but was most attracted to Elwell-Parker Electric Company, a manufacturer of heavy-duty electric lift trucks, family-owned and operated for 102 years.

The company was in serious trouble and the family was losing money. Still, Sue had to face the attachment the seller held for his grandfather's business. "He had a hard time letting go. Every emotion you can possibly have, I worked through with him." Eventually, a bond was formed that allowed the company to pass out of the family: "He justified it by saying I was the Chinese daughter he never had," Sue says, laughing. Sue's investment group, she says, was the only potential buyer of thirty-six that refused to liquidate the assets, move the company, or change the name.

The union, however, could not be won over, and Sue found herself in a game of hardball that still troubles her. She says she asked for no pay cuts or layoffs, but rather a donation of one week of vacation from everyone in the company. She offered profit-sharing, but says the union workers wanted a 40 percent raise to make up for the raises they didn't get under the previous owner. Not even the support of the union leaders could win the workers over, Sue says. She recalls it as "the most ego-destroying experience I'd ever had."

Sue's $500,000 bill for accounting and legal expenses convinced her she was already committed. She swallowed hard and circumvented the union by purchasing the company with no workforce. She says she isn't proud of what she did, but was capable: "I'm no angel. I can be pretty bad, too." A full-page ad in the *Cleveland Plain Dealer* announced to the workers that their jobs were available. Applicants' appointments were staggered to create a long, visible line leading into the plant. New hires were widely announced. By the end, a third of the old staff was with her. Sue says she is still puzzled about her rejection by the union: "I thought I did a lot of cutting and pasting in trying to turn this business around in a softer way. But the gap was too wide."

Through these twists, turns, and tough choices, Sue has come out on top. After opening with sixty-five employees, she's expanded to eighty-two, and hopes to hire another ten. Sales have gone from $16 million per year to $25 million in 1997, and Sue sees no reason why they can't hit $100 million in ten years. Her employees are all on profit-sharing, all on salary, and all known to her by name. And now that daily routine isn't just "fighting fires," Sue has been allowing herself to spend more time out of the office on education and serving on boards, just to figure something out: "I still want to know what I want to be when I grow up."

M. Denise Kuprionis, Esq.

Fotohaus / Sally Chester

CORPORATE SECRETARY
The E. W. Scripps Company
Cincinnati, Ohio

WORK HISTORY

1978–1980   Secretary to the Editor, *The Kentucky Post*, Covington, Kentucky.

1980–1985   Secretary to the Executive Vice President and President of The E. W. Scripps Company, Cincinnati, Ohio.

1985–1987   Executive Assistant, The E. W. Scripps Company, Cincinnati, Ohio.

1987–present   Corporate Secretary, The E. W. Scripps Company, Cincinnati, Ohio.

EDUCATION

1985   B.S. in management and organizational behavior, Northern Kentucky University, Highland Heights, Kentucky.

1994   J. D., Salmon P. Chase College of Law, Northern Kentucky University.

FIRST JOB

Handing out locker room keys at the YMCA at age thirteen.

ASSOCIATIONS AND NETWORKS

Member, American Society of Corporate Secretaries, and Vice President of regional chapter; Member, American Corporate Counsel Association; Member, American, Ohio, and Cincinnati Bar Associations; Member, Women's Capital Club; Member, Leadership Cincinnati Alumni Association, a program affiliated with the Greater Cincinnati Chamber of Commerce.

COMMUNITY SERVICE

Member, United Way 1997 campaign cabinet (Business II section leader); Member, Board of Trustees and Executive Committee, Children's Hospital Medical Center; Member, Board of Directors and Executive Committee, Northern Kentucky University Foundation; Member, Board of Trustees and Executive Committee, Work and Rehabilitation Centers of Greater Cincinnati.

AWARDS AND HONORS

One of Cincinnati's "Forty Under 40," *Cincinnati Business Courier,* 1995; honored for "commitment to greater Cincinnati community," National Philanthropy Day Annual Luncheon, 1996.

FAMILY

Married, two stepsons, two grandchildren.

GREATEST OBSTACLES OVERCOME

Myself—lack of confidence in early career.

DRIVING FORCE

The need to give 100 percent, to always do better.

DEFINITION OF SUCCESS

Being happy and having fun most of the time, both professionally and personally.

GREATEST REWARD FROM CAREER

Becoming the first female officer at The E. W. Scripps Company.

WAYS OF DEALING WITH PRESSURE AND STRESS

I am lucky to have the most wonderful husband. I can talk with him about anything.

ADVICE TO ASPIRING BUSINESSWOMEN

Never stop learning. Nurture all kinds of relationships—with role models, mentors, and personal supporters.

i think I've been so successful at Scripps because I give one hundred percent to each new project I start, and once that project is completed, I look for new challenges. Fortunately, we have many executives at Scripps who ask good questions about our future challenges, which is why Scripps is such a successful company.

Denise Kuprionis became a pioneer while staying at the company she calls home. Nine years after she joined a Scripps's subsidiary, *The Kentucky Post*, as a secretary, she was elected the company's first woman officer. Her appointment to Corporate Secretary came as a result of her timing, her drive, and two CEOs she calls her mentors.

"It is because of them that I have stayed at Scripps for so long," Denise says of Lawrence A. Leser, former CEO and now Chairman of the Board for Scripps, and William R. Burleigh, now CEO. "They clearly wanted people to succeed and be successful." Both were her supervisors at one point or other as Denise grew in the company, and when the offer to be an officer was presented, she says, "I immediately said yes." There was plenty to do—Denise was elected Corporate Secretary in 1987, and the family-owned company went public in 1988. Today, Scripps is a $1.2 billion company with newspaper and broadcast operations in sixteen states and Washington, D.C.

As Secretary of the company, Denise's responsibilities include working closely with the Board of Directors and preparing the annual proxy statement and other meeting documents. She is also responsible for executive compensation plans and the company's ethics program. However, in 1990, she started looking for even more to do. There was at the time no in-house legal counsel, and she saw this as a clear opening. With her mentors backing her decision, she became Corporate Secretary by day, law school student by night. "When I felt I needed to quit, like I couldn't do this any longer, they both urged me to hang on, take some time off, and keep at it." Even though it wasn't the route she had originally planned, Denise now is a complete convert to the perspective law school can offer: "Law overlaps everything. Everything you do, whether it's in human resources, finance, managing projects, there's always legal ramifications."

An example is Scripps's ethics program, formally instituted three years ago and covering everything from proper use of e-mail to political contributions. To ensure that this program is understood and not just a directive from on high, Denise worked with employee groups to draft the ethics policy, planned training sessions for all employees, and established a toll-free hot line. Every one of Scripps's 8,100 employees has access to this number for advice on compliance with the law and company policy. Questions from this line will be incorporated into the review and redesign of the ethics and compliance program, and keep Denise constantly aware of what the company might need in the area of additional training.

In her experience at corporate headquarters, Denise says she rarely felt held back, patronized, or mistreated because she is a woman. Even as the first female officer, she never felt out of place: "I was always welcomed into management meetings, I always felt like part of the group and that the others were glad that I was there. Maybe I was lucky, but I've always been given more responsibility, and as long as you can do the job, you get treated equally here."

Working for the same company for twenty years, Denise says, has a few drawbacks, but many more advantages. The surroundings, people, and history are familiar; all that's left is to do her job well. But it's also difficult to compartmentalize the personal and professional: "It's hard to define when you're working for the company and when you're not. So your life just kind of blends together."

However, Denise takes this as an almost insignificant downside to a job she loves and a career that only makes her look ahead. "I can't believe where I am right now," she says. "Would I like to start over and do some things differently? Yes. There are some things I could have done better. But I still am where I am, working with great people and working for a great company, and I don't have much time to look backward. I'd rather look forward, and see where I'm going."

Cheryl R. Cohenour

Motophoto

PRESIDENT

CRC & Associates, Inc.

Tulsa, Oklahoma

WORK HISTORY

1982–1985   Research Assistant, C. E. Natco, Tulsa, Oklahoma.

1985–1988   Laboratory Director, Williams Brothers Engineering Company, Tulsa, Oklahoma.

1988–present   President, CRC & Associates, Inc., and Cherokee America Drilling.

EDUCATION

1985   B.S. in Chemistry and Biology, Tulsa University, Tulsa, Oklahoma.

1989   Hazardous Materials Management, Oklahoma State University, Tulsa.

1990   Graduate work in environmental engineering; Oklahoma State University—Tulsa.

Certifications: Certified Hazardous Materials Manager (CHMM), Hazardous Materials Institute, Rockville, Maryland; Registered Environmental Professional (REP), National Registry of Environmental Professionals; groundwater professional, State of Iowa; Oklahoma Underground Storage Tank Professional Oklahoma Corporation Commission; certified SBA-8(a) small business.

FIRST JOB

Working at the local Frostee-Freeze at age fourteen.

ASSOCIATIONS AND NETWORKS

Board Member, Metropolitan Tulsa Chamber of Commerce; Member, Tulsa Economic Development Foundation; Member, Leadership Tulsa; Board Member, Leadership Oklahoma; Member, Cherokee Nation; Board Member, Environmental Quality Board, State of Oklahoma.

COMMUNITY SERVICE

Oklahoma Commission on the Status of Women; Tulsa Authority for Recovery of Energy; Chair, Tulsa Recycling Committee.

AWARDS AND HONORS

Business Woman of the Year, Metropolitan Tulsa Chamber of Commerce, 1992; Highlighted as a community business leader, *Tulsa World*, 1996; featured on cover of *Tulsa People* as one of five successful entrepreneurs.

FAMILY

One daughter.

GREATEST OBSTACLES OVERCOME

Being female and trying to procure financing. There were also prejudices about Native Americans to be overcome—that we're lazy, that we're drunks.

DRIVING FORCE

Initially it was the need to survive—to support myself and my daughter. Now it is because I love what I do and I strive to do it well.

DEFINITION OF SUCCESS

I think really accomplished people never achieve it. They're always striving for it.

WAYS OF DEALING WITH PRESSURE AND STRESS

Humor. Humor. Humor.

ADVICE TO ASPIRING BUSINESSWOMEN

I'm not sure if knowing how much time and commitment this would take might have scared me off, but I think a lot of people don't realize just how hard it is. It looks good from the outside, but the actual responsibility is very heavy.

i think when I first got started in this business I was seen as a novelty. I was a woman with a strong background in science, and very analytical, not something these guys had seen very much. Especially when I wanted to work with hazardous waste sites—they certainly didn't want to fool with that stuff.

For ten of her fifteen years in hazardous waste management, Cheryl Cohenour has been out on her own, but the first five, she says, were critical in developing her dreams and goals. It's still unusual to find a woman in this field, but even more unusual to find one who was so actively encouraged by her male colleagues when she started out. "At my first job out of college, at an R&D facility, I worked with a group of thirty engineers, all with their Ph.D.s, all men," Cheryl recalls. "It was the best work environment I'd ever had. They constantly pushed me to do more, to use my mind, to think." They also helped build a solid foundation for a successful hazardous materials management firm: Cheryl's CRC & Associates.

After Cheryl's divorce in 1981, she knew she was faced with two choices—go back to work or go back to school. She did both: "My father always wanted me to go back to school, and I don't know how he came up with the first semester's tuition, but he did, and I knew this was the only way to provide a better life for my daughter, so I went." Having experienced dry and repetitive laboratory jobs in college, Cheryl says she was drawn to the challenge and variety of environmental work while she was being pushed forward by the R&D engineers: "Every site is different. I'm never stuck behind a desk doing the same thing over and over again. It all goes back to those guys who encouraged me in my first job. Everything they sent me contained a new problem to work on."

But this department was cut back during a slowdown in the industry, and while the next job she had presented plenty of challenge, she didn't see the opportunity for advancement. That's when she pondered starting her own consulting company. "Again it was my father who encouraged me, this time to strike out on my own. He asked me what was the worst thing that could happen. 'You could fail. And then what would you do? You'd get a job.' It doesn't sound so bad when you vocalize it." The timing was right; Cheryl says a new batch of regulations came down just as she was getting started, and she got her first contract two days after her doors opened.

CRC & Associates provides a full range of laboratory, drilling, and cleanup services to industrial and governmental clients, including emergency response to leaks and spills, bioremediation, and regulatory compliance. It's often gritty work, and despite the fact that CRC now employs fifteen, it still takes Cheryl out into the field, where she's still a novelty: "You can tell as soon as you get to a job site if this is going to be a problem. They'll look you up and down like they don't know what to think, as if they're wondering '*She's* going to tell me what to do?' " Cheryl still regularly has to prove herself, but has found a better way to deal with this apprehension: "I think that one thing I've learned through business is that you have to be pretty good-humored about it."

Humor's gotten Cheryl through more than the prejudice of others. Building her business took an effort she'd never known, a strength she never knew she had. "I used to wake up in the middle of the night and wonder if I'd gone insane for quitting my job." Her daughter had to exhibit a sense of humor about the early days of the business as well. According to Cheryl, "There were many times when I had to wake her up in the middle of the night, put her in the back of a car, and take her out to a site. There was no choice, she just had to come along with me." The result, Cheryl says proudly, is a young woman sure of herself and what she can do. "I have to laugh sometimes, she's so independent. I think I might have created a monster."

But perhaps the greatest benefit of succeeding on her own has been the opportunity to create a work environment that reflects the boss's own personality. "It's not like the corporate structures I came from," she says. "We have a very professional organization, but it's a very relaxed atmosphere. We joke, we have fun. I can see how that helps people think outside the box and enjoy their jobs." If the environment could be even more casual, Cheryl would welcome it, but there are limits. "I'd love to run this out of my home," she jokes, "but I don't think the neighbors would like the drilling rigs."

Debi Coleman

CHAIR, PRESIDENT, AND
CHIEF EXECUTIVE OFFICER

Merix Corp.
Forest Grove, Oregon

Kent Derek Photography

WORK HISTORY

1978–1981	General Accounting Supervisor, then Financial Systems Analyst, then Cost Accounting Supervisor, then Financial Manager, Hewlett-Packard Corporation, Palo Alto and Cupertino, California.
1981–1983	Controller, Macintosh Management Team, Apple Computer, Cupertino, California.
1983–1984	Group Controller, Apple 32 Group, Apple Computer, Cupertino, California.
1984–1985	Director, Apple 32 Group Manufacturing and Operations, Fremont, California.
1985–1987	Vice President of Operations, Apple Computer, Cupertino, California.

1987–1989 CFO, Apple Computer, Cupertino, California.

1990–1992 Vice President, IS&T, Cupertino, California.

1992–1994 Vice President, Materials Operations, Tektronix, Inc., Wilsonville, Oregon.

1994–present Chair, President, and CEO, Merix Corp.

EDUCATION

1974 B.A. in English, Brown University, Providence, Rhode Island.

1978 M.B.A., Graduate School of Business, Stanford University, Stanford, California.

FIRST JOB

Supermarket clerk.

ASSOCIATIONS AND NETWORKS

Committee of 200; Business for Social Responsibility; International Women's Forum; Oregon Business Council; Board of Directors, Applied Materials and Synopsys; former Board Member, Octel Communications and Software Publishing Co.

COMMUNITY SERVICE

Board of Trustees, Oregon Symphony; Board of Trustees, Oregon Museum of Science and Industry; Northwest Business Committee for the Arts; Board of Trustees, Marylhurst University; Board of Trustees, Brown University; Advisory Council, Stanford Graduate School of Business; former Member, Harvard Business School Visiting Committee.

AWARDS AND HONORS

Honorary Ph.D. in Engineering, Worcester Polytechnic Institute, 1987; Woman of Achievement, Santa Clara County Commission on the Status of

Women, 1987; named as one of five women likely to become a Fortune 500 CEO, 1987; Tribute to Women in Industry Award, YWCA, 1988; American Society of Women CPAs Honoree, 1988; Woman of Vision Award, Career Action Center, 1989; Women of the Year Award, Financial Women's Association, 1989; Hall of Fame, *Upside Magazine,* 1990; Women of Achievement, *San Jose Mercury News* / The Women's Fund 1990 and 1991; Top 100 List, *CIO,* 1990, 1991, 1992; nominee, CIO of the year, 1992; Manufacturing Entrepreneur of the Year, Oregon Enterprise Forum, 1995; Start-up CEO of the Year, *Upside Magazine,* 1995.

GREATEST OBSTACLES OVERCOME

Lack of an engineering degree.

DRIVING FORCE

I don't want to fail. I'm also trying to prove that a business executive can have a good life and can also make a contribution to society.

WAYS OF DEALING WITH PRESSURE AND STRESS

Having a good support system, including a housekeeper, personal trainer, bookkeeper, and personal assistant.

ADVICE TO ASPIRING BUSINESSWOMEN

It's really important to have one area where you are the best. What's most important is to establish a beachhead in your career where you are known for your skills. But then if you want to move into the executive suites, you have to supplement that with organizational skills and being able to drive results across a variety of departments and functions.

*i*f you have a curiosity and a thirst for knowledge, you can get it refreshed very quickly in this business.

Debi Coleman has been on a steep learning curve of her own making throughout her twenty-four years in high technology, and ascending through some of the best corporations in the business. She helped make history as a member of the Apple Macintosh team, created a legacy of her own at Apple as the youngest Fortune 200 CFO at the age of thirty-four, and most recently took Merix, a small operating unit of oscilloscope manufacturer Tektronix, and spun it off into a separate and profitable company. After more than doubling Merix's business in three years, Debi's even more in demand, serving on several boards, scooping up awards and honors from top industry watchers, and even taking calls from the White House.

High technology wasn't even a blip on Debi's personal radar when she graduated from Brown as an English and liberal arts major. Even in business school she knew she was going places, but says she had no idea electronics would take her there: "I thought I would probably end up with a consumer company, in product marketing." Instead she ended up first at Hewlett-Packard, and then at Apple, where Steve Jobs was heading up a secretive project that would forever change personal computing. "At the time," Debi recalls, "the project didn't even have official blessing or anything. We just kind of hatched this business plan for a revolutionary desktop appliance that became the Macintosh. It was a real exciting ride."

Debi's role, when she first came to the team at age twenty-eight was project controller, but her interests and responsibilities quickly expanded. Debi soon found herself drawn to manufacturing and helped plan, and later manage, the state-of-the-art Macintosh manufacturing plant. "It was a chance to build the machine that was going to build the machine," Debi says, paraphrasing Steve Jobs. "Everyone always writes about the Macintosh design and marketing teams," Debi continues, "but the finance and manufacturing teams played an equal role. The first year, if you count the associated peripherals, we sold about three quarters of a billion dollars. If this were the automobile industry, it would have been similar to the launch of the Mustang."

After rising to CFO, and seeing Apple through its largest growth period ever, Debi left for new challenges. When Tektronix started a major restructuring program in 1993, she took a long look at the Merix subsidiary, which supplied circuit boards to its parent, and other companies such as AT&T and Motorola. Her report gave several options, and the most appealing was spinning it off into a separate company. "This was kind of risky," Debi says "because about four customers, including Tektronix, accounted for about 90 percent of the revenue." But there was also an overwhelming sense of excitement about the possibilities, excitement that peaked when Debi was asked to be CEO of the operation. "Obviously we were a little anxious about going out on our own, but people seemed to be very positive and really thought we could grow the operation. And grow it we did."

Building the team that would build the company was key, Debi says. The one stipulation she put forth was that Terry Timberman, who was an executive in human resources at Tektronix, would join her. In an industry known for high turnover and bidding wars for top executives, Merix has managed to cultivate employee loyalty through achievement awards, stock options, and an average of fifty-four hours of training per employee per year. As a result, it has been named among the best twenty companies to work for in Oregon two years in a row by *Oregon Business*. In return, Debi's executives are asked to share Debi's commitment to volunteer service: "It's really important, not just for the CEO, but for the executives of a company, which is obviously enjoying the benefits of the community, to be a part of the community."

When she was a CFO in her early thirties, Debi was told by her elders that things would get easier when she hit her forties. She didn't believe them then, but says they turned out to be right: "I don't know if it happened on the very day I turned forty, but certainly now I don't have to work as hard. I know how to do this," she says. Looking back on the days when she was making up for her lack of a science and math background, she says she's reached a point where everything's come together: "My experiences are much better integrated now. I've learned how to roll with the punches."

Gun Denhart

FOUNDER AND CHAIR

Hanna Andersson Corporation
Portland, Oregon

WORK HISTORY

1969–1971   Comptroller, American Can Company, Lund, Sweden.

1971–1972   Business and Business Law Teacher, Landskrona, Sweden.

1972–1973   Systems Analyst, Scandinavian Touring, Malmoe, Sweden.

1973–1975   Assistant to the Secretary General, Business Industry
Advisory Committee to the OECD, Paris, France.

1977–1983   Board Member and Area Financial Manager, Educational
Foundation for Foreign Study, Greenwich, Connecticut.

1983–present   Founder, Hanna Andersson Corporation.

EDUCATION

1967   Equivalent of M.B.A. from Lund University, Sweden.

FIRST JOB

Swimming teacher in the Swedish town of Torekov, summers of 1963 and 1964.

ASSOCIATIONS AND NETWORKS

Social Venture Network; Businesses for Social Responsibility; Young Presidents Organization; Committee of 200; Natural Step Network.

COMMUNITY SERVICE

Board Member, Children First for Oregon; Chairperson, Steering Committee, Children's Museum of Portland.

AWARDS AND HONORS

Business Enterprise Trust Award, 1992; American Business Ethics Award, 1994; Best 100 Companies for Working Mothers, *Working Woman*, 1990–1995. 100 Best Companies to Work for in Oregon, *Oregon Business*. 1995–1998; Marketing Top 100, *Advertising Age*, 1996.

FAMILY

Married, three children.

GREATEST OBSTACLES OVERCOME

I grew up and was educated in Sweden and did not know much about the U.S. when I moved here. Much of what I studied in Sweden was not relevant here so I have had to learn a lot.

DRIVING FORCE

I have always been curious about life. This curiosity drives me forward.

BUSINESS MAXIM

Do the right thing and money will come.

WAYS OF DEALING WITH PRESSURE AND STRESS

I do yoga almost every day and hike when the weather allows. I also take one month in the summer to go to Sweden and recharge.

ADVICE TO ASPIRING BUSINESSWOMEN

Follow your heart. When you work with something you have a passion for, it isn't work. It has to be with a company or product that you believe in. It is also very important to have either a good boss or, if you are the boss, a good mentor.

*b*usinesses, like people, don't live in a vacuum. You can't have a healthy company in an unhealthy community. If you're not involved to help keep your community healthy, your company will suffer in the long run.

Weaving her company into the fabric of her community is only one element of Gun Denhart's success with Hanna Andersson. The company has been devoted to producing quality clothing for children, committed to serving its employees, and expanding its markets and suppliers since Gun founded the company in 1983. Since then, Hanna Andersson has grown to over $50 million in annual sales, expanded into the Japanese market, and won press recognition and awards for its innovative charitable work. Still, the founder and now Chair remains down-to-earth and composed as she deals with the attention. As she told one interviewer, "I just try to be myself, so it's not like I'm playing a role."

Gun and her husband, Tom, left behind their careers, high salaries, and Tom's hectic commute to a worldwide ad agency when they moved to Oregon from Connecticut in 1983, searching for a simpler life. It didn't quite turn out that way for Gun: "I definitely don't have any regrets, but it's not exactly simpler for me. Maybe for Tom. The big difference is that we see each other." While Tom freelanced, Gun contemplated starting a business.

She says she didn't set out to design children's clothes until she found herself disappointed with what most American stores had to offer for her young son, Christian. Remembering the clothes she wore growing up in Sweden—made of strong, durable, natural fibers—Gun and Tom formed a mail-order company devoted to quality clothing for children. The first catalog was assembled in their home, with a small fabric sample hand-glued into each of the first 75,000 catalogs. The bright colors and bold patterns that Gun says "let children be children" caught on almost immediately. Within six months, they had $53,000 in sales.

As the business evolved, so did Gun's social commitment. Among the most headline-grabbing programs she initiated was "Hannadowns," whereby the company would give a credit to customers for donating their used "Hannas," which Gun says are designed to be handed down. The program was perhaps too successful—the cost of the credits and the distribution of over one million articles of donated clothing proved to be a drain, and now the credit has been discontinued. But loyal customers are still sending in their clothes, and Hanna Andersson is still sending them to organizations such as the local Community Transitional School, a school for homeless children, and Teen Insights, a program that teaches parenting skills to teen parents.

Other initiatives are so much a part of the organization that they will never be lost. Five percent of Hanna Andersson's pretax profits are donated, and employees are still given a childcare credit, one of the reasons Hanna Andersson appeared on *Working Woman*'s list of the best companies for working mothers five years in a row. The company touches the lives of its employees' children past the age of day care through its Cash for Kids program, which has an impact beyond the financial gift of one hundred dollars for each employee's school-age child each year. The checks are to be used only in the child's classroom, and the children work with parents and teachers to decide how the money will be spent. "I didn't know how a small amount of money could make such a difference," Gun says, "and the teachers are unbelievably grateful. But a wonderful surprise is how the kids get behind it. They learn how they can have an effect on their world."

What started as a dream of a simpler life has by now touched so many other lives that Gun thinks the original plan may be getting closer. She's let go of the President's chair to head the Board, takes a month in her native Sweden each year to "recharge," and says she's accepted the fact that while she can do plenty, she can't do everything: "Unfortunately, or not, I've had to learn the word 'no.'"

Rebecca Matthias

PRESIDENT AND FOUNDER

Mothers Work, Inc.
Philadelphia, Pennsylvania

WORK HISTORY

1979–1980 Construction Engineer, Gilbane Building Company, Providence, Rhode Island.

1980–1982 Manager, Finance and Administration, Board Member, SOLVation, Waltham, Massachusetts.

1982–present President, Founder, and Board Member, Mothers Work, Inc., Philadelphia, Pennsylvania.

EDUCATION

1975 B.A. (cum laude), University of Pennsylvania, Philadelphia.

1978 *Master's* in Architecture, Columbia University, New York City.

1979 *Master's* in Civil Engineering, Massachusetts Institute of Technology, Boston.

FIRST JOB

Construction Engineer for Gilbane Building Company.

COMMUNITY SERVICE

Board of Trustees, Drexel University; Co-founder, Independence Apparel, a welfare-to-work initiative.

AWARDS AND HONORS

Inc. Entrepreneur of the Year, 1992; NASBIC Portfolio Company of the Year, 1995; Best 50 Women in Business, State of Pennsylvania Department of Economic Development, 1997.

FAMILY

Married, three children.

PROFESSIONAL GOALS

To see Mothers Work make $1 billion in revenue by 2005.

DRIVING FORCE

My husband has been my friend, my mentor, and my inspiration.

DEFINITION OF SUCCESS

Setting an ambitious goal and achieving it.

BUSINESS MAXIM

Focus on your goal and never give up.

WAYS OF DEALING WITH PRESSURE AND STRESS

My family is my relief.

ADVICE TO ASPIRING BUSINESSWOMEN

Set a large goal for yourself and focus on it. Don't let anything stand in your way and never, never give up.

*N*ever give up. Somehow you just have to stay in business, keep thinking creatively, keep trying new strategies, and eventually you will get there. It sounds easy, and I know it's not, but it's the truth.

For Rebecca Matthias, never giving up has meant never growing too attached to a single plan if it wasn't working. This has been as true for her maternity clothing business, Mothers Work, as it was for her early life's ambition: "I spent nine years in college and graduate school studying to be an architect and civil engineer," she recalls. "One year afterward, I realized I really wanted to start a business, and totally switched direction."

But what sort of business remained unclear until she was pregnant with her first child in 1982 and working with her husband in his start-up software company. The need for acceptable office wear for pregnant women became painfully obvious, and Mothers Work was born. Rebecca first envisioned the company as a high-end mail-order catalog, and placed ads in *The New Yorker* and *The Wall Street Journal.* The need was obvious to many women besides herself, and she sent out even more catalogs than expected.

She hit her first stumbling block immediately—only a handful of orders were placed. Here was Rebecca's first opportunity to give up, but she didn't, and hasn't since. Instead, she went to one hundred of the women who requested her catalog, and asked what was wrong. "It was the best thing I could have done. I was ready to quit, but when I realized all the things I could have done better, I decided to try one more time."

For the next two years, Rebecca steadily restructured the catalog in response to her customers' comments. Finally, it became clear that mail order would never work for this niche market, and she started selling franchises. Shortly afterward, she realized that she couldn't devote herself wholly to high-price professional clothes, and opened two lower-price shops. By 1985, there were eleven Mothers Work franchises across the country. The growth was explosive, but still, the margins weren't great. It was time to change plans again. Rebecca started buying back franchises and opening new company-owned stores. Steadily growing through redefining her company and focus, Mothers Work moved into manufacturing, went public in 1993, and had increased sales tenfold by 1998.

Much of the credit for the success of this company can be traced back to the first lesson learned. Rebecca and her husband, Dan, who serves as Chairman and CEO, have integrated the process of customer feedback through a sophisticated computer inventory system called TrendTrack, which they developed themselves. The system offers real-time sales figures, takes into account factors such as store location and volume, and gives each product a rating. Customer feedback goes low-tech when Rebecca visits her stores and talks directly to the customers. Either way, it's a process of gathering as much information as possible for decision making, something of a carryover from Rebecca's engineering training: "We've structured a very rational and scientific way of being in the garment business, which is a very chaotic business, often done on gut feeling. We try to analyze every piece, and determine what the customers like. Not what we like—we don't design things we like. We design things the customers like."

While her education helped her think like an engineer, Rebecca credits her husband with helping her be more focused and businesslike or, in her half-joking words, "to think like a man." If there was a business plan to write, or a project to complete, she says, "he was the one who said, 'You don't have time to make dinner. Put that pan away.' He helped me think that way myself, so that I would value my own time." Rebecca and Dan share their lives and their work; Dan wakes her every morning with the latest sales data. "We spend every moment together," Rebecca says. "It's a very intense way of life, but we like it that way."

As if life weren't intense enough, Rebecca has embarked on two major projects related to but just outside of Mothers Work: a book that she hopes will teach other entrepreneurs through her example, and Independence Apparel, a welfare-to-work program that will not only offer a hand up to Philadelphia's poor but will hopefully help bring the garment indus-try back to the city from overseas. But these projects don't represent Rebecca slowing down at her company; her latest goal is to see Mothers Work earn one billion dollars by 2005. For her, never giving up means never standing still.

Maureen Greichen Kielbasa

PRESIDENT AND DIRECTOR
Bright Ideas, Inc.
Middletown, Rhode Island

WORK HISTORY

1979–1986   Speech and Language Pathologist, Warwick School
Department, Warwick, Rhode Island.

1983–1986   Speech and Language Pathologist, Visiting Nurse Service,
Newport, Rhode Island.

1986–1987   Educator and Speech Pathologist, Early Intervention
Program, Fall River, Massachusetts.

1986–1990   First and Second Grade Classroom Teacher, Warwick
School Department, Warwick, Rhode Island.

1989–1993   Speech and Language Pathologist, Portsmouth School
Department, Portsmouth, Rhode Island.

1996–present Faculty Member, Early Childhood Department, Salve
Regina University, Newport, Rhode Island.

1991–present   President and Director, Bright Ideas, Inc., Middletown, Rhode Island.

EDUCATION

1977   B.A. in Speech and Language Pathology and Elementary Education, University of Rhode Island, Kingston.

1979   M.S. in Speech and Language Pathology, University of Rhode Island, Kingston Rhode Island.

1995   Early Childhood Certification, Rhode Island Department of Education.

FIRST JOB

At fourteen, I baby-sat; at sixteen, I worked in a card shop; and through college and grad school, I waited tables.

ASSOCIATIONS AND NETWORKS

Rhode Island Speech and Hearing Association; American Speech and Hearing Association; National Association for Education of Young Children; Rhode Island Association for Education of Young Children; Women's Business Network; Aquidneck Island Director's Association; Newport County Chamber of Commerce; International Reading Association; Rhode Island State Reading Council.

COMMUNITY SERVICE

Volunteer, Lucy's Hearth Shelter for Women and Children; founding Member and past Chairman, Aquidneck Collaborative for Education; Founding Member and past Chairman, Aquidneck Island Director's Association; Volunteer at Elmhurst Public School—classroom tutor, member of Strategic Planning Committee, Principal Selection Committee, School Improvement Team; Eucharist Minister at St. Barnabas Church.

FAMILY

Married, two daughters.

DRIVING FORCE

A desire to keep things interesting—to avoid becoming stale.

DEFINITION OF SUCCESS

I define success not by my bank account, but by my children.

BUSINESS MAXIM

Relationships first.

WAYS OF DEALING WITH PRESSURE AND STRESS

I run or walk. I have a strong support system in my husband, family, and friends. I ask myself if the stress is over something that will be significant in a month. I separate inconveniences from true problems. I admit I am not always successful avoiding stress. Chocolate also helps!

ADVICE TO ASPIRING BUSINESSWOMEN

Do something that makes a difference. Do something you enjoy. Make sure you can look yourself in the mirror each day. If you forfeit your reputation, all the money in the world won't buy it back. Read.

*m*y husband and I sat down and came up with the worst-case scenario if the business failed. We figured that it would be living on the third floor with cinder-block bookcases, and we'd been there, done that, and it wasn't so bad. So we took the plunge.

Bright Ideas, Inc., was a bright idea that came about as if by accident. Maureen Kielbasa was feeling that her current job had grown "stale" at the same time she had to pull her daughters out of their day care center. Then she learned that an ideal space for a preschool had become available. Maureen says, "The way I looked at it, it was meant to be." The worst case never came about—today Bright Ideas' twenty-two employees care for 124 children, and the preschool is among the 5 percent in the nation to be accredited by the National Academy of Early Childhood Programs. But Maureen is still amazed at how close they came.

No worst-case analysis could have anticipated what happened after Maureen and her husband committed to the risk of starting the school. First, she says, she was attacked by the competition, even before opening, with a letter campaign. Then came phone calls while the space was remodeled, threatening to burn it down. "I had to get a lawyer to address the issue from a slander standpoint," Maureen says. "We had to have a policeman stand by while we were under construction. It was incredible. But I had to believe that I had a finite amount of time to do this, and they're not going to get any of that time. So I weathered that without getting into the fray."

Then, in the week before opening and before remodeling was complete, Maureen had to weather hurricane Bob. "I was very discouraged and depressed," Maureen recalls, "and worried about the people I had hired. I decided to treat it as an adventure." The final early disappointment was the loss of her partner. Although they broke amicably, it was at an inopportune time: "It totally took me by surprise, and meant that I had to continue with a job I held prior to opening." As with her other early obstacles, the solution was found in working harder and being better, and the ability to do this, Maureen says, came directly from her family.

"I have always said that my biggest asset is my family. I have a remarkable family with an incredible work ethic." Maureen's maternal grandfather was a pole climber for the telephone company and worked until he was seventy-five. Her paternal grandmother supported four children by taking in laundry after she was widowed. "I never felt like I needed a mentor outside my family," Maureen explains. "My father always said we weren't a Walton family, meaning we weren't perfect, but we were absolutely a team." An example was the loans Maureen started her business with—she borrowed the money from family members, and paid them back in five years with interest.

These days, working in a family-oriented business has meant Maureen had to develop another side of her personality: "In dealing with children you have to have a personality that is nurturing and creative—that's willing to be fun or silly, and comfortable with getting down on the floor. But as an administrator, I have to balance that with the need to run things efficiently. So I have to walk a fine line between being warm and nurturing and being an employer." She started, she says, with absolutely no business experience and learned about running her business "the hard way, by the seat of my pants. It's clearly been a process of learning from my mistakes."

But the rewards are outstanding, she says. Besides having a business that allowed her to be around her young children throughout the day, she gets to watch other young children develop through a critical time. She helps them along with a solid curriculum, a staff that's certified, and a teacher-student ratio that exceeds state standards. She's got a pediatric nurse on staff, and computers in the three-year-olds' room. But Maureen denies that her program puts pressure on the children: "We have a more academic focus, but I don't mean to say it's a high-stress place where the kids work all day long—there's a great emphasis on play. We try to give them a mind-set that they can try anything, and that school is a great place to be."

As for her own development, Maureen has reached a point in her forties where she feels entirely comfortable with her abilities and achievements. Turning forty wasn't traumatic, she says, but "somewhat depressing because there were some things that hadn't happened." She looked to her grandmother to put things in perspective: "I had a grandmother who lived to be almost ninety-six, and she always said her goal in life was to keep getting older. It's kind of hard to worry about turning forty when your ninety-six-year-old grandmother's still living independently and enjoying life."

Barbara Langford Davis

CFP

American Express Financial Advisors Inc.

Columbia, South Carolina

WORK HISTORY

1979–1982   Customer Service Manager, then Knitwear Department Manager, Riegel Textile, Johnston, South Carolina.

1982–present   Financial Advisor, American Express Financial Advisors Inc.

EDUCATION

1979   B.A. (magna cum laude) in sociology, Newberry College, Newberry, South Carolina.

1990   Certified Financial Planner designation, College of Financial Planning, Denver, Colorado.

FIRST JOB

Customer Service Manager, Riegel Textile Corporation.

ASSOCIATIONS AND NETWORKS

Institute of Certified Financial Planners; International Association of Financial Planners; South Carolina Society of ICFP; National Association of Community Leadership; Leadership Columbia Alumni Association.

COMMUNITY SERVICE

Former Member, Board of Directors, Greater Columbia Chamber of Commerce; Board of Directors, Family Shelter; Board of Directors, Midlands Technical College Foundation Board; Board of Directors, Leadership South Carolina Board of Trustees; Board of Directors, Junior Achievement of Central South Carolina; Board of Directors, Greater Columbia Community Relations Council; Board of Directors, Columbia Metropolitan Convention and Visitors Bureau.

AWARDS AND HONORS

DALBAR Seal for Financial Professionals, 1998; Leadership Columbia Alumni's Five for the Future, 1997; YWCA Twin Honoree, 1995; "Doer's Profile" for community service *Greater Columbia Business Monthly,* 1996; Richland County School District One Service Award, 1995; Greater Columbia Chamber of Commerce Volunteer of the Month, 1994; Leadership USA, 1996; Leadership South Carolina Graduate, 1995; Leadership Columbia Graduate, 1993.

FAMILY

Married, two sons.

DRIVING FORCE

The desire to be at the top of my profession, the desire to be recognized as a true professional, to be recognized among my peers as a leader in the profession, to be recognized in the business community as a top financial professional.

DEFINITION OF SUCCESS

Success means reaching daily goals and rewarding yourself. The feeling of greatness when you visualize the ultimate goal. Not worrying, but seeing, believing, doing, and thus achieving.

BUSINESS MAXIM

As you soar to new heights in life, remember that the altitude you reach will be determined not by your aptitude, but rather by your attitude.

WAYS OF DEALING WITH PRESSURE AND STRESS

By taking a special break each day, enjoying sporting events like football and basketball, playing racquetball and basketball, reading books and magazines.

ADVICE TO ASPIRING BUSINESSWOMEN

Be true to yourself, have fun being whatever you want to be, take some time for yourself each day, set realistic daily goals to measure your progress, look forward to life's challenges, don't be afraid to learn from others but keep your identity. Once you achieve, help someone else.

*W*ith the latitude I have right now, I don't think there's any limit to what I can do.

Sixteen years ago, Barbara Davis became a financial advisor with American Express Financial Advisors Inc. (formerly IDS Financial Services). This choice meant leaving behind opportunities in the field of sociology, and a promising career within a company that might have taken her anywhere. What did she get in return? Freedom and a rewarding career. "No one's looking over my shoulder. I don't have to feel guilty if I have to be away from my office to take my son to the dentist. If I work better between one and three A.M. that's what I do. I can never go back to a nine to five job."

On her own terms, Barbara has built a practice of over 340 clients from all walks of life: "I have millionaire clients, clients who are just starting their careers and families, schoolteachers who don't make a lot of money, clients who have achieved very prominent status in the community." Her clients are also varied in terms of race and are of both sexes, but Barbara never felt her own race or gender has been an issue, even back when the profession was dominated by white men. "I really think this is one of the greatest careers a woman can have," she says. "More and more women are entering this field and really outperforming their male counterparts." The occasional difficulties Barbara dealt with by turning them into challenges: "All through my life I've always set my goals high and always wanted to be among the leaders. Therefore, I look at everything as a challenge, not as an obstacle. *Obstacle* is, I guess, just not a word I want be a part of my vocabulary."

Barbara's most recent achievement was her high DALBAR rating and award. DALBAR was created in 1997 as an independent survey of the top financial advisors in the country. Barbara was among the first selected for review, which proved her to be one of the best. This amounted to a national recognition of what her community has known for quite some time. Barbara's work with the local Chamber of Commerce and her participation in financial planning articles and projects for local newspapers had already established her as one of the best in her area.

On the job, Barbara cites the rapidly changing financial markets, the variety of challenges she faces daily, and above all, the bond of trust between herself and her clients as incentives to stick with her career. The fact that she is an independent contractor for American Express Financial Advisors means that she has total control over her schedule and what she will do with her day. Oftentimes, that means she will devote herself to community service.

Prominent and active in the local Chamber of Commerce, Barbara was asked to help restart the inactive Minority Business Council and to chair the Financing Local Government Task Force. The Minority Business Council is once again active, with majority-minority partnerships as a main focus. The policy statement created by the task force will hopefully help improve local government structure and spending. Through the local school district's mentoring program, she guided her mentee to college, and was then asked by the girl's younger brother if Barbara could be his mentor next.

Barbara's family still . comes first. With her sons approaching their teenage years, it has become even more important for her to retain the flexibility that drew her to the financial planning profession, and to ensure that they will always have her as a mother, mentor, and friend. "My life will probably never be as completely balanced as I want it to be," she says, "but I always want to maintain that close relationship and never be too busy to talk to them."

Georgie Olson Harper

VICE PRESIDENT,
CORPORATE SALES

Dakotah, Inc.
Webster, South Dakota

WORK HISTORY

1973–1975 Production worker, Dakotah, Inc.

1975–1986 Customer Service Manager, Dakotah, Inc.

1986–1992 Contract Sales Manager, Dakotah, Inc.

1992–present Vice President, Corporate Sales, Dakotah, Inc.

EDUCATION

1974–1975 Attended Northern State University, Aberdeen, South
Dakota.

FIRST JOB

At a dry cleaner in Sioux Falls.

ASSOCIATIONS AND NETWORKS

Past Member, Network of Executive Women in Hospitality; past Member, Quality Assurance Board, American Hotel and Motel Association.

COMMUNITY SERVICE

Webster, South Dakota Chamber of Commerce; Co-President, Webster Booster Club; Church council United Methodist Church, Webster, South Dakota.

FAMILY

Married, three children.

PERSONAL GOALS

To raise my children and get them educated. After that, to find a great place to live, maybe near a beach.

PROFESSIONAL GOALS

To find a good job near that beach.

DRIVING FORCE

The desire to please people. No matter what I'm selling, I want them to be happy with the transaction.

DEFINITION OF SUCCESS

Happiness. I would love to be rich and happy, but happiness comes first.

BUSINESS MAXIM

Be fair and honest. People respect you for being fair and honest, even if you don't know it.

WAYS OF DEALING WITH PRESSURE AND STRESS

Being at home, cooking, exercising. I know my job's important, but some days I have to pull back, just turn it off when I get home.

ADVICE TO ASPIRING BUSINESSWOMEN

Get a good education—it's trite but true. Always feel good about yourself. Never make people feel like you're better than they are. Be sure to give to your personal life; it so easy to leave that behind.

*l*iving in a small town really helps balancing work and family. I travel all the time, but when I get back from New York or San Francisco, I come back to a life. That stability has made all the difference.

✤

Georgie Harper works for a small company that's a big part of a small town. Dakotah, Inc., employs four hundred in the region, and is headquartered in a town of 2,500. One of the bedding manufacturer's main purposes when it started in 1971 was to bring jobs to northeastern South Dakota, and after expanding into the hospitality market in the late 1980s and going public in 1993, its succeeded. Dakotah now has five factories in the area and licenses brands from the Elvis Presley estate, Harley-Davidson, Roy Rogers Enterprises, and Walt Disney, among others. Georgie, who started when the company was two years old, has been along for the entire ride: "Twenty-five years," she points out, "that's over half my life! It's pretty amazing."

Her rise to Vice President of Corporate Sales was truly from the ranks. When she and her husband first came to Webster, South Dakota, it was supposedly just a stop on the way to Minneapolis, where Georgie says she was looking at a very different career: "Of all things, I wanted to be a flight attendant. Don't ask me why; I really don't know. I fly all the time now, and you can keep it." Dakotah was one of the few employers in the area, so Georgie signed up to work the night shift on the factory floor. "I don't know what you would call that job. I would mark chalk lines on the quilts—they were all handmade—before the quilters got to them. That's how I started."

As the company grew, Georgie moved into an opening in customer service, and from there saw an opportunity to sell to national hotel and motel chains. Her plan and initial success got her promoted to contract sales manager, responsible for Dakotah's new market in hospitality bedding. "It was really just picking up the phone book, calling corporate headquarters, and networking to find out how we could be a player in that market and it worked," Georgie remembers. Before long, she was managing sixty sales reps, found buyers among the largest hotel chains, and created, she says, "the only area of growth for our company at that time." So they made her a VP.

Georgie was the company's first female Vice President, just thirty-seven at the time, and felt she did have to take extra steps to gain acceptance. But she absolutely refuses to dwell on this fact: "You have to take these things seriously, but you can't let it bother you. You can't resent your male counterparts for whatever reason; it just makes you less effective." Taking the extra steps came naturally, and produced stunning results. National contract sales went from $15 million when she started as VP to $42 million in just three years, mostly due to her belief in the company and commitment to the product. "I have to believe in what I'm selling, and I was able to get that across to the reps. A lot of the success was due to travel, talking to customers and sales people and getting everyone enthused and excited, even anxious, to sell the product."

Returning from these trips is Georgie's favorite part of the job. That's when she returns to where she started, the women who make the product, and tell them what happened. Dakotah employees own about 35 percent of the company, so they're eager to hear about her accomplishments, but Georgie says there's something more that keeps them interested in her reports from the field. "The spirit of the people who work here is amazing," Georgie says. "They're thrilled to hear about where I traveled to, they love to have me come back and share what my latest project is. It might be a midwestern thing, but they're so proud of what they do, proud of their company and their jobs."

Betty DeVinney

VICE PRESIDENT, COMMUNICATIONS AND PUBLIC AFFAIRS

Eastman Chemical Company
Kingsport, Tennessee

WORK HISTORY

1973–present   Eastman Chemical Company, Kingsport, Tennessee.

EDUCATION

1964   B.S. in English and History, University of Southern Mississippi, Hattiesburg.

FIRST JOB

Dorm Receptionist, University of Southern Mississippi.

ASSOCIATIONS AND NETWORKS

Chair, Number One Committee; Board Member, Eastman Credit Union.

COMMUNITY SERVICE

Board Member of Model City Coalition; Paramount Theatre; East Tennessee State University Foundation; Northeast State Technical College Foundation;

University of Tennessee–Knoxville Chancellor's Advisory Board; Kingsport Chamber of Foundation Board; past President, Kingsport Chamber of Commerce.

AWARDS AND HONORS

Alvah K. Borman Award, American Society for Engineering Education, Cooperative Education Division, 1989.

FAMILY

Married, one son, one granddaughter.

PROFESSIONAL GOALS

To demonstrate the value of communicating face-to-face in a high-tech world.

DRIVING FORCE

The determination to prove that a nonengineer can achieve, can learn the technical information needed. The drive to prove to myself and then to others.

BUSINESS MAXIM

Gentle with people, ruthless with time.

GREATEST REWARD FROM CAREER

Recognition by Eastman management and the ability to "sit at the table" of the executive team, made up of senior executives who report to the CEO.

GREATEST DOWNSIDE TO CAREER

Not having an even playing field. Gender issues have been the biggest downside. Having to work harder, having to prove yourself more often and more frequently because of gender.

WAYS OF DEALING WITH PRESSURE AND STRESS

Humor and quiet time. I'm an introvert in an extroverted world, so I have to have the quiet time to reenergize.

ADVICE TO ASPIRING BUSINESSWOMEN

Don't expect anything to come to you without a lot of hard work. There will be all kinds of barriers in front of you, some self-imposed, some external. Get creative and work around them.

i'm an English major in a chemical company. That can be a major barrier, if you let it become one.

✻

Betty DeVinney started at the University of Southern Mississippi as a physics major, but says she was told point-blank that science wasn't for her: "I got talked out of it because I was a girl. If I was going to be a mother, I was told, I needed to teach." She did as she was told—for a while. Betty taught in Mississippi, Florida, and Georgia, following her husband, who was completing his service in the air force. She might never have regretted those lost physics courses if she hadn't later taken a sales job at the chemical company where her husband worked.

That job was the beginning of a twenty-five-year career in what is now a nearly five-billion-dollar company, Eastman Chemical Company. From sales, Betty moved to the treasurer's office, then to the human resources department, and then into communications. "I've had a different job every two years with this company," Betty says, "each one very different and very challenging. The only place I haven't been is manufacturing." Now she sits on the ten-member executive team, reporting directly to the CEO as the Vice President of Communications and Public Affairs.

But the first step she took was to make up for the science she was steered away from as a teen. "I set out to learn the language of the chemical company," Betty says. "I took engineering courses and chemistry courses—reactions, chemical transformations—it was all very interesting. If you set your mind to it, you can learn just about anything." Moving to the financial side presented new learning opportunities in corporate policy, and her time in human resources gave Betty a chance to learn "the people flow process."

After her first twenty years, Betty was witness to a major change in the one-hundred-year-old company. In 1994, Eastman was spun off from Eastman Kodak Company and went public. Shortly after, as the newly independent Eastman was going global, Betty was working close to home as manager of community relations. The latest challenge was keeping the lines open with the community advisory panel, made up entirely of non-Eastman employees. The challenge turned out to be Betty's favorite part of the job as she watched respect run both ways: "There's a lot of community support for the company and a lot of company support for the community," she says. Adjusting to public ownership and a new department, Betty decided it was once again time to further her education. "I was lucky enough to attend the executive development program at the University of Tennessee, building a very solid base for management." A move to corporate relations was the next outlet for her unfolding skill set, and less than a year later, she became part of the executive team.

There were few women role models for Betty as she furthered her positions, and she would like to see that change. "I feel I have to be a role model in this company and community," she says, "whether working as coach or mentor for other women in the company, or working and speaking to women's groups." Giving talks to organizations such as the National Association of Women Business Owners and helping Girls Incorporated raise funds are a couple of ways, but actions speak louder, and becoming President of the Kingsport Chamber of Commerce was one of her louder statements. While she was proud to accept this post, she adds, "I'm not particularly proud that I was the first female President in the fifty-year history of the organization. Nor do I think they were very proud of that either."

If she had to do it all over again, Betty says she wouldn't listen to those who told her that science isn't for girls. But she's also found that being an exception in her company offers ways to be exceptional: "My educational background has been an advantage just from the aspect of being conceptual as opposed to being linear. This is a company of engineers—very data-based, very quality focused. I can bring to the table a different way of thinking."

Sharon Meehan

PRESIDENT, CHIEF
EXECUTIVE OFFICER

Ham I Am!
Enterprises Limited
Richardson, Texas

WORK HISTORY

Lamaze instructor for fifteen years, had a gift basket business for three years before the Ham business took off.

EDUCATION

No college—traveled instead.

FIRST JOB

Worked in a specialty food and cooking store with a great wine section. Did yacht provisioning and gift baskets.

ASSOCIATIONS AND NETWORKS

Board Member, National Association for the Specialty Food Trade; Les Dames d' Escoffier; International Association for Culinary Professionals.

COMMUNITY SERVICE

Volunteer at children's schools; Volunteer, Meals on Wheels; hiring women on the mend from Nexus, a local substance abuse program.

AWARDS AND HONORS

Numerous awards from the National Association for the Specialty Food Trade's International Fancy Food Show in 1992, 1995, and 1997; various awards for packaging designs.

FAMILY

Four children.

GREATEST OBSTACLES OVERCOME

Having no money, being divorced and raising four children, not having a college degree or business experience. Each was an obstacle and each has also contributed to my success.

DRIVING FORCE

My four children and their needs. My own need to contribute and to have a full life. My own drive to create and own a profitable company.

DEFINITION OF SUCCESS

Managing the balancing act of life—to raise children with the desire to contribute to the community and to be in charge of their destiny, to be profitable and to provide a work environment that gives opportunities for my employees to create success in their own lives.

BUSINESS MAXIM

Never compromise quality and customer service. Find a way to do what they want.

WAYS OF DEALING WITH PRESSURE AND STRESS

With a sense of humor. I remind everyone that we sell ham—not vital organs.

ADVICE TO ASPIRING BUSINESSWOMEN

Write a business plan. Get a support network going. Do something special to reward yourself once a year—a vacation, a spiritual retreat, or a time indulgence of some type.

i've had to learn how to walk away from entrepreneurship and become a businesswoman. I could no longer do everything. I had to admit that I wasn't good at certain things, and I had to fill those gaps with people I trust. It's hard to see your faults, but I saw that while we were doing okay, we could be doing a heck of a lot better.

Ham I Am! started as the ultimate one-woman show. While looking for a way to extend her Christmas budget in 1986, Sharon Meehan remembered the taste of a smoked ham she'd sampled in Arkansas, and hit on the idea of distributing the product in Texas. With a loan of $1,250 and her family car, a new business was born. Twelve years of hard work moved Ham I Am! from her garage to an office park, from obscurity to a spot in the Neiman's Christmas catalog, and from a hobby to a million-dollar-plus business venture.

Today, after years of "incremental" growth, Sharon is preparing for an explosion. After the *Dallas Morning News* featured Ham I Am!, investors took notice, and a restaurateur bought out her silent partner. Sharon's hams will now be the centerpiece of a twenty-thousand-square-foot restaurant in the heart of Dallas's business district. She's hired a financial advisor, a marketing consultant, and a mail-order manager, and is making ready to expand her own company through the purchase of another. In 1997, Ham I Am! shipped twenty tons of ham, forty tons of turkey, and 100,000 jars of Sharon's own Hogwash, a sauce she cooked up to complement the hams she sold. Sharon's current plans will, she says, allow those figures to increase "exponentially."

Sharon credits her humble beginnings for much of her present business sense: "Having no money has taught me how to run a lean operation," Sharon says. "We never have to worry about downsizing, because with the seasonal nature of the business, we're always in downsizing mode." Having no college degree, Sharon says, has also had it's upside: "I'm in a constant state of needing to know more—I have a hunger for knowledge. It's opened me up to the whole mentoring process. Education is something I should have done, but didn't, and so I'm in a continual mode of learning." Even being the single mother of four children while running her business has informed her about how her business should be run: "Families have to come first around here—you have to make your job work around your life. This is part of my being a single mom, leading the company with a family-first attitude." Her employees get the benefit of flexible time for family life, and if they can't do it on their own, Sharon gives them a gentle push: "The accountant who took work home—she got in a little bit of trouble with me. I had to let her know that her time was her own."

Sharon makes the same efforts herself, but also realizes that her company is a part of her persona: " "I have a driving need for fun. I have to implement it every day, in every part of my life, and my business is a true extension of my life. I'm a very hospitable person—I love to entertain, to make people feel welcome, to cook for people." When her personal life was in crisis, she realized her business had another purpose, one that she now extends to her employees: "When I went through my divorce, I was a wreck, but my business was a safe haven for me. I decided my business would be a safe haven for my employees as well, a place for people to come and get their feet on the ground." So Sharon hired three drug addicts from a local program for women in recovery. "The only rule was that you had to tell the truth. Everyone knew they were junkies, and everyone knew we had an opportunity to help them."

With all the changes at Ham I Am! and Sharon's new sense of professionalism, keeping her work and personal time separate is more of a challenge than ever: "I now integrate business thinking into a lot of what I do, but one of the things I definitely don't do is bring a lot of work home with me. I have to be jealous of that time and really watch it." She knows that on a deeper level, she is changing as well, but vows to hold on to the person who got her to where she is today: "As much as I fought it in the beginning, it really is hard to keep work and home life separate. I used to define myself as a friend and mother, but being a businesswoman is now part of that makeup. I now have to add that to my definition of myself, but it's not my only definition."

Cheryl L. Thompson-Draper

Custom Images

CHAIRMAN OF THE BOARD
AND CHIEF EXECUTIVE
OFFICER

Warren Electric Group
Houston, Texas

WORK HISTORY

1970–1985   Order filler, file clerk, administrative assistant, expediter, will call department, shipping and receiving clerk, credit and collections, billing department, and accounting for Warren Electric Company.

1985–1989   Manager, Marketing and Public Relations and Treasurer of the Board, Warren Electric Company.

1990–1992   Vice President, Marketing and Secretary of the Board, Warren Electric Company.

1992–present   Chairman of the Board, Warren Electric Group.

1993–present   CEO, Warren Electric Group.

EDUCATION

1971–1972   Houston Community College.

FIRST JOB

Sweeping floors, cleaning toilets, and dusting warehouse shelves for Warren Electric at age nineteen.

ASSOCIATIONS AND NETWORKS

Vice President, National Association of Electrical Distributors; President (to 1999), Houston Electrical League; Director, All Those Texans; Director, Houston Livestock Show and Rodeo; Member, National Association of Female Executives; Member of Advisory Councils of Texas A&M College of Veterinary Medicine and College of Engineering / Technology; Member, American Alliance of Family Business; Member, National Association of Corporate Directors; Member, Texas Executive Women; Member, Executive Women International; Member, Petroleum Club of Houston; Executive Committee and Director, Greater Houston Partnership; International Committee, U.S. Chamber of Commerce.

COMMUNITY SERVICE

Director, Theater Under the Stars; Director / VP San Jacinto Girl Scouts; past Director, Rotary Club of Houston; Director, Junior Achievement.

AWARDS AND HONORS

Paul Harris Fellow, Rotary Club of Houston; Texan of the Year, All Those Texans, 1994; Marketing Excellence Award—Industrial Sales, Affiliated Distributors, 1994; Woman on the Move, City of Houston, 1995; Outstanding Family-Owned Business, State of Texas, 1995; Second-Largest Woman-Owned Houston Business (based on revenue), *Houston Business Journal,* 1996 and 1997; Third-largest Woman-Owned Business in the State of Texas (based on revenue), *Woman Enterprise Magazine,* 1996 and 1997; Runner-up, Cora Bacon Award for Outstanding Business Leadership, National Association of Women Business Owners, 1997 and 1998; ranked #19 in *Entrepreneur Magazine*'s Hot 100 Companies, 1998; ranked 89th among women-owned business, *Working Woman Magazine,* 1998; finalist, Ernst & Young Entrepreneur of the Year, 1998; International Executive of the Year, U.S. Chamber of Commerce, 1998.

FAMILY

Remarried, three children, two daughters-in-law, three grandchildren.

DRIVING FORCE

No one can tell me I *can't* do something. It's always been my "hot" button.

DEFINITION OF SUCCESS

I will be successful when I can pass on a growing, dynamic company to my children—when they are ready to take it on and I am young enough to enjoy retirement.

BUSINESS MAXIM

Life is 10 percent what happens to me and 90 percent what I do with it.

GREATEST REWARD FROM CAREER

To have my family tell me they are proud of me and agree with the way I have handled the family business.

GREATEST DOWNSIDE TO CAREER

It *is* lonely at the top. There is really no one to talk to about the overall plans and problems internally—not even my husband, as he is the President of Warren Electric Telecom & Utility, and reports to me.

WAYS OF DEALING WITH PRESSURE AND STRESS

I try to get away from Warren Electric at least quarterly to the ranch. I need to think about *anything* else every once in a while.

ADVICE TO ASPIRING BUSINESSWOMEN

Believe in your own instincts; most women don't and should. Risk it all—if you don't try, it won't happen. Be yourself, don't be a "make believe" man, but don't let anyone run over you either.

i couldn't wait to turn forty. I figured if I was at least forty, if I had a few gray hairs, people would listen to me a little bit more. It was a real passing of youth, but in a good way.

☀

Cheryl Thompson-Draper was thirty-five when she realized she would someday pass from under her father's broad shadow. J. R. Thompson had run Warren Electric, a wholesale distributor of electrical products, in his own way—there was only one Vice President, and no middle management. Everyone reported directly to "J.R.," and Cheryl started reporting to him at work at the age of nineteen. She was recently divorced, had no college degree, and had a child to support, so he gave her a job. Her first assignment at Warren was sweeping floors and scrubbing toilets.

At age thirty-five, Cheryl announced that she wanted to continue in his footsteps and received a nod of approval, but no direct encouragement: "His reaction was something like 'That's nice.' He wasn't really willing to let go of the company." He did, however, help her move onto the Board of Directors as Treasurer, where her confidence and ability grew, even as she was typically thought of as J.R.'s "little girl" first and foremost, by both her father and other employees.

Years after their conversation, Cheryl's father passed away, setting the stage for a lengthy court battle in which Cheryl and her mother fought to keep the company in the family. When it was finally over, Cheryl faced the issue of winning the respect of her employees: "Winning the lawsuit helped. They realized that I really do care about them, the company, our business, and our customers." It was another year, Cheryl claims, before she felt her employees were completely comfortable with her at the helm, and she gave them good reason.

When Cheryl took over, Warren Electric Group had six locations. They now have thirty-six. In her four years of leadership, she has taken the company from $93 million in 1993 sales to $210 million in 1997, and has secured vendors such as Rockwell Automation, Hubble, Hoffman, and

Crouse Hinds, and clients such as BASF, Shell Oil, Amoco, and HL&P. Warren now has locations in Texas, Louisiana, Alabama, Florida, Puerto Rico, the Dominican Republic, and Trinidad, and employs 625 people, including much of Cheryl's immediate, merged, and extended family.

Cheryl is certain that Warren will remain a family business for generations to come. Her husband is one of the two Presidents and COOS who reports to her, her son serves on the Board of Directors and works in Warren's corporate marketing department, her daughter is on the Board, and her husband's son and daughter-in-law both work for Warren. Her eighty-five-year-old mother is on the Board, as well as one of Cheryl's first cousins, who's been with Warren for twenty-five years. "It's an interesting mixture around here," Cheryl says. "During family holidays, we talk about Warren constantly. Even weekend family meals turn into mini Board meetings." Although she admits that she has had difficulty separating family life from professional life, she wouldn't have it any other way: "I've been able to keep a seventy-nine-year-old family business together and growing and still keep a family feeling, and keep it employee-friendly."

To give employees a sense of being part of a family, Cheryl invests time in "small" gestures whenever she can—showing up at the hospital to celebrate a birth, or attending a funeral to mourn the death of an employee's loved one. Warren's last company picnic drew over a thousand employees and their families to Houston. Warren also emphasizes higher education, something Cheryl still regrets she didn't complete, with tuition assistance and classes through Warren University, an Internet-based program developed in conjunction with the National Association of Electrical Distributors and the American Management Association. "I try to do more than big corporate America does," Cheryl says. "I want my employees to understand that they are very important to me. I couldn't do this by myself, and I know it."

Cheryl also knows that keeping the company employee- and family-friendly will place limits on its future growth. In five years, she predicts, Warren's rapid expansion will have to slow if she is to continue to be active in the community and proactive toward her employees. There are still, however, plans for Warren to move into Alabama and Mississippi, and in the meantime, Cheryl says that she can't wait to turn fifty.

Maxine Turner

PRESIDENT

Cuisine Unlimited, Inc.
Salt Lake City, Utah

WORK HISTORY

1967–1970   Utah Marketing Division Assistant Secretary, First Security
Bank, Salt Lake City, Utah.

1970–1972   Secretary, U.S. Borax, Los Angeles, California.

1972–1975   Division Marketing Department Secretary, First Security
Bank, Salt Lake City, Utah.

1980–present   President, Cuisine Unlimited Deli and Catering.

EDUCATION

1967–1970   University of Utah, coursework in business management
and special education.

FIRST JOB

Checker at a Safeway during my junior year in high school.

ASSOCIATIONS AND NETWORKS

Board of Directors, National Caterers Association; Member, National Association of Women Business Owners; Salt Lake City and Park City Chambers of Commerce; National Association of Catering Executives; Member, Utah Economic Development Corporation; Member, International Special Event Society; Member, Meeting Planners International.

COMMUNITY SERVICE

Board of Directors, American Red Cross, Salt Lake City chapter; Board of Directors, Utah Microenterprise Loan.

AWARDS AND HONORS

Small Business Administration Advisory Counsel Award for the State of Utah, 1995; Woman Business Owner of the Year, 1995; Nominee, Avon Women of Enterprise, 1993.

FAMILY

Married, three children.

GREATEST OBSTACLES OVERCOME

Lack of financial stability in the early years. Operating a high-end catering service in a conservative community.

DRIVING FORCE

Entrepreneurial spirit.

DEFINITION OF SUCCESS

The ability to balance career, family, and personal goals.

WAYS OF DEALING WITH PRESSURE AND STRESS

Through keeping a journal and the support of colleagues.

ADVICE TO ASPIRING BUSINESSWOMEN

Let the passion come from the heart and the business sense from the head.

i learned how to manage my company not from a lesson taught by a terrific professor but from the everyday experiences of running my business. I am most fortunate to have had generous people along the way who were advisors and mentors. I know they have had a profound effect on our success.

Maxine Turner started small. In the beginning she didn't plan to own a catering company that would eventually employ her husband as well as two of her children, that would be capable of hosting events of up to ten thousand people, and that would grow to become, according to the local Chamber of Commerce, one of the largest women-owned businesses in the state. Maxine was primarily looking for a way to make extra money while raising her kids, but a series of opportunities, a number of shrewd business decisions, a powerful support network, and her own dedication formed a thriving and growing company.

Just a few months after she left her job at a Salt Lake City bank, Maxine was approached by a local Jewish women's organization and asked to coordinate the catering for a synagogue. "As I started working on developing kosher menus and cooking meals," Maxine says, "I found that it sparked an interest in me, and I fell in love with the catering business." At the same time, word spread about what Maxine was cooking up, and other offers started coming in. She got her business license, and started making plans.

It was then that she was offered a contract to provide lunches for a private school of about four hundred students. Seeing an opportunity to use their facilities to help launch her business, she struck a deal with the school, cleared up the zoning issues with the city, and was on her way. Cuisine Unlimited was housed for six years in this incubator-type environment, allowing Maxine to develop a loyal following of corporate and individual clients. She could sense, even then, that she was on to something big; everything she made, she poured back into the business: "In the first five years of business, I didn't even draw a salary."

Five years after she started in the synagogue, Maxine had grown beyond the confines of both this location and the school. Her client base was large enough, she felt, to take a chance on a small business loan and move out on her own. "I guess that was my first rude awakening," she remembers. "I was very protected working first in the synagogue and then in the school. All of a sudden I had overhead, employees, and monthly rent in our new location. I learned very quickly how easy it can be to lose a company."

Small businesses never succeed just because of one person, Maxine says. In her case, having the school's facilities in the early years was critical, as was the advisory board she assembled from contacts in the community. "They didn't have to be in the food business," she says, "but they had to be small business owners." The group met once a week for three months, giving Maxine a crash course on running her own show: "I took the strength and the ideas of each of these individuals and started incorporating those into my own business. I found I learned very fast."

Today, Cuisine Unlimited employs forty full- and part-time staff, does over $1.6 million in yearly business, and boasts of being the best caterer in the market. Maxine's distinctive menus, which blend her Greek background with her husband's Jewish heritage, have become nationally recognized. Her deli, located in Salt Lake City's business district, has been rated the best Greek restaurant in town by Zagat's Survey, and has been named the twenty-fifth largest women-owned business in the State by the *Utah Business Journal*. Maxine has served dinner to President and Mrs. Bush, dined with Julia Child in New York, and been appointed treasurer of the National Caterers Association. But still, Maxine says, it's the customer's opinion that really makes her job satisfying: "Nothing is more delightful to me than when someone receives our name over and over again as the premier Salt Lake City caterer."

Joyce Flower Hugg

VICE PRESIDENT, SENIOR
ACCOUNT EXECUTIVE

Walter W. Cribbins Co.
Ogden, Utah

WORK HISTORY

1970–1971   Receptionist, John Bolles Associates, San Francisco, California.

1971–1976   Secretary, then Product Researcher, Walter W. Cribbins Co., San Francisco, California.

1976–1981   Legal Secretary, Keil, Conolly & Barbieri, San Francisco, California.

1982–1983   Clerk, Southern Pacific Railroad, Ogden, Utah.

1983–1984   Secretary, Ogden City Corporation, Ogden, Utah.

1984–1985   Clerk, Southern Pacific Railroad, Ogden, Utah.

1985   Started as a Sales Representative, Walter W. Cribbins Co., Ogden, Utah.

EDUCATION

1967–1970   Weber State University, Weber, Utah.

1994–present Continuing education courses, Promotional Products
Association International.

FIRST JOB

Carhop at a drive-in. But I didn't do rollerskates.

ASSOCIATIONS AND NETWORKS

Member and past President, Utah Idaho Promotional Products Association;
Board of Directors (1994–1996), Ogden Weber Chamber of Commerce.

COMMUNITY SERVICE

Member, P.E.O. Sisterhood, Chapter M, Ogden, Utah; Member, Small
Business Advisory Council, State of Utah, 1993–1994.

AWARDS AND HONORS

Spirit of the American Woman Award, Your Community Connection, 1990;
Nominee, Athena Award, Ogden/Weber Chamber of Commerce, 1994;
Award of Merit, American Advertising Federation, 1972 and 1976; Gold
Pyramid Award, Promotional Products Association, 1998.

FAMILY

Married.

GREATEST OBSTACLES OVERCOME

My own denial.

PERSONAL GOALS

To help others as much as I can. I've also thought about running for public office, but of course, I'd have to stand up and say, "Whatever you've heard about me is true. Believe everything you hear!"

PROFESSIONAL GOALS

To continue to strive to give my customers what they want. To work *only* with people I want to work with.

DEFINITION OF SUCCESS

Always making progress.

BUSINESS MAXIM

Be honest, be yourself, be brave, step forward, include God as your guide, listen to your inner voice.

GREATEST REWARD FROM CAREER

Last year when I was given business cards showing my new title as "Queen."

ADVICE TO ASPIRING BUSINESSWOMEN

Don't let anyone or anything stand between you and your sunlight. If something diverts you from your purpose, revise, delete, and proceed. If you fail, move on. If you succeed, take credit and then move on.

*S*ome things in my life have been serendipitous, but to succeed I had to rely on determination and design. I knew that I had to be very self-disciplined, reliable, consistent and, of course, offer first-class service.

Joyce Flower Hugg is more than grateful for the opportunities she's been given. From where she stood, they were not just a chance to succeed in business, but to save her own life. In 1985, she returned to Walter W. Cribbins, a company she had left eleven years before, not to ask for a job, but to make amends. Joyce was admitting to her former boss and co-workers that she was an alcoholic. At that meeting, her former boss, Carl Rosenfeld, saw something in Joyce that let him take a chance. With no experience in outside sales, just a few business cards and catalogs, she became the company's sole sales rep in Utah.

Today, Joyce is a Vice President with one of the best sales records in the company. Her Utah operation employs eighteen people in Salt Lake City and Ogden, and her 1997 sales record of $1 million accounted for a twelfth of the company's annual take. Walter W. Cribbins sells promotional items—when a company wants its logo on just about anything, Cribbins is one of the companies they can call. With $2 million in revenue being generated out of Joyce's office in 1998, she says, "that means an awful lot of ballpoint pens, calendars, and coffee mugs."

It was a long road to this point, and Joyce says it was made only more difficult by her own choices earlier in her life. After dropping out of a Utah college, she says, "I finally did what hippies do in the late sixties: I moved to San Francisco to pursue an existence in the school of hard knocks." While she emphasizes that not all her experiences there were negative, they culminated years later in a slide into alcoholism. Finally, after terminating her first stay at Walter W. Cribbins, she took at job at a legal firm and it wasn't until 1981 when, she recalls, "I could see the writing on the wall." Still, she was fired for coming into work drunk.

"The world came crashing down on me all at once. I got fired, I got a DUI, and my husband of seven years threatened divorce if I didn't give up my bottle," Joyce says. "I literally felt like I was sliding off the face of the earth." She contacted her family, left her husband, and returned to Utah for a treatment program. With the help of her parents, she says she started to turn around: "I was thirty-two years old when my second life began. I was spiritually lifted from my previously hopeless state and this happened when I surrendered. When I gave up, I won the war."

Working through her recovery, Joyce supported herself (her parents were "wisely" charging her rent) with various low-paying jobs. When she was furloughed and given a severance package, she made the trip back to California, where she was welcomed back into Walter W. Cribbins as a commission-only sales rep. Back in Ogden, she set up an office in a one-bedroom apartment. "My files were cardboard boxes on top of an old closet door. I had an answering machine, a box of business cards, and a 1972 Volkswagen van. I started to cold call."

Looking back at what she had conquered pushed Joyce forward as she struggled to build a customer base from cold calls: "I had nothing to lose. I kept telling myself that the worst thing that could happen in my life had already happened. So I kept making phone calls based on that." In her first year she worked a second job part time and sold $12,000 gross. In her second year, after applying herself to contacts at the local Chamber of Commerce and its Women in Business subgroup, she sold $60,000 in promotional products and $200,000 in signs. "In my third year," Joyce continues, "I took a leap of faith and bought a brand-new car. My boss was thrilled because he knew I would push myself to make the payments." Joyce really didn't need the push—she had hit her stride, found her career, and found herself.

Joyce has remarried and has recently learned to live with rheumatoid arthritis. This latest challenge—she calls it her "new" disease—has slowed her down, but hasn't gotten her down: "I've come to appreciate family and friends like I never had before. I had to learn to do more business from my desk than I previously did in front of customers. I probably worked less in 1997 and had a larger volume in sales than any year before." Having learned lessons from her earlier, self-inflicted disease, she rarely dwells on this one, following the advice she gives as a mentor to other women suffering from addiction: "No matter how bleak and dark their lives may be at the moment, there is always hope if you are determined enough. If you ask for guidance, it will be there for you. It's always been there for me."

Elisabeth B. Robert

CHIEF EXECUTIVE OFFICER, CHIEF FINANCIAL OFFICER, DIRECTOR, TREASURER

*The Vermont
Teddy Bear Co.®, Inc.*

Shelburne, Vermont

WORK HISTORY

1979–1980   Trainee, First National Bank of Boston, Boston, Massachusetts.

1984–1989   Assistant to the President, the Director of Gas Supply, Rates, and Planning, Vermont Gas Systems, South Burlington, Vermont.

1989–1990   Campaign Manager, McCarren for Lieutenant Governor, Burlington, Vermont.

1991–1995   Vice President, Finance, then Founding Partner, Executive Vice President and CFO Air Mouse Remote Controls, Williston, Vermont.

EDUCATION

1978   A.B. (magna cum laude, Phi Beta Kappa, and Highest
        Departmental Honors), Middlebury College, Middlebury,
        Vermont.

1984   M.B.A., University of Vermont, Burlington.

FIRST JOB

Working in the packaging department of my father's precision tool manufacturing company.

ASSOCIATIONS AND NETWORKS

Vermont Business Roundtable; Lake Champlain Chamber of Commerce; New England Direct Marketers Association; Vermont Attractions Association; Vermont Businesses for Social Responsibility.

COMMUNITY SERVICE

Coach seventh and eighth grade girls basketball team for Mater Christi School, Burlington.

AWARDS AND HONORS

Zimel Resnick Prize for outstanding scholarship and leadership from UVM School of Business; 1979–1980 Outstanding Contributor, Greater Boston Chamber of Commerce.

FAMILY

Two daughters.

GREATEST OBSTACLES OVERCOME

Balancing family commitments with job responsibilities and opportunities for career growth. Balancing sensitivity to human nature and need with the ability to be fair, firm, and even tough in the interest of the company. Keeping up with relevant detail while commanding a bigger and bigger picture and exercising a broader perspective.

DRIVING FORCE

Myself. Something that I was born with. An intense desire to make sure that every moment is productive, to achieve my full potential, to live life to its fullest, to evolve both mentally and spiritually.

GREATEST REWARD FROM CAREER

Achieving a turnaround of The Vermont Teddy Bear Co. and realizing the faith its 170 employees have invested in me to now lead it into a new era of opportunity and growth.

GREATEST DOWNSIDE TO CAREER

Social sacrifices. Sometimes I feel alone.

ADVICE TO ASPIRING BUSINESSWOMEN

Never outwardly invoke your gender to further your career in business. Stay closely connected to your family, particularly your children; they force you to develop and maintain balance and perspective that's critical to developing leadership qualities and to learning how to cope with and manage change. Be genuine, direct, and honest at all times; people must have respect for you and trust you. Never give in to the silver bullet mentality. Stay personally and professionally grounded in reality.

*t*he fact is that, in the experience I've had, the dog-eat-dog part of business has definitely been the primary atmosphere, the primary mode I've had to operate in. That takes a tremendous amount of psychological energy, and it doesn't just come naturally to people. I think it only comes with the kind of exposure I've had to it.

The bears The Vermont Teddy Bear Co. makes are cuddly, but Elisabeth Robert has had to be tough. From the moment she joined the company as CFO, she saw them through one financial crisis to the next. Finally, when the CEO stepped down in 1997 during a particularly harrowing year-end audit, Elisabeth knew it was time to step up to the plate and put the company in turnaround mode. First order of business: raise enough cash in two weeks to pass an independent audit with a clean opinion. Second, bring the company back to its core market—direct response radio—in time for Valentine's Day, the make-or-break season for teddy bears.

"It was certainly hair-raising for the four months. We were very, very short of cash, and had to very quickly transition the entire business strategy away from retail and the expanded catalog that my predecessor had initiated. We focused on the peak holiday, and Valentine's Day, as being our opportunity, basically, to save the company. It was harrowing. I lost fifteen pounds." That year, the new CEO was down on the packing line at two A.M. getting out Bear-Grams®. Thanks to a team effort and long hours, Elisabeth says, Valentine's Day 1998 was the best the company had ever seen. "That was the beginning of our recovery," she says.

Driving this company forward hasn't been the only thing on Elisabeth's mind. Working through the lean years, Elisabeth realized she needed to balance a hard-nosed business perspective with sensitivity. "I would feel terrible about people in the company who weren't able to get raises for two years, and struggled along with the company believing in it. You get into a mode where you are saying, 'no, no, no, no, no,' and then you realize 'oh my God, these are real people out there.' " This drove her to take over as CEO in the middle of a crisis situation as much as her "dog-eat-dog" sensibility: "It was this intense feeling of wanting to save the place, basically, for the employees that caused me to want to step into it. I wasn't thinking of it as a personal challenge at first. I was in survival mode."

The way forward for Elisabeth is to take small steps. Both in her management style and her overall strategy for The Vermont Teddy Bear Company, a balance between pushing and waiting, dictating and listening, has to be found at each advance. "It's easy to get overwhelmed," she says with the authority of experience. "I've found that you make much better progress when you take small steps because the feedback loops are much shorter." With coaching managers, the balance is between granting autonomy and getting too involved: "I move in and out of a micromanaging role. I'm not going to deny that I micromanage things—I do. But I don't just take the problem and fix it myself. I will always keep the individuals responsible for that process involved."

And although she prefers to manage as "the person in the upstairs office," rather than as a "pal," Elisabeth says she learned the importance of listening to employees from her children. "They are their own individuals, and as a result, they teach you how to listen. They teach you to respect other people's opinions and perspectives. In a company like this one, where employees are making a contribution much larger than what they're getting paid for, it's so important to listen to them, and respect their perspectives." Children have other lessons, Elisabeth laughs. "Certainly my kids have taught me time management as well."

Through small steps, Elisabeth hopes to internationalize The Vermont Teddy Bear Co. The company is already, for the first time, working with off-shore vendors for certain raw materials, and the determined CEO hopes that selling overseas won't be far behind: "I see the possibility of becoming an international Bear-Gram® company in a very seamless way. To advertise and to ship to Tokyo should be no different from advertising in and shipping to St. Louis." But the heart and soul of the business and manufacturing will, she says, remain in the brightly painted Shelburne factory: "I deeply love this company. You can't work for The Vermont Teddy Bear Company for three years and not just grow to absolutely love the place, and love the people."

Janet C. Wylie

PRESIDENT AND CHIEF
EXECUTIVE OFFICER

HCL James Martin, Inc.
Fairfax, Virginia

WORK HISTORY

1977–1978   Project Engineer, Exxon Company, New Orleans,
Louisiana.

1979–1980   Regional Engineering Consultant, McDonnell Douglas
Automation Company, Atlanta, Georgia.

1980–1986   National Product Sales Manager, Boeing Computer
Services Company, Vienna, Virginia.

1986–1988   Manager, Marketing and Strategic Planning; then
Director, Advanced Programs, Martin Marietta I&CS,
Bethesda, Maryland.

1988–1994   Director, Applications Marketing; then Director,
Advanced Programs; then Vice President and General
Manager, Engineering Document Management Systems;
then Vice President, International and Indirect
Operations, Xerox Corporation, Herndon, Virginia.

1994–1996   Vice President, Commercial and Civil Operations; then Vice President, Commercial Outsourcing, Computer Sciences Corporation, Falls Church, Virginia.

1997–present   President and CEO, HCL James Martin, Inc.

EDUCATION

1977   Bachelor of Civil Engineering (highest honors), Georgia Institute of Technology, Atlanta, Georgia.

1977   Graduate work in Structural Engineering, Georgia Institute of Technology.

1988–1989   Graduate work in Marketing, University of Chicago.

FIRST JOB

Production Engineer for Exxon in the Gulf of Mexico.

ASSOCIATIONS AND NETWORKS

President-Elect, Women in Technology; Board Member, Northern Virginia Technology Council; National Capitol Speaker's Association; Professional Services Council; The Tower Club.

COMMUNITY SERVICE

Senior Mentor, Women in Technology; volunteer work for MADD, Children's Hospital, Special Olympics.

AWARDS AND HONORS

Featured in the Yearbook of Experts, Authorities, and Spokespersons; CSC Eagle Award for Meeting All Business Unit Goals for 1994, 1995, and 1996; Xerox President's Club 1988–1993; Boeing Quota Club Qualifier for each year on quota; Boeing Computer Services Employee of the Year, 1981; Chi Epsilon Award for Most Outstanding Civil Engineering Student of 1976–1977.

GREATEST OBSTACLES OVERCOME

Stereotypes about women. The glass ceiling still exists.

DRIVING FORCE

A desire to challenge myself in every way.

DEFINITION OF SUCCESS

Happiness in every aspect of my life—personal, professional, spiritual.

BUSINESS MAXIM

Stay focused on your goals, but never sacrifice your principles.

WAYS OF DEALING WITH PRESSURE AND STRESS

Working out each day. Lots of good friends to talk to.

ADVICE TO ASPIRING BUSINESSWOMEN

Be true to yourself and play to your strengths as a woman.

i don't feel women should have to go through what I went through. It shouldn't be such an uphill battle. Working, getting a job, and being competitive in a field is difficult enough as it is.

Janet Wylie makes this statement without a hint of bitterness. She has been determined enough and, in her words, stubborn enough to create success on her own terms, even while working for some of America's largest companies, even after being directly discouraged from joining a field in which women were rare.

Janet now heads HCL James Martin, Inc., a joint venture between the multimillion-dollar, multinational HCL Corporation and James Martin & Co., a U.S.-based consulting firm. HCL James Martin's focus is on helping companies redesign, restructure, and rethink their vast computer systems when they are faced with sweeping changes such as the millennium bug, the conversion to a single European currency, or a corporate merger. Janet took the reins of HCL James Martin when it was a fledging venture in desperate need of a new approach. Four months later, it was breaking even. Six months later, the company had twenty-six major clients—including NCR, Air Products, and 20th-Century Fox—when before they had three. For fiscal 1997, profits went from a negative $3 million to a positive $1.4 million. But what pleases Janet most is that an outside review of their clients revealed that all of them would do business with HCL James Martin again.

This rapid turnaround is only the latest in a career of challenges met and overcome. From her days at Georgia Tech, where she was one of two women graduates out of a class of 632 from the engineering department, to her first job on an offshore oil rig, where she slept in the tool shed next to the diesel generators and posted a guard when she used the showers, Janet has taken her uphill battles as a chance to learn valuable lessons, reinventing herself along the way.

Although she claims she didn't realize it at first, Janet now sees engineering as a perfect training for management: "It teaches you how to think. It teaches you how to sift through reams of data, take out the things that are important, and act on them. I think it's really fundamental and basic in business to be able to deal with that volume of data." When she realized that engineering didn't teach her about the arts or cultures, she took it upon herself to learn about life's finer points through independent study and night classes.

Despite the conditions aboard the oil rig, where she was the first woman sent by Exxon to the Gulf of Mexico, Janet not only got the job done and gained the respect of her team, she also realized some valuable things about herself: "It was such a rough-and-tumble environment, and I really didn't know how to relate to these guys. Finally, after a few months of this I figured out that trying to be one of them was not working. So I tried to be myself." Years later, she continues, she finally figured out what that meant: "There were no female models, so the question was 'How feminine can you afford to be?' Can you have flowers in your office? Can you wear dresses to work instead of suits? How feminine can you be without compromising respect or your performance?"

As it turns out, Janet says, women can be as feminine as they want to be, as long as they capitalize on their strengths as women: "Women are better at doing multiple tasks at the same time. Women are typically better communicators than men. Women are typically more sensitive to the personal aspects of business than men." Janet can back these claims up—she gathered evidence from women in business and the latest research on brain structure differences between genders for her book, *Chances & Choices: How Women Can Succeed in Today's Knowledge-Based Businesses,* published in 1996.

Janet's most recent reinvention of herself happened when she turned forty. "I use every birthday as a chance to reflect," she recalls. "It turned out that I didn't want to be in a bureaucratic structure. I didn't want to be in a large corporation, unless I was running it." Five months later, she got her chance at HCL James Martin, and ran with it. Now she continually reinvents a corporation, from the top down.

Phyllis J. Campbell

PRESIDENT

U.S. Bank, Washington
Seattle, Washington

WORK HISTORY

1972–1980   Management Trainee, Operations Manager, Commercial
Loan Officer, Branch Manager, Old National Bank,
Spokane, Washington.

1980–1988   Vice President and Area Manager, U.S. Bank (formerly
Old National Bank).

1988–1989   Senior Vice President and Area Market Manager, Eastern
Washington, U.S. Bank.

1989–1991   Executive Vice President and Manager, Retail Branch
Banking, U.S. Bank.

1992–1993   Area President, Seattle/King County, U.S. Bank.

1993–present   President, U.S. Bank, Washington and Regional Manager,
Private Financial Services—Washington and Northern
Idaho, U.S. Bank.

EDUCATION

1973   B.A. in Business Administration, Washington State University.

1981   Professional degree, Pacific Coast Banking School at the University of Washington.

1987   M.B.A., University of Washington.

1992   Executive Marketing Program, Stanford University.

1997   Executive Management Program, Stanford University.

FIRST JOB

ASSOCIATIONS AND NETWORKS

Boards of Directors, SAFECO; Board of Directors, Puget Sound Energy; Board of Regents, Washington State University; Board of Trustees, Greater Seattle Chamber of Commerce; Vice Chair and Board of Directors, Washington Roundtable; Board of Governors, Washington Athletic Club.

COMMUNITY SERVICE

Campaign Chair, United Way of King County; Seattle Foundation, Vice Chair and Trustee; Board of Directors, Pacific Science Center; Director, National Center for Nonprofit Boards.

AWARDS AND HONORS

Fabulous Five Award, Business and Professional Women of Washington, 1998; Human Relations Award, American Jewish Committee, 1996; Distinguished Citizen Award, Alpha Gamma Delta, 1995; honorary doctorate degree, Whitworth College, 1994; honored at *Northwest Asian Weekly* "Diversity at the Top" banquet, 1993; Puget Sound Woman of Achievement, Matrix Table, 1992; Alumni Achievement Award, Washington State University, 1989.

DRIVING FORCE

Strong work ethic and persistence. Pride in my work. Results orientation.

DEFINITION OF SUCCESS

Leaving a situation—workplace, corporation, etc.—better off than if you had never been there. Maximizing one's potential. Being a lifelong learner.

BUSINESS MAXIM

Always give back more than you take out of any situation, whether it is in the context of business or community.

WAYS OF DEALING WITH PRESSURE AND STRESS

Living a balanced lifestyle.

ADVICE TO ASPIRING BUSINESSWOMEN

View education as a lifelong pursuit, give back by helping others along the way, take informal risks and learn from mistakes, have a sense of humor, especially about oneself.

*b*eing in a position where I've enjoyed success means that I'm able to help others who don't have or haven't had the same advantages. It's an obligation of leaders to step forward and help those who aren't able to help themselves.

There is no distinction for Phyllis Campbell between community service and business success. One leads to the other, and back to itself again. Her commitment runs deep, and has been reinforced throughout her life—by her family, her cultural background, her company, and personal experiences, including a high-stakes struggle with cancer when she was thirty-two. Throughout it all, she has stayed with the same company and risen to the top.

In addition to her own determination, Phyllis credits the working environment at U.S. Bank for much of her growth: "I was very fortunate to be with a company that believes in promoting based on ability and promoting from within. I had mentors who opened doors and moved me along to places I didn't know I could go." Her career path was not without snags: there was the occasional supervisor who felt a woman would not be appropriate for this or another position, but Phyllis was undeterred: "At those times I had to make a decision, and I decided that door is closed. I told my supervisors that I didn't like it, but I knew I had to go another route. I had to go around it, above it, or through it, but I persisted."

Fortunately, those times were rare, allowing Phyllis to remain in a company that she feels has always had a conscience: "I've been very fortunate in that an explicit value of the company I have worked for is the fact that community service and community involvement is just a part of who we are as a company. It's the right thing to do, but we also realize that the social fabric of the community is intricately intertwined with our success as a business. The two are one." As President of U.S. Bank, Washington, Phyllis promotes this philosophy not only through her bank's decisions and actions, but by directly encouraging her employees to serve the community. Her employees are given time off for volunteer work, and her company gives to those charities favored by her employees. Phyllis is open about the fact that community service is essential to advancement within the ranks of U.S. Bank: "We look at the whole person, not just what they've done in their business life. We want to know what they've done to make their community better."

In turn, Phyllis says, she treats her employees as volunteers. "In a tight labor market, our best and brightest can go anywhere. It takes time, but we have to make our employees feel as if they are included and valued. It's the same thing one would do while working with a volunteer board." In her case, good works also go well beyond recognition—in spite of her work for major charities and her company policies, Phyllis says that "the service I'm most proud of isn't the one that's going to get a big headline. Mentoring, the time I've spent with individuals, being a sounding board for their own careers won't get a lot of attention, but it's what I enjoy most."

Phyllis came to U.S. Bank with many of these ideals firmly in place. Her grandfather, who moved from Japan to Seattle when he was in his twenties and converted to Catholicism, passed on to Phyllis a carefully crafted blend of Eastern and Western philosophy and spirituality. Her family on her father's side, who suffered forced internment during World War II, passed on a sense of compassion for the wronged. While she worked in her father's dry cleaning business as a teen, he challenged her to remember customers' names and laundry preferences, giving Phyllis her first experience in customer service. Now her cultural background and independent study of Asian culture give her an advantage on business trips to Japan, China, and Hong Kong.

It was on one of these trips that Phyllis was reminded of one of her own pieces of advice—not to take one's self too seriously—and at the same time was reminded that as far as she and other women have come, there is still much to be accomplished. While waiting in a hotel lobby for her group to arrive, she says, she became reflective: "I was thinking, 'Here I am meeting with clients in the financial capital of Asia. I've really arrived,' and just at that moment a woman grabbed my left arm and loudly exclaimed, 'I'm so glad you're here, you must be our tour guide.' " Phyllis says she laughed with her colleagues and helped the woman find her guide, suddenly recalling the lessons of humility taught by her parents and grandfather. She knew then, as she does now, that in her career, her marriage, and her struggle against disease, she has been blessed as well as driven: "Sometimes it's better to be lucky than good. I've been both."

Gail Ann Lione, Esq.

VICE PRESIDENT, GENERAL COUNSEL, AND SECRETARY

Harley-Davidson. Inc.
Milwaukee, Wisconsin

WORK HISTORY

1974–1975   Attorney, Morgan Lewis & Bockius, Philadelphia, Pennsylvania.

1975–1980   Attorney, Hansell & Post, Atlanta, Georgia.

1980–1986   Vice President, The First National Bank of Atlanta, Atlanta, Georgia.

1986–1989   Senior Vice President, Corporate Secretary, and General Counsel, Sun Life Group of America, Inc., Atlanta, Georgia.

1989–1990   Vice President, Maryland National Bank, Baltimore, Maryland.

1990–1997   General Counsel, U.S. News and World Report, L.P., The Atlantic Monthly Company, Applied Printing.

Technologies, L.P., and Applied Graphics Technologies, Inc., Washington, D.C.

1997–present   Vice President, General Counsel, and Secretary, Harley-Davidson, Inc.

EDUCATION

1971   B.A. (magna cum laude, Phi Beta Kappa) in Political Science, University of Rochester, Rochester, New York.

1974   J.D., University of Pennsylvania Law School, Philadelphia.

FIRST JOB

Working for my Congressman, Seymour Halpern, in high school. I had to write to him almost every week until I finally got a call from him, saying I had been so persistent that he had to meet me.

ASSOCIATIONS AND NETWORKS

Member, ABA Standing Committees on Publishing Oversight and Strategic Communications; Trustee, Copyright Society of USA; Member, ABA Litigation Section Judiciary Task Force. Past ABA activities include: Regional Co-Chair, Forum on Communications Law; Chair, Standing Committee on Association Communications; Co-Chair, Litigation Section Committee on Federal Legislation; Member, ABA House of Delegates.

COMMUNITY SERVICE

Trustee, University of Rochester; Advisory Board, Cardiovascular Research Center, Medical College of Wisconsin; former Member, Finance Committee, National Symphony Ball; former Member, Board of Directors, YMCA of Baltimore; former Vice Chairman, Metro Atlanta United Way Campaign; former Chairman of the Board and fourteen-year Board Member, Atlanta Ballet; former Chairman of the Board, Special Audiences, Inc.; former Member, Board of Directors, Metro Atlanta YMCA; former Member, Board of Atlanta Legal Aid Society.

AWARDS AND HONORS

Teaching Fellow, Salzburg Institute, Austria, 1989; Leadership Atlanta, 1988; Top 20 Women in Atlanta, Atlanta Business Chronicle, 1987; Top 40 Under 40, *Atlanta Magazine,* 1984; Outstanding Volunteer (JC Penney Golden Rule Award), 1984; Outstanding Young People of Atlanta, TOYPA, 1982.

FAMILY

Recently remarried, one daughter.

GREATEST OBSTACLES OVERCOME

The biggest hurdle for women, especially today, is not necessarily attaining the position but being successful in the position.

DRIVING FORCE

My mother gave me the confidence to do whatever I wanted to do. She probably wouldn't think of herself as a feminist, but clearly she was the first and most important feminist I knew. I was a single mom for eight years, and my daughter really inspired me to move forward, knowing that I was totally responsible for her.

DEFINITION OF SUCCESS

Having the ability to create luck.

WAYS OF DEALING WITH PRESSURE AND STRESS

I take a hot bath every night.

ADVICE TO ASPIRING BUSINESSWOMEN

Relax. Take each day as it comes. Younger women sometimes seem to be so busy pursuing their goals that they miss opportunities. People should do what they enjoy doing, even if it means taking a lower salary. What you want is to be able to look back on your life and say, I did a good job, I had a lot of fun, and I made good friends in the process.

a common thread in my business success has been the friends I have made and worked with. Just in the year I've been at Harley-Davidson, I've made such wonderful friends, people who will be with me for the rest of my life.

✹

Gail Lione's richly varied career owes almost as much to her friends as it does to her ability to see the common elements in diverse industries. Her friends and her skills had already taken her from real estate to banking to publishing when one day a headhunter, who she also considers a friend, asked her if she would be interested in another big change—becoming General Counsel and Secretary for motorcycle manufacturer Harley-Davidson. "When she called, she called on the premise that this was absolutely the perfect job for me, both career-wise and personality-wise," Gail remembers. "And when she started describing it, of course I was interested."

Taking the job meant taking a few risks. Gail was then General Counsel of U.S. News & World Report and its affiliates. She had never been to Milwaukee before her interview. She had never worked in heavy manufacturing. But she also knew that fresh opportunities were what she had been seeking ever since she entered law school. "The thing that interested me about law," she says, "was that it could take you into different industries, that it would always be varied. There's always a newness, a freshness about what's before you, and you aren't bound to one city, state, or even country. To me that had a lot of appeal."

Gail says her career gave her better results than she could have expected: "I had the extremely good fortune of being in industries when the industries were hot." She started in real estate law at a prime time and location: the seventies in Atlanta. She moved into financial services in 1980, at a time when "everything was expanding and the consolidations were just starting. The eighties was just the time to be in banking." In 1990 she switched to publishing at a critical juncture for that industry. Gail experienced the initial excitement about the Internet, growth of online services, new developments in graphics, and new problems about intellectual property while working for two respected magazines and their associated printing and graphics companies. Now she's in motorcycle manufacturing as the entire culture surrounding the bikes is being redefined. "This is really fun," she says. "What we are actually in is the entertainment business. We're not so much providing transportation as we are fulfilling dreams."

After settling in at Harley-Davidson, Gail took her first motorcycle safety course as soon as the weather would allow. It wasn't just for fun. She wanted to learn about the motorcycle, which will help her work with Harley's trademarks and patents and understand issues about motorcycle performance to help her supervise the product liability group. She's also gained an appreciation for the machine itself and the culture around it: "The bikes are just beautiful. You can't look at one and not think about what a magnificent object it is—objects of art as well as objects of fun."

Harley-Davidson would like more riders like Gail. More women, and more families, are becoming involved with the Harley Owners Group (HOG), which organizes rallies and tours. No one should be surprised, therefore, at how Gail sees her company's products: "They represent freedom, power, and independence, and all of those things are as important to women as they are to men." Gail is just one of many female officers at the company, and she wasn't at all surprised to sit between two female dealership owners at a recent dealer meeting. She says the corporate culture at Harley is far from the macho image some might associate with the bikes: "It's not even hierarchical. The company is run by a functional leadership group working with our CEO, and you really have to be able to play on a team. It's the kind of working environment that's very important to me."

Gail's career and experience have given her plenty of freedom and independence. She's moved assuredly from one industry to the next. She's had the means and confidence to raise her daughter on her own. She's relocated four times with a spirit of adventure. But she also knows that she's needed her friends. A friend recruited her into Sun Life in Atlanta, another invited her into publishing in Washington, D.C., and a third "played matchmaker" between her and Harley-Davidson. Gail knows that independence allows for possibilities, but real strength comes from friendships: "One of my favorite quotes is from Yeats," she says. " 'Think where glory most begins and ends/I say my glory is I have such friends.' "

Catherine Colan Muth

PRESIDENT AND CHIEF
EXECUTIVE OFFICER

O. R. Colan Associates, Inc.

South Charleston,
West Virginia

WORK HISTORY

1973–present   O. R. Colan Associates.

EDUCATION

1969   B.S. in Political Science and English, West Virginia
University, Morgantown.

1971   Graduate Course, Harvard University.

1979–1981   Additional undergraduate work in accounting and
computer science, Bluefield State College.

FIRST JOB

Tennis instructor during eighth grade summer.

ASSOCIATIONS AND NETWORKS

International Right of Way Association; Environmental Assessment Association; TEC 2004; United Methodist Church; American Association of University Women.

COMMUNITY SERVICE

Past President, United Methodist Church; Market Advisory Committee, Bluefield State College.

AWARDS AND HONORS

West Virginia Entrepreneur of the Year finalist, Ernst & Young, 1996.

FAMILY

Married, two children, two stepchildren.

GREATEST OBSTACLES OVERCOME

Establishing and maintaining a line of credit for start-up costs of new contracts. Repurchasing stock of other stockholders of the company.

PERSONAL GOALS

To organize my business well enough to allow more time with my family. To reduce the amount of time that I need to travel.

PROFESSIONAL GOALS

To put in place a team of top-level professional staff so the business depends more on my vision and less on my implementation.

DRIVING FORCE

After watching my mother and her friends go through "empty nest syndrome," I resolved to be prepared to do something interesting after my children left home. I substantially overachieved this goal.

DEFINITION OF SUCCESS

Not caring what other people think about you.. Looking at life as a gift. Believing that all things work together for good.

BUSINESS MAXIM

Never base decisions on fear.

WAYS OF DEALING WITH PRESSURE AND STRESS

I remind myself that in the grand scheme of things my success or failure means very little. It helps to keep this in perspective.

ADVICE TO ASPIRING BUSINESSWOMEN

It is more important to make a timely decision than to make the best decision. When you fail, don't waste energy thinking about it. There is usually a bigger opportunity around the corner. Put people ahead of money.

My father and I worked together for some time before he died. When I was working I felt like he was still in the next room, looking over my shoulder, or working with me. I still do.

Richard Owen Colan founded his company in 1969 and built it into an organization strong enough to pass on to his daughter, Catherine Muth, who started working part time in the family business in 1972. Catherine became an integral part of the company over the years, writing a complete accounting software package in 1982 that's still in use today. But as she followed in her father's footsteps, she never felt he was dragging her along: "If I was being groomed, he was very subtle about it. He always encouraged me to study what I liked and to do what I liked. I never once felt forced into this business at all."

Mr. Colan was carving out a farsighted niche for his daughter to fill. The company is the nation's oldest firm specializing in right-of-way acquisition and relocation advisory services for public projects. When a convention center, a highway, or an airport expansion project is slated for occupied property, O. R. Colan handles the human factor, buying the land and finding new homes or business location for the displaced. As government agencies have downsized, O. R. Colan has grown and, Catherine says, has added a new level of quality and integrity to a delicate and sometimes traumatic process.

"We don't think it's appropriate for the public to be inconvenienced more than they already are," Catherine says. "We work very hard to get the people moved in a humanitarian fashion." Her employees are the ones who actually work with the public as intermediaries between the government and the residents, making sure the acquisition and relocation plans meet federal standards and occur within the project's timeframe. Catherine says it's a challenging position: "Right of way is often called the stepchild of the industry. Plans are always completed late, and the construction companies' schedules are set in concrete. We're always expected to catch up."

Catherine inherited a company poised for growth. "Like many entrepreneurs," she explains, "my father believed that he needed to closely manage every problem. I realized, however, that our employees were technically proficient people who knew as much as or more than I did, and I was willing to give them a level of independence my father was hesitant to give. That's what allowed us to grow." Since she took over in 1989, Catherine has seen revenues triple and has extended west of the Mississippi, establishing branches in Seattle and adding a marketing professional in California to her over one hundred employees. They've handled high-profile projects for thirty-five airport clients and now train personnel for both the FAA and the Federal Highway Administration. Handing more responsibility to her employees also gained their respect, creating a smooth transition into her father's leadership role: "No one questioned my taking over; the loyalty and support I received was absolutely amazing."

It's support she clearly needs. O. R. Colan wades into some level of controversy with every project. "We've found that in every population you have about five percent of the people who are never happy," she says, adding that these are the ones who get the attention. "The press always focuses on the people who are discontented with the process, so the public perception of our industry is very poor. But we have files of all kinds of thank-you letters from people and businesses thanking us for helping them work through a very stressful time." Because of the federal standards for relocation, Catherine points out, many residents are moved to larger, safer, and more sanitary situations. And although they can't exceed guidelines for relocation, her company does push for updates and improvements to existing regulations and laws. If the residents are happier, after all, Catherine's job is easier.

Not that it will ever be made easy—Catherine's travel schedule is a job in itself, and her expansion plans will consume her days for years to come. But she says she can always turn to home for support: "I can't see how a woman in business could attempt this level of that responsibility without the kind of encouragement I get from my husband. If he were ever to say anything complaining about my schedule, it would really take away from the energy level I have to have. But he never does."

Kathryn L. Bibbey

PRESIDENT

National Business Systems
Cheyenne, Wyoming

WORK HISTORY

1972–1975   Greeley National Bank, Greeley, Colorado.

1975–1989   Larimer County Youth Services, Fort Collins, Colorado.

1979–1985   Trader's Printing and Publishing, Cheyenne, Wyoming.

1985–present   National Business Systems, Cheyenne, Wyoming.

EDUCATION

1970   B.A. in Social Sciences and Business, University of Northern Colorado, Greeley.

1973   M.A. in Vocational Rehabilitation, University of Northern Colorado, Greeley.

FIRST JOB

Working at a refreshment stand.

ASSOCIATIONS AND NETWORKS

Capitol City Business and Professional Women's Club.

COMMUNITY SERVICE

Director, Greater Cheyenne Chamber of Commerce; Chairman, Leadership Cheyenne; President, Leadership Unlimited; Wyoming State Board of Business and Professional Women; Hebard, Cole & Goins Neighborhood Oversight Committee; Norris Viaduct Reconstruction Steering Committee.

FAMILY

Many nieces and nephews.

DRIVING FORCE

Dreams.

DEFINITION OF SUCCESS

Reaching a point where you are at peace with who you are and what you are doing.

BUSINESS MAXIM

Do what you say you are going to do.

WAYS OF DEALING WITH PRESSURE AND STRESS

In addition to the many familiar methods—listening to music, massage, visiting with friends—I find the most effective manner of dealing with the world of human invention is to place my consciousness in the world that operates naturally without human direction. Native American religion refers to this as the Second World of Being.

ADVICE TO ASPIRING BUSINESSWOMEN

For people who live in areas like mine and don't want to live in a city: take a look at all the opportunities out there because of technology and gear the business in that direction.

'm not a city person, and didn't want to go to a city just to get a job. One of the best ways to avoid that is to start a company that can support you.

Kathryn Bibbey grew up surrounded by rural entrepreneurs. "Everyone was in business for themselves, from having a farm or ranch to having a dress shop," she remembers. Trucks hauling cattle from her small northern Colorado town carried the name of her father's trucking company, a constant reminder that she could make it on her own. "We had a very good business name," she says, "and seeing those trucks going down the highway was an emotional experience. I guess that's what put it in the can."

After graduating with her M.A., Kathryn worked in vocational training, at a bank, and finally for a printing company. "I was fascinated with the printing process. How did they get these images on paper? I started asking questions at a print shop, and by the time I was done, they said they would teach me," she says. Years later, it turned out that the experience she gained in printing was a perfect fit for the business she started with her nephew in 1985. "We were looking for a business to help the family," she says, "and secondly, we really didn't want to live in the city."

Kathryn and her family had by that time moved to Wyoming after watching their hometown of 27,000 grow to about 80,000 and lose much of its character along the way. The challenge of starting a company without going urban lay in finding a niche that would attract business from all corners of the country. The challenge was met with National Business Systems, specializing in medical forms, charts, and office supplies. The company is small enough, Kathryn says, and the market specific enough, that orders come from as far away as New York and Florida. "No one else does exactly what we do. For one thing, we know the filing codes used by insurance companies and Medicare and can catch a mistake a printer wouldn't be able to. We mostly sell to single-doctor practices, while bigger printers sell huge quantities to hospitals. We want the small guy. They don't."

With an 800 number and a UPS account, Kathryn says that her business is just as effective in a remote location as it would be in a larger city. Forms are designed in-house and transmitted to the printer best equipped to deal with the order. A vendors' group in Denver extends the reach of NBS by batching their products with other items doctors need, and Kathryn says she's past the point where generating business meant "wearing out several cars." Advantages to working out of Wyoming were clear from the beginning. There is no corporate income tax, no personal income tax, and few regulatory hurdles to getting started: "We just hung up a sign," she says. "We didn't have to get a license or a license to get a license or anything like that."

In fact, Kathryn makes starting a business sound easy. "We didn't go for any loans," she says. "I was at an age where I could live on nothing for any length of time, so I rented my house in Colorado and moved to a 'modest side of town' in Cheyenne." Even though her business grew to about a million in sales a year, she never left that side of town, and now serves on the neighborhood oversight committee and Cinco-de-Mayo committee.

Her civic commitment extends to the larger Cheyenne area through her Chamber of Commerce directorship, and statewide through the State Board of Business and Professional Women. The community and the state need new businesses, she says, but her first commitment is to the people and businesses already there: "The big issue is how to maintain who we are as Westerners as we take on this growth banner." One part of this identity that can't be lost, Kathryn adds, has been the acceptance of women in all manner of trades and businesses. "When I first came here, I was surprised to see how much women were involved in everything, from putting up telephone wires to running dump trucks and cattle trucks. Even one third of the state legislature were women." She got over her surprise very quickly, and learned to appreciate her adopted home state even more.

There's no better place to be a woman in business, she says, and no better place to be a part of a community. "People need each other up here. When you don't have the population and you have our weather, everybody counts. You have to be nice to people, because you never know who's going to pull you out of a ditch someday."

Bonnie Stern

Peter Bugg, Maclean's

The Bonnie Stern School of Cooking
Toronto, Ontario

WORK HISTORY

1970–1971   Restaurant Coordinator, Ontario Place, Toronto.

1971   Assistant Manager, The Doctor's House, Kleinburg, Ontario.

1971–1973   Gourmet Consultant, Eaton's, Toronto.

1973–present   Owner, The Bonnie Stern School of Cooking.

EDUCATION

1969   B.A. in English literature, University of Toronto.

1971   Studied Hotel and Restaurant Administration, George Brown College, Toronto.

1975   Attended Simone Beck School of Cooking, Grasse, France.

1976   Attended La Varenne, Paris, France.

1977   Attended the School of Classic Italian Cooking, Bologna.

1980   Attended the Greenbrier Cooking School, West Virginia.

1981   Attended the Wei Chuan School of Cooking, Taipei, Taiwan.

1990   Attended the Giuliano Bugialli School of Cooking, Florence, Italy.

1993   Attended the Ballymoloe Cookery School, Shanagarry, Ireland.

1998   Attended the Oriental Hotel Cooking School, Bangkok, Thailand.

FIRST JOB

Working at a dry cleaners.

ASSOCIATIONS AND NETWORKS

International Association of Cooking Professionals; The American Institute of Wine and Food; The James Beard Foundation; Cuisine Canada; Women's Culinary Network.

COMMUNITY SERVICE

Organizer, Taste of the Nation event for Share Our Strength; Advisory Board Member, Second Harvest (a perishable food recovery program); Author of *CKFM Cookbook,* which raised money for the Hospital for Sick Children; Author, with the Heart and Stroke Foundation, of *Simply Heart-Smart* and *More HeartSmart Cooking,* raising money for the Foundation.

AWARDS AND HONORS

Silver Ladle Award, Toronto Culinary Guild, 1988; Gold Award for the Media, Ontario Hostelry Institute, 1996; Cuisine Canada Award (for *More HeartSmart Cooking*), 1998.

FAMILY

Married, three children.

GREATEST OBSTACLES OVERCOME

Sometimes it's hard to separate being professional from being generous.

DRIVING FORCE

My desire to reach other people, to give them an opportunity to have food and cooking as a part of their lives.

BUSINESS MAXIM

My father always said that the harder you work, the more luck you seem to have.

GREATEST REWARD FROM CAREER

Because I love what I do, I can be just as happy writing successful cookbooks or appearing on a TV show as I am reaching just one person in my class.

WAYS OF DEALING WITH PRESSURE AND STRESS

By keeping in mind how lucky I am. By helping others. Exercise.

ADVICE TO ASPIRING BUSINESSWOMEN

Try to find something you really love to do. The more honest you are, the more you concentrate on things you love, the more you just be yourself, the better you will feel about what you do.

i would love to say that I had this groundbreaking plan, that I was a great visionary, but it wasn't like that at all. It's almost a Pollyanna story. I just wanted to do good deeds and be happy.

By the time she graduated from college, Bonnie Stern knew she wouldn't be happy if she wasn't working with food. At the time, she says this was a highly unusual career move: "In 1968, we didn't have celebrity chefs, there were few great restaurants in Toronto, there wasn't much happening in food the way there is now. I was lucky to get into the business when I did." Today, of course, fine food is big business, and in Canada, Bonnie plays a big role.

The cooking school she started in 1973 has expanded twice and welcomed international experts such as Madhur Jaffrey, Giuliano Bugialli, and Jacques Pepin to teach classes. Bonnie has written eight cookbooks, writes a weekly *Toronto Star* column, and contributes regularly to *Canadian Living*. In addition to her guest spots and regular segments on Canadian broadcast television and radio, she has her own cable show on the Women's Television Network. Her reach is greater than she ever thought it would be when she set out to support herself "not in a glamorous way, but simply, and by doing what I really cared about."

Keeping her life simple would seem to be a challenge these days. From Florence to Bangkok, Bonnie has continued her education at internationally renowned cooking schools and brings what she learns back to Toronto. But she takes a humble view of her extensive travels: "I'm really more of a homebody, but I love to have traveled. I love coming home having tasted the food and having seen it cooked in its country of origin. It's really important just to be able to relate it to people here in my classes." Even as television demands more of her time, Bonnie says she never wants to give up teaching small groups in person. For one thing, she loves it. For another, it keeps the program fresh. "My experiences in the classroom are very important for the TV show. I have to make sure I'm still talking to people in person." When she's finished with a class, she helps with the least glamorous part of her business—washing dishes and general cleanup: "In a small business, you never stop paying dues, and we are still very much a small business."

Although she didn't know it at the time, Bonnie's cooking career started in her parents' kitchen when she was just five years old. "My mother loved it when I cooked, and never cared if I made a mess, or if she cared, she didn't stop me. And my parents always ate my food, no matter what it was." During college, her repertoire expanded beyond spaghetti and meatballs as she saved money to eat in the few fine restaurants Toronto had to offer. Still, she never saw herself standing before large groups or television audiences until she tried it. "Before I went into food," she says, "I was very shy and withdrawn. When I did a couple of years of training for a department store,

I realized I really had something I could offer people. It brought me out of myself and enabled me to talk to people and share. That made me very happy." With this new-found confidence she took on two partners—"wonderful people who just wanted me to succeed"—and started her cooking school. She bought out her partners after three years, was invited to start a weekly radio spot after five years, and took on a newspaper column after six years in business. The way she describes this progression of her success makes it seem almost by fate: "These things just happened along the way, they weren't things I planned, but opportunities that developed. Behind it all was just the idea of helping make people's lives happier and healthier. That was my idea of success."

Bonnie calls the food industry "a very warm and loving business, a business of generosity," so it's not surprising to find her giving through her business. Her first cookbook for charity raised approximately $100,000 Canadian for the local Hospital for Sick Children, and her collaborations with the Heart and Stroke Foundation have raised awareness about healthy diets, not to mention approximately $500,000 Canadian for the foundation. Her efforts with Share Our Strength and Second Harvest, which fights hunger with reclaimed food, has united Toronto's food industry. "It brought us together," she says, "and knocked down competition barriers between us in a way that really allowed us to give back."

After over twenty-five years in business, Bonnie isn't even close to slowing down. The opportunities and challenges of food, she says, will always be her life: "Every time I open a door, there's a thousand more doors behind it. There are so many cultures in the world, so many ways of cooking right. If I ever think I know it all, I soon realize I haven't even started."

Micheline Bouchard, P. Eng., CM

CHAIRMAN, PRESIDENT, AND CHIEF EXECUTIVE OFFICER

Motorola Canada Limited
North York, Ontario

WORK HISTORY

1969–1987	Engineer, then Assistant to the Vice President of Communication, then Assistant to the President and CEO, the Commercial Delegate, Hydro-Quebec, Montreal, Quebec.
1987–1988	Vice President, Management Consulting Services, CGI Group Inc., Montreal, Quebec.
1988–1995	Vice President, Business Development, DMR Group, Inc., Montreal, Quebec.
1996–1998	Vice President, Quebec Operations, then Vice President, Business Development, Hewlett-Packard (Canada) Limited, Montreal, Quebec.
1998–present	Chairman, President, and CEO, Motorola Canada Limited.
1998–present	Vice President, Motorola, Inc.

EDUCATION

1969 B.S. in applied sciences and physics engineering, École Polytechnique de Montreal.

1978 M.S. in applied sciences and electrical engineering, École Polytechnique de Montreal.

ASSOCIATIONS AND NETWORKS

Current board directorships: Sears Canada, Alliance Forest Products, Banque Nationale de Paris, Corby Distilleries. Member, Business Council on National Issues; Board of Directors, Information Technology Association of Canada; President, International Women's Forum–Canada; Vice President, Canadian Academy of Engineering; past Chairman and Founding Member, Canadian Engineering Public Awareness Board; former Member, Advisory Council to the Prime Minister on Canada's Public Service Renewal; former President, Canadian Council of Professional Engineers; former Founding Member of the Board of Directors, Canadian Engineering Memorial Foundation; former Founding Member, Board Member, Honorary Member, Public Policy Forum; former Member of the Board of Directors, Official Residences Council (to Canadian Prime Minister); former Member of Advisory Committee on Science and Technology, Canadian Broadcasting Corporation; former President, Executive Committee Member, Member of the Board of Directors, Committee Chair, Order of Engineers of Quebec.

COMMUNITY SERVICE

Former Member of the Board of Directors, Advisory Council on Quebec Sciences and Technology; former Vice President, Executive Committee, Montreal Board of Trade; former Vice President, Secretary, Member of the Board, Committee Chair, Montreal Chamber of Commerce; former Member of the Board of Directors, Chambre de Commerce Française au Canada; former Member of the Board of Directors, Quebec Learning Centre; former Honorary President, Member of the Board, Committee Chair, Montreal Metropolitan Orchestra; former Member of the Board of Directors Quebec Youth Orchestra. Fundraising campaigns include: Marie-Vincent Foundation (1998), President; United Way (High-tech Industry Committee), (1996 to 1997); National Engineering Week (1994), President; Saint-Charles-Barromée Foundation (1993); Espace Go Theatre (1993); Women's Information Centre (1984); Engineering 100th Anniversary Celebration Committee (1983); Second Conference of Women Engineers in Canada (1982).

AWARDS AND HONORS

Honorary Chair, National Engineering Week, 1999; Polytechnique University Alumni Association, Merit Award, 1999; Polytechnique University Engineering Personality of the 125th Anniversary of the Polytechnique Foundation, 1998; Honorary Member, Golden Key Society, University of Toronto; Honorary Doctorate of Engineering, Ryerson Polytechnic University, Toronto, 1998; Honorary Member, Golden Key Society, University of Toronto, 1998; Member, Order of Canada, 1995; Woman of Distinction, YWCA, 1994; Fellow of the Canadian Academy of Engineering, 1993; Canada 125th Anniversary Memorial Medal, 1993; Woman of the Year in Business, Salon de la Femme, 1981; Honorary Member of the Order of Engineers of Quebec, 1990; Honorary Member of the South Shore Chamber of Commerce, 1986; Honorary Member of the Montreal Chamber of Commerce, 1983.

FAMILY

Married, two children.

GREATEST OBSTACLES OVERCOME

Having been the first woman in a number of my positions. Dealing with people who were getting used to that.

DRIVING FORCE

The satisfaction of contributing to the success of someone else or the success of an organization.

DEFINITION OF SUCCESS

Being in a position to help and support others.

BUSINESS MAXIM

Attitude is more important than aptitude.

WAYS OF DEALING WITH PRESSURE AND STRESS

By trusting people and empowering them. It relieves you from the pressure of wondering if the job will be done well.

ADVICE TO ASPIRING BUSINESSWOMEN

You must be visibly competent. You must find promoters and mentors, people who will actually speak about your values and aptitudes. Never hesitate to ask for help—no one succeeds alone.

*b*ecoming CEO of Motorola Canada was not something I had ever envisioned. But strangely enough, every new challenge I've met in my career has had very little to do with the previous one.

⁂

At age fourteen, Micheline Bouchard thought she wanted to become a lawyer. A single trip to the local engineering school quickly changed that, and she's never looked back. "I didn't even know what an engineer was," she recalls, "but I knew I wanted to be one at that very moment. I was still incredibly motivated when I returned to attend school there a few years later." Micheline found that her degree and years of technical experience opened more doors than she could imagine: "I went into the IT consulting services industry without any knowledge of that industry. I moved to Hewlett-Packard without much knowledge of computer products. And then to Motorola Canada, when, frankly, I'm not an expert in telecom."

She doesn't have to be, she adds. Trust, delegation, high-level strategic planning, and committed teamwork define her management style, and she pays close attention to how these elements are valued by the corporation. "A large part of my success has been in that I have operated in various environments that were very reflective of my own personal values," she explains, "corporations like Motorola that believe in their people and respect the value one person can bring to their company. For me, it all comes down to respect."

Micheline joined Motorola Canada in early 1998, at a time that would test her skills to the limit. The Asian financial crisis, the worldwide partial collapse of the semiconductor industry, and Canada's falling dollar all hit her company harder than expected. "I understood that I was coming on board to work with the team on a five-year strategic plan, but we were suddenly called upon to measure up to greater challenges," she says. The scale of the issues that now require her daily attention are far removed from her training and original career path, as an engineer for Canada's largest utility company. How she made the move from technology worker to management reflects her commitment to finding partnerships between the private and nonprofit sector. In her case, community involvement spurred professional growth.

As an engineer, Micheline admits, her contact with the world was limited; "I really developed my management skills working outside of my own field. Being involved with various associations and organizations and community work, I realized that I had to work with people from different disciplines, with different backgrounds, different experiences, people who were not seeing things in the same way." After she realized that she was good at dealing with diversity, Micheline threw her hat in the ring to become President of the Order of Engineers of Quebec. "That was the turning point of my career," she says. "Suddenly, I became excited with other matters outside technical challenges and wanted to get involved in areas like management, strategic planning, political areas. I had to develop those just to get elected." She was elected to a two-year term at age thirty.

Ever since that eye-opening experience, Micheline has been committed to keeping her view very broad. Serving on company boards as diverse as Sears Canada and Corby Distilleries, she says, "has been a tremendous experience from the standpoint of being exposed to other industry sectors, other leaders, and working at a very high strategic level." As President of the Canadian chapter of the International Women's Forum, she has found a truly global "community of interests" among professional women. "We all travel a lot and look up members in other countries. We exchange and compare notes and, surprisingly, we have the same observations about the progress we've made so far and what needs to be done, especially with being more supportive of younger talented women, being role models to those women."

Helping others is what Micheline believes success is all about. The greatest reward of her career, she says, had little to do with her career. In 1995, the father of a rape and murder victim contacted her after reading about her YWCA Woman of Distinction Award. The prime suspect in the case wouldn't give a DNA sample, as was his right under Canadian law. Micheline's intensive and tough three-month campaign to alter the Canadian charter of rights changed, in her words, "the course of justice in this country," and convicted the young woman's killer. "This, I think, was my most rewarding contribution," she says. "But I didn't do it, or anything, alone. I pooled resources and strategized. But other people made it happen. I always achieve with others."

WOMEN WHO MEAN BUSINESS